100 Beautiful Pieces of
FURNITURE *You Can Build*

Prepared by
The Craftsman Editors,
Popular Mechanics Magazine

~

WITH A COMPLETE INDEX

~

Copyright 1950
Printed in U.S.A.

POPULAR MECHANICS COMPANY
200 East Ontario • Chicago 11, Ill.

Styled exclusively for Popular Mechanics by John Bergen, furniture designer

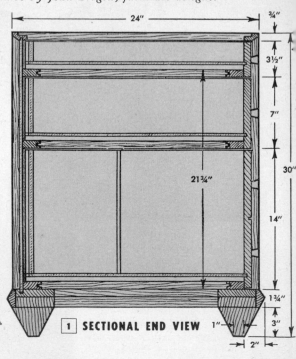

1 SECTIONAL END VIEW

24"
3/4"
3½"
7"
21¾"
30"
14"
1¾"
3"
1"
2"

Living-Room FURNITURE

Story by Wayne C. Leckey

Part I

M ODERN as tomorrow, here's a smartly styled ensemble that will transform your living room into a room of distinction. It's exclusive, colorful and, to top it off, this furniture is easy to build. Designed expressly with the home craftsman in mind, all the pieces of the group can be duplicated with just a jointer and a saw. Combining plywood with solid stock further simplifies construction, and the use of separate upholstered units enables the inexperienced worker to do a first-class job of upholstering the sectional units and easy chair.

The suite, most of which is shown in full color on preceding pages, includes a sectional sofa, easy chair, hostess chair, step table, commode, cocktail table, corner table, desk, table lamp and floor lamp. The desk chair shown was an extra piece and is not included in the group. However, a dining chair of the style presented in the dining-room furniture suite illustrated in another part of this book will provide a

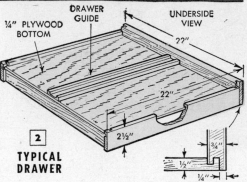

DRAWER GUIDE

¼" PLYWOOD BOTTOM

UNDERSIDE VIEW

22"

22"

2½"

¾"

½"

¼"

2

TYPICAL DRAWER

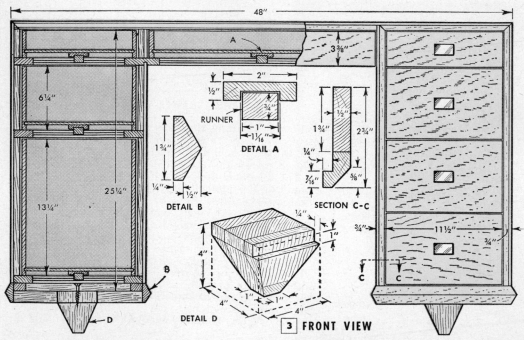

48"

A

3⅜"

6¼"

2"

½"

¾"

RUNNER

1"

1 1/16"

DETAIL A

1¾"

½"

1¾"

¼"

2¾"

7/16"

5/8"

SECTION C-C

25¼"

13¼"

1¾"

¼"

½"

DETAIL B

¼"

1"

4"

B

D

4"

1"

1"

4"

DETAIL D

¾"

11½"

¾"

C

C

3 **FRONT VIEW**

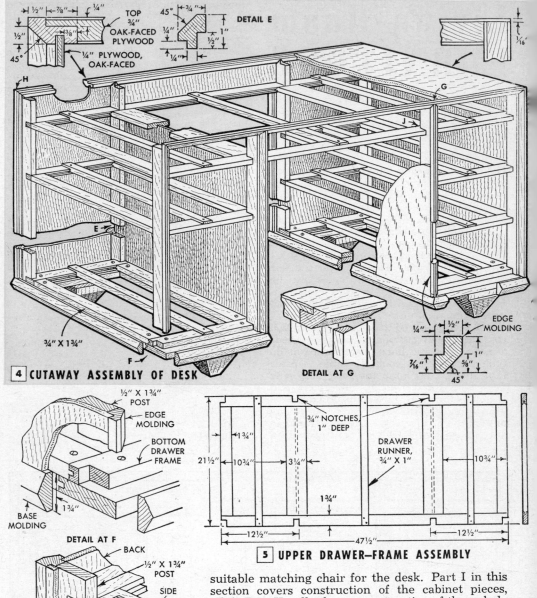

½" ⅞" ¼"
TOP ¾" OAK-FACED PLYWOOD
½"
45°
¼" PLYWOOD, OAK-FACED
³⁄₁₆"

45° ¾"
DETAIL E
¼"
½"
1"
¼"

¹⁄₁₆"

H

G

J

E

4 CUTAWAY ASSEMBLY OF DESK

¾" X 1¾"

F

DETAIL AT G

EDGE MOLDING

¼" ½"
³⁄₁₆" ⁵⁄₈" 1"
45°

½" X 1¾" POST
EDGE MOLDING
BOTTOM DRAWER FRAME
BASE MOLDING
1¾"

DETAIL AT F

BACK
½" X 1¾" POST
SIDE
EDGE MOLDING

DETAIL AT H

PLYWOOD PANEL
½" X 1¾" POST
TOP DRAWER FRAME
EDGE MOLDING

DETAIL AT J **6**

¾" NOTCHES, 1" DEEP
DRAWER RUNNER, ¾" X 1"
21½"
1¾"
10¾"
3¼"
10¾"
1¾"
12½"
47½"
12½"

5 UPPER DRAWER—FRAME ASSEMBLY

suitable matching chair for the desk. Part I in this section covers construction of the cabinet pieces, while Part II will take up construction of the upholstered pieces and the two lamps.

The kneehole desk, which may be considered optional, is the most detailed piece of the group and, therefore, requires the most explanation. Figs. 1 and 3 show sectional views, while the cutaway view in Fig. 4 gives a general idea of the assembly. The original furniture was made of oak-faced plywood and solid stock and finished in limed oak, but birch, maple or other hardwood can be used. The upper drawer frame of the desk is made first, Fig. 5, and although the drawer runners are shown in place, these can be added later. The dotted lines represent ¼-in. grooves which are made on the underside. As no part of this frame is exposed, it can be made of inexpensive wood. The built-up bases at the bottom of each drawer unit are made exactly alike, consisting of a drawer frame, screwed to a bottom frame. The two frames must fit flush at the sides. The front member of the bottom frame should be about 4 in. wide and cut from finished stock. Note in Fig. 6, detail F, that the drawer frame is notched at the corners for ½-in. posts which also are notched. Next, the posts are joined to the upper and lower frames, and intermediate drawer frames are installed.

Now, a molding is applied around the base of each drawer unit, as in Fig. 3, detail B. This is mitered at the corners, and is glued and screwed to the bottom frame to bring it flush with the top. When this is done, the four tapered legs can be fitted. Fig. 3, detail D, shows how they are built up and rabbeted across the front edge to come flush with the face of the base molding. Glue and a long, flat-headed screw are used to attach each leg. Next, a rabbeted molding is applied to the edge of the front posts. This is detailed in section C-C, Fig. 3, and is edge-glued to the posts. A similar molding cut according to detail E, Fig. 4, is edge-glued to the back posts. Note that the molding strips on the inner posts, at both front and back, are notched at the upper ends in the manner shown in detail G, Fig. 4. The ¼-in. plywood panels on the inside of the kneehole are fitted next. These are cut to fit the rabbeted edge molding and the grooves in the underside of the upper drawer frame. You'll notice in Fig. 6,

detail J, that the plywood is cut L-shaped at the top to continue it to the top of the front posts. In gluing and clamping in place, the panels are pushed up into the grooves so that the lower edge rests flush on the edge of the base molding. The panels covering the outside of the drawer units are installed similarly, except that they run to a point about 1/16 in. down from the mitered end of the edge molding. This permits the desk top to overlap the end plywood and conceal the plies in a rabbeted joint. Plywood panels which enclose the rear ends of the drawer units are slid into grooves in the edge molding, and then strips of rabbeted molding are run across the top of the desk at the front and back. Note that the rear strip differs slightly from the front one. The top, which is ¾ in. thick, is rabbeted all around, leaving about the thickness of one ply at the ends and ¼ in. at the sides.

Fig. 2 details drawer construction. The bottom left-hand one is a deep single drawer which is grooved across the face to represent two smaller drawers. Guides are detailed in Fig. 3, A.

The commode, detailed in Figs. 7 and 8,

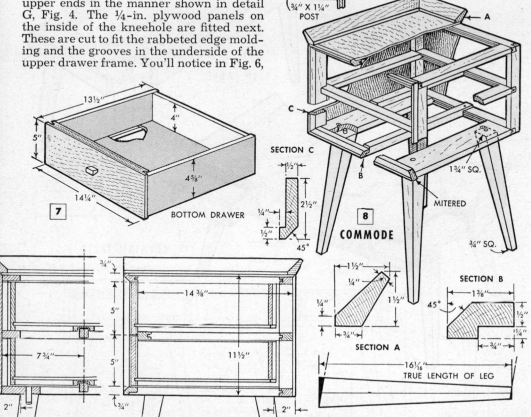

13½"

4"

5"

14¼"

4⅝"

7

BOTTOM DRAWER

TOP VIEW AT REAR CORNERS

¾" X 1¼" POST

A

C

B

1¾" SQ.

MITERED

8

COMMODE

¾" SQ.

SECTION C

½"

2½"

¼"

½"

45°

¾"

5"

14⅜"

5"

11½"

2"

¾"

2"

1½"

¼"

¼"

1½"

45°

¾"

SECTION A

1⅜"

½"

1¼"

¾"

SECTION B

16 1/16"
TRUE LENGTH OF LEG

5

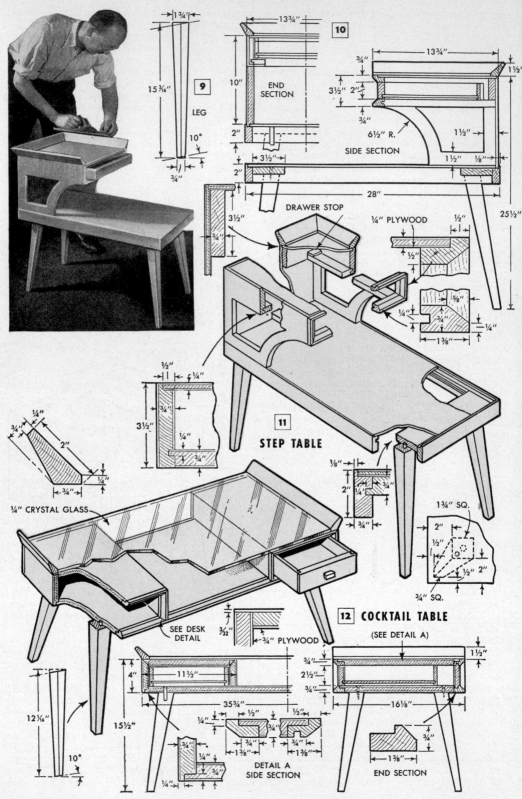

9
LEG
1 3⁄4″
15 3⁄16″
10°
3⁄4″

10
END SECTION
13 3⁄4″
10″
2″
2″
3 1⁄2″

SIDE SECTION
13 3⁄4″
3⁄4″
1 1⁄2″
3 1⁄2″ 2″
3⁄4″
6 1⁄2″ R.
1 1⁄2″
1 1⁄2″ 1⁄8″
28″
25 1⁄2″

DRAWER STOP
3 1⁄2″
3⁄4″

1⁄4″ PLYWOOD
1⁄2″
1⁄2″
5⁄8″
1⁄4″ 3⁄4″
1⁄4″
1 3⁄8″

11
STEP TABLE
1⁄2″ 1⁄4″
3⁄4″
3 1⁄2″
1⁄4″
3⁄4″

1⁄8″
2″
1⁄4″ 3⁄4″
3⁄4″

1 3⁄4″ SQ.
2″
1⁄2″
1⁄2″ 2″
3⁄4″ SQ.

1⁄4″
3⁄4″
2″
1⁄4″
3⁄4″
1⁄4″ CRYSTAL GLASS

SEE DESK DETAIL

3⁄32″
3⁄4″ PLYWOOD

12 COCKTAIL TABLE
(SEE DETAIL A)
1 1⁄2″
3⁄4″
2 1⁄2″
3⁄4″
16 1⁄8″
3⁄4″
1 3⁄8″
END SECTION

4″
11 1⁄2″
35 3⁄4″
1⁄4″ 1⁄2″ 1⁄2″
3⁄4″
3⁄4″ 3⁄4″
1⁄4″ 1 3⁄8″ 1 3⁄8″
3⁄4″
DETAIL A
SIDE SECTION

12 1⁄16″
15 1⁄2″
10°

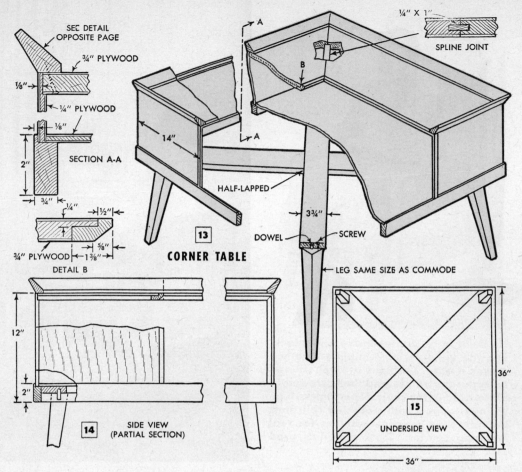

SEE DETAIL
OPPOSITE PAGE

¾" PLYWOOD

⅛"

¼" PLYWOOD

SECTION A-A

2"

¾"

¼"

½"

⅝"

¾" PLYWOOD   1⅜"

DETAIL B

A

B

A

A

14"

SPLINE JOINT

¼" X 1"

HALF-LAPPED

3¾"

DOWEL   SCREW

13

CORNER TABLE

LEG SAME SIZE AS COMMODE

12"

2"

14   SIDE VIEW
(PARTIAL SECTION)

36"

36"

15

UNDERSIDE VIEW

is built up around a rough framework which has a mitered molding edge-glued around the front. The tapered legs are doweled and screwed 2 in. in each way from the corners. The framework is covered with ¼-in. plywood which is rabbeted, as shown, to conceal the plies at the rear corners and around the top. The top is finished off on three sides with a slanting molding and, finally, two drawers are made and installed.

The step table, detailed in Figs. 9 to 11 inclusive, is made by grooving and rabbeting solid stock and then assembling it on edge to form a mitered frame. The grooves house tenons on two crosspieces to which the legs are fastened and the rabbet around the top edge receives a ¼-in. plywood panel. The latter is glued flush with the top of the frame. The scrollsawed sides, which are cut from solid stock, are rabbeted along the top and bottom edges and grooved to take the drawer frame. An edging glued around the front frames a shallow drawer. After the top of the table is covered, edging is added on three sides.

The cocktail table, detailed in Fig. 12, features a glass top, a center pocket for magazines and two small drawers. Except for the legs and molding, the table is made of ¾-in. plywood. The bottom board is rabbeted all around the edges, the rabbets at the ends being a reverse of those along the sides. The outer sides of the drawer compartments are likewise rabbeted and are glued and nailed from the bottom. Then the endpieces for the backs of the compartments are tenoned and rabbeted to take a rabbeted edge molding which frames both front and back.

The corner table for the sectional sofa is detailed in Figs. 13, 14 and 15. The top is made of ¾-in. plywood while sides and bottom of the table are ¼-in. plywood. Construction is apparent from the drawings. The base is similar to that of the step table, and the legs are the same size as those on the commode. The mitered joint in the top is fitted with a spline and an edge molding, detail B, Fig. 13, is used to conceal the laminations. Here again, a slanting molding is added to finish off the top.

No need to be apprehensive about tackling the upholstering—simplified method makes it easy. Cushions are upholstered on separate frames and then screwed in place right in the chair. New sagless-type springs topped with pocketed coil units provide deep oversize cushions for real lounging comfort. Stock materials used

Your Living-Room

Furniture

Styled by John Bergen, noted furniture designer

Part II

WITH THE cabinet pieces of the living-room group completed as described in Part I, you can begin the sectional sofa and chairs. Normally, conventional upholstering that requires tying springs and sewing welt seams is a job for the experienced worker, but here, through the use of sagless-type springs and "box" cushions, the work is simplified to the point where an amateur can do a first-class job. The upholstered pieces of the group include a three-piece sectional sofa, an easy chair and a hostess chair, the latter being made with either wooden or padded arms. The two photos on the opposite page show how

Here's how units of the sectional sofa can be used in conjunction with a living-room fireplace and cocktail table. End units of the sofa are placed together and the center unit is used opposite as a separate chair

the hostess chair will look in each case. Basically, the easy chair, shown at the top of the same page, is a duplicate of the sectional units, except that it is fitted with two arms. Seat and back cushions of each unit are built up on separate frames which are then screwed to the chair frame. In the case of the hostess chair, the upholstering method differs in that the seat and back are sprung and padded right on the chair.

The sectional sofa is highly functional and can be arranged in a number of ways. The units may be grouped around a corner table as pictured on the title page, or they may be used side by side and flanked with a pair of end tables as shown on the preceding page. Still another suggested arrangement is given in the photo above. Here, the two end units having the arms are placed together and the center unit is used as an individual chair. In addition to the upholstered pieces, Part II covers the construction of two distinctive lamps.

Frames for the sectional sofa, easy chair and the hostess chair are detailed in Figs. 18 to 22 inclusive. The original pieces were made of solid oak to match the rest of the furniture. Parts of the frames not exposed can be made of any scrap hardwood. Both end units of the sofa are made as pictured

in Fig. 19, one being built with a right and the other with a left-hand arm. The center unit of the sofa, and the easy chair, are exact duplicates of the others, the center unit, of course having no arms. Construction of the hostess chair, Fig. 21, is basically the same, differing primarily in size and the addition of a tacking rail across the back. As previously mentioned, this chair can be fitted with either wooden or padded arms. In both cases, the arms are made up separately and doweled through the holes in the fabric and into the frame after the upholstering has been completed. Then screws are driven into each arm from the inside. Fig. 18 details the framework for the padded arms and Fig. 17 shows them being trial-fitted, registering holes being made for the dowels. Note that the seat corner joints of all the frames are glued and doweled and then drawn up rigidly with lag screws. The front legs of the frames are half-lapped into the side rails, glued and screwed. The arms on the easy chair and the end units of the sectional sofa are screwed permanently to the frames before upholstering. Holes for the screws are counterbored through the width of the arms. When the frames are completed, all exposed surfaces of the chairs are sanded and finished as desired. The rear

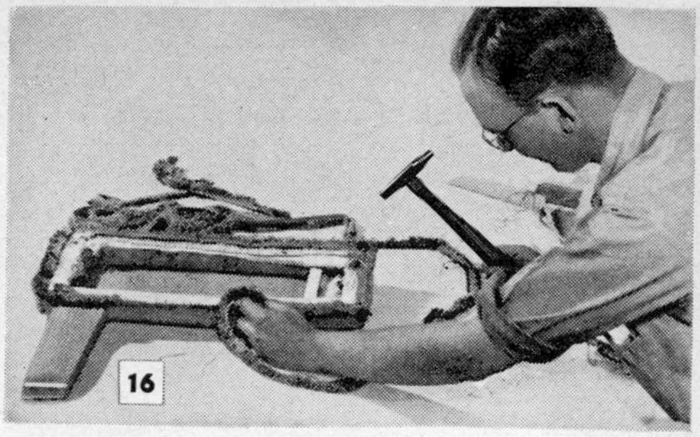

16

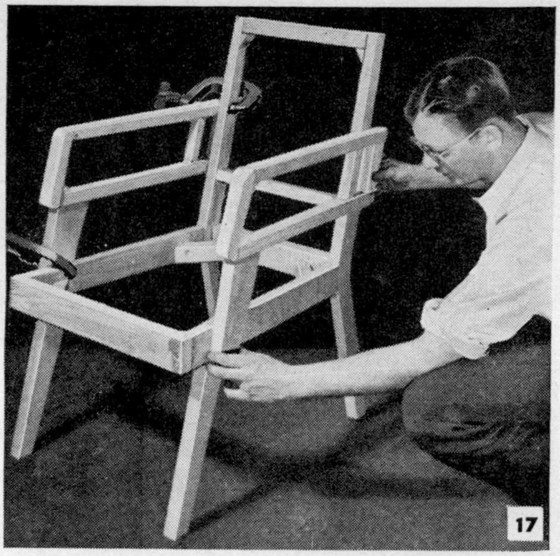

17

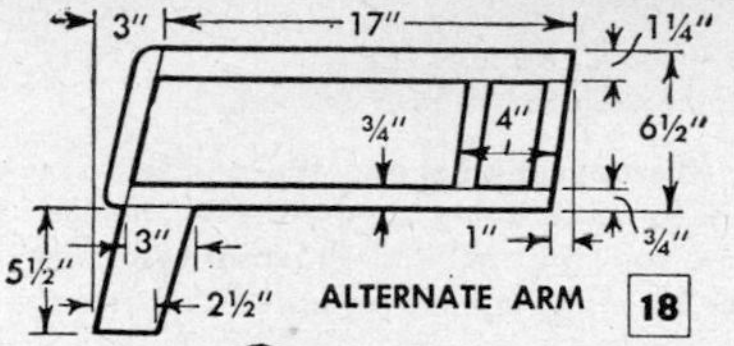

3"
17"
1¼"
¾"
4"
6½"
5½"
3"
1"
¾"
2½"

ALTERNATE ARM 18

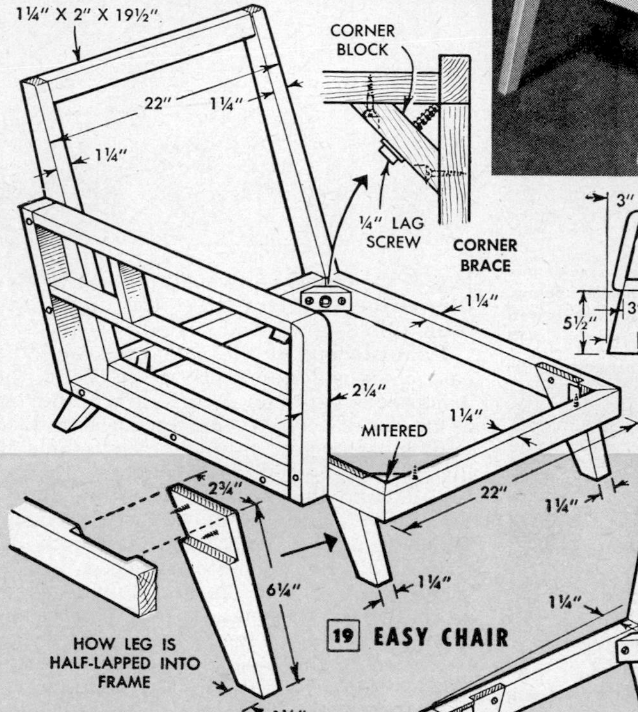

1¼" X 2" X 19½"
22"
1¼"
1¼"
CORNER BLOCK
¼" LAG SCREW
CORNER BRACE
1¼"
2¼"
1¼"
MITERED
22"
1¼"
1¼"
2¾"
6¼"
1½"
HOW LEG IS HALF-LAPPED INTO FRAME

19 EASY CHAIR

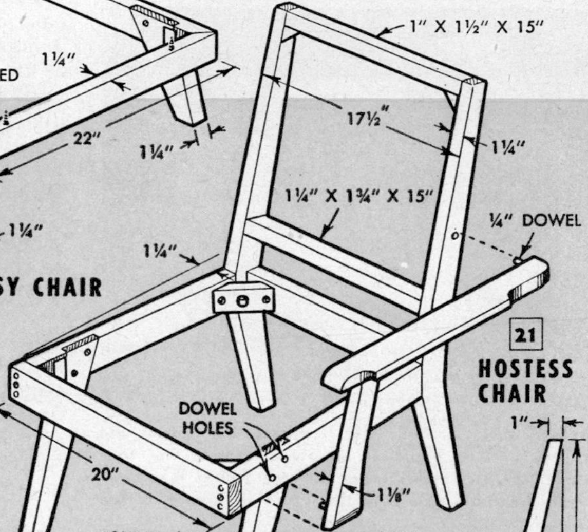

1" X 1½" X 15"
17½"
1¼"
1¼" X 1¾" X 15"
¼" DOWEL
1¼"
DOWEL HOLES
20"
1⅛"

21 HOSTESS CHAIR

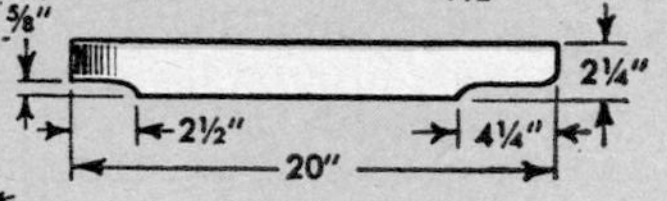

⅝"
2¼"
2½"
4¼"
20"

HOSTESS-CHAIR ARM

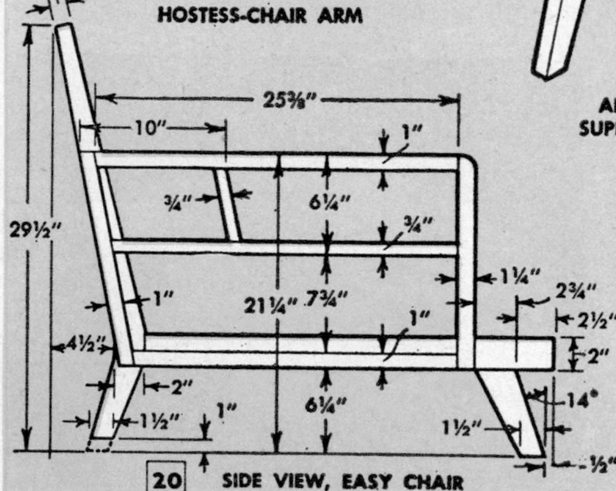

1¼"
29½"
25⅜"
10"
1"
¾"
6¼"
¾"
1¼"
2¾"
1"
21¼"
7¾"
2½"
1"
4½"
2"
2"
14°
1½"
1"
6¼"
1½"
½"

20 SIDE VIEW, EASY CHAIR

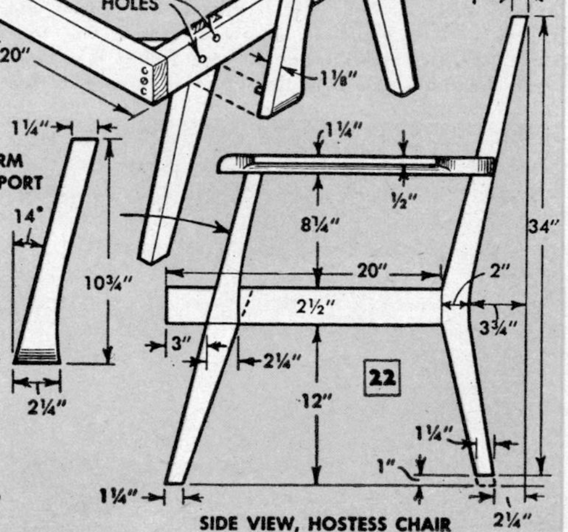

1"
1¼"
ARM SUPPORT
14°
10¾"
2¼"
1¼"
½"
8¼"
34"
20"
2"
2½"
3¾"
3"
2¼"
12"
1¼"
1"
1¼"
2¼"

22

SIDE VIEW, HOSTESS CHAIR

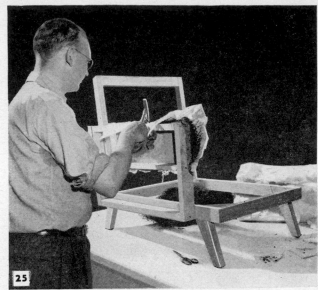

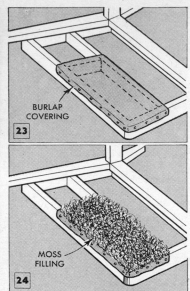

BURLAP
COVERING

23

MOSS
FILLING

24

25

Above, this operation shows the padded arm of one of the sofa units being covered with muslin. Below, pocketed coil springs sold in strip form are sewed together to make up the required-size marshall unit

26

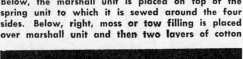

Below, the marshall unit is placed on top of the spring unit to which it is sewed around the four sides. Below, right, moss or tow filling is placed over marshall unit and then two layers of cotton

27

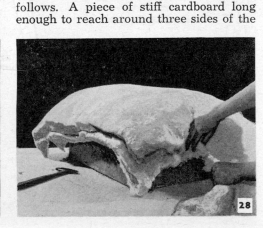

28

legs of the chairs can be cut off now to give the correct slant or after the units have been upholstered and tested.

Upholstering of the sofa units and the easy chair is done exactly alike. First, the arms are covered on the inside with burlap as in Fig. 23. Next, the burlap is padded with moss or tow filling which is held in place with long stitches through the burlap, Fig. 24, and then a layer of cotton placed over the filling is covered with muslin which is pulled firmly and tacked to the arm, Fig. 25. Edging material called "brush" is applied to the inside and outside edges of the arms. The details in Fig. 31 show how this is done. On the inside, the brush is tacked to the face of the arm on three sides so that it overhangs the padding. On the outside, the material is tacked to the edge of the arm on all four sides so it stands upright. The space around the edge of the arm between the brush trim is covered as follows. A piece of stiff cardboard long enough to reach around three sides of the arm is padded with cotton and covered with fabric. Gimp nails are used to tack the strip in place, driving them along each edge and then concealing the heads by pulling the fabric up over them. This leaves the outside of the arm which is covered similarly with a cardboard panel, tacking it in the same manner as just described.

Cushions for the seat and back of the sofa and easy chair are built up separately on flat hardwood frames, half-lapped at the corners, Fig. 32. The frames are made the same size as the over-all size of the chair frames. The seat frames require five 8-ga. sagless-type springs, 26 in. long, while the back frames take five, 12-ga. springs 16½ in. long. The springs are anchored to the front and rear edges of the frame with special clips made for the purpose. These are first nailed to the wood and then crimped over the spring wire before renailing. Note that the ends of the springs are bent back to prevent them from slipping out of the clips. In all installations, it is

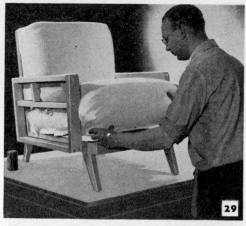

29

Above, here the seat and back cushions of the easy chair are being tested for satisfactory fit prior to covering with fabric. Screws hold cushions in place

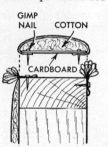

GIMP NAIL   COTTON

CARDBOARD

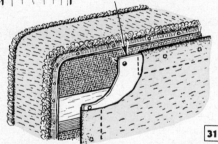

CARDBOARD

31

METHOD OF ATTACHING FABRIC TO SIDE OF CHAIR

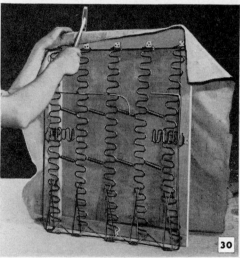

30

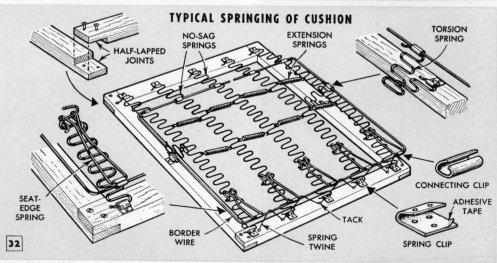

TYPICAL SPRINGING OF CUSHION

HALF-LAPPED JOINTS

NO-SAG SPRINGS

EXTENSION SPRINGS

TORSION SPRING

CONNECTING CLIP

SEAT-EDGE SPRING

ADHESIVE TAPE

BORDER WIRE

SPRING TWINE

TACK

SPRING CLIP

32

33

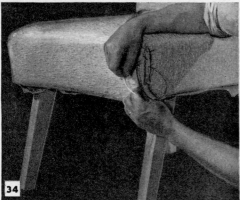

34

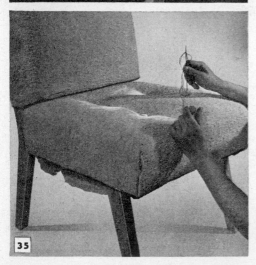

35

recommended that the direction of the bent ends be alternated. If the bent end of the first spring points to the right, the bent end of the next spring should point to the left. This permits the connecting extension springs to be applied in a straight line. The springs are applied bowed and are cross-tied with eight extension springs. Edge springs are hooked into the sagless springs across the front and these serve to support an 8-ga. border wire which forms the box shape of the spring unit. The border wire is attached to the edge springs with special clips which are crimped over the two parts. This type of clip also is used to fasten the rear edge of the border wire to the sagless springs. At each side, a torsion spring is used to support the border wire, clips being applied as before to anchor it to the wire and the wooden frame. You'll note that the border wire does not extend to the rear of the frame but stops about 8 in. or so from it. This is done to allow room for the back cushion to fit neatly into the seat cushion. Finally, the border wire across the front edge is pulled down under tension with regular spring twine and tacked securely to the wooden frame. The back cushions are sprung in exactly the same manner, the front edge of the seat becoming the top edge of the back.

The next step is to cover the spring unit with burlap as shown in Fig. 30. This is pulled firmly over the border wire and tacked to the edges of the frame. Now, the spring unit is covered with a marshall unit which is made up of a number of individual coil springs encased in cloth pockets. These are purchased in strips and you merely build up the unit to the required size by sewing them together as in Fig. 26. The seat requires a unit seven coils wide and nine coils deep, while the back takes seven wide and five deep. The completed unit is sewed to the spring unit, using a curved upholsterer's needle and sewing around the border wire and the base of each individual coil spring, Fig. 27. Next, moss or tow filling is placed on top of the marshall unit and then two layers of cotton, Fig. 28. This is followed by covering the cotton with muslin, pulling it down smoothly and tacking it to the underside of the wooden frame. Fig. 29 shows checking the cushions for fit after the muslin covering has been finished. Box corners are formed at the front corners of the seat and at the top corners of the back cushion by hand-stitching the fabric covering as shown in Fig. 34. The cushions are held in place in the chair with flat-headed screws. In the case of the seat, the screws are driven up from below in counterbored holes in the rails. The back cushion is held with four screws which are driven through holes in the back of the chair frame and capped with regular wooden screw plugs or short lengths of dowel rod. The back cushion differs from the seat in one respect. With the underside of the frame exposed, the back must be fitted with a fabric-covered cardboard panel before fastening the cushion to the chair frame.

The hostess chair is upholstered in the same general manner, except that the springing is done right on the chair frame as indicated in Fig. 37. Five 9-ga. sagless springs, 20½ in. long, are required for the seat and five 12-ga. springs, 14½ in. long, are needed for the back cushion. Also, 10 additional seat-edge springs are required as these are installed at both front and back, Fig. 37. The fabric covering is brought down over the rails of the seat and tacked to the underside. The back is covered similarly, Fig. 33. The rear of the back is enclosed with a fabric-covered panel in the same manner as previously described, nailing it with gimp nails and then pulling the material up over the heads. If padded arms are to be used on the chair, brush edging is applied around the outside edge of the arms, Fig. 16, and a cardboard panel is used on the outside.

Tufting the seat and back cushions gives them a professional touch. Four buttons are placed in the seat cushions of all the pieces and two in the back cushions. Plain wooden buttons made for this purpose are covered with scraps of fabric and then stitched through to the springs, Fig. 35. The tufts are made by pulling down on the buttons and tying the sewing twine securely to the sagless springs, Fig. 36. Finally, cambric dust covers are tacked to the underside of each seat cushion.

The lamps are detailed in Figs. 38 and 39. The table lamp features four 6-in.-sq. ceramic tiles framed in a box-shaped base. These can be purchased in any large department store and, as the exact size of the tile varies somewhat, buy them first and build the base around them. The sectional view shows how the wooden members are grooved for the tiles which are installed as the assembly progresses. Corners of the base are mitered and holes are provided for a 30-in. length of ⅛-in. threaded pipe. The exposed portion of the pipe is covered with ½-in. brass tubing as indicated. Then, with a standard cap and canopy attached to the top, a locknut concealed in the base of the lamp ties the assembly together.

The wooden column of the floor lamp, Fig. 38, is made up of two separate pieces to provide a center hole for the lamp-cord pipe. A ¼ x ½-in. groove is run lengthwise in each piece and then the two are glued and clamped together before tapering. Assembly of the top portion of the standard is shown in the detail above Fig.

36

Upholstery of the hostess chair differs from the others in that springs are fastened directly to the chair frame, instead of a separate frame. Also, seat-edge springs are placed across both front and back as indicated below. Fabric is brought down over rails and tacked to underside

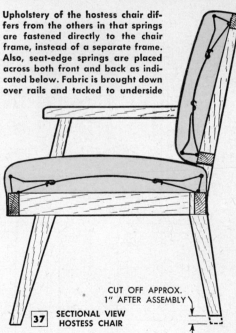

CUT OFF APPROX.
1" AFTER ASSEMBLY

37 SECTIONAL VIEW
HOSTESS CHAIR

38. The brass fixture at the top of the wooden column is not a stock item but is made up specially from lengths of brass tubing soldered together.

The fixture is designed to take a standard mogul-type socket which is screwed to the upper end of the ⅛-in. pipe. A hole is provided in the side of the fixture to accommodate the socket turn button and the top ring is fitted with three thumbscrews to support a standard 10-in. glass bowl. The base of the lamp consists of four 1¾-in.-thick pieces planed to ¾ in. at the edge and mitered at each corner. These are glued together and then a flat surface is planed at the apex of the four pieces to receive a ¾ x 2⁵⁄₁₆-in.-sq. block. Then a ½-in. hole is bored through the center and the hole is counterbored on the underside of the base to take a washer and nut. A small tapered leg is glued and screwed to each corner of the base and then the lamp column is tightened securely to the base by means of the nut in the bottom.

Plans detailing the entire living-room set are available for those who prefer to work from larger drawings.

10" GLASS BOWL

⅛" IRON PIPE

2¾" SQ.

2⅛" SQ.

¼" X 2½" SQ.

2⅛" SQ. AT TOP

3" DIA. BRASS TUBING

2½" DIA. BRASS TUBING

1" DIA. BRASS TUBING

3"

¾"

4"

4"

4¾"

¼"

38

53"

36"

TABLE LAMP

FLOOR LAMP

1½" SQ.

2¹⁵⁄₁₆" SQ.

¾"

LEG

½" DIA. BRASS TUBING

½" HOLE

⅛" IRON PIPE

1" HOLE

39

3½"

¾"

6"

1¼"

6"

¾"

1¼"

16"

¼"

6"

¾"

10½"

6½"

A

½"

⅛"

¾"

1¼"

1" HOLE, ⅞" DEEP

DETAIL A

⁵⁄₁₆"

¼"

⅝"

⁵⁄₁₆" HOLE

1⅛" SQ.

2⁵⁄₁₆" SQ.

¾"

1"

¾"

¾"

12"

16

OCCASIONAL FURNITURE

Includes a drop-leaf table, made to order for a combination living-dining room, and a sectional wall ensemble, the units of which can be interchanged to form varied groupings

Story by Wayne C. Leckey

DESIGNED as companion pieces to harmonize with the dining and living-room furniture suites presented in other sections of this book, the attractive occasional pieces as pictured here can be used to augment the other pieces or used by themselves in any particular arrangement you desire. The drop-leaf table pictured above is designed especially for a dining alcove where limited space does not permit room for even a dinette set. Such is the case in the latest trend toward eliminating a separate dining room in favor of a combination living-dining room. This table adequately fills the requirement for a piece that takes little space

1 TABLE OPEN

2 TABLE FULLY EXTENDED

against the wall when not in use, and yet has big-table capacity when needed. To seat four persons comfortably, the leaves of the table are raised to a horizontal position and the whole top is rotated 90 deg. on a center pivot. In this position, the base of the table supports the drop leaves as shown in Fig. 1. Retractable brackets in each end of the table pull out to support the leaves when the table is fully extended. A lazy-tong mechanism, taking the place of the usual extension slide, extends to permit insertion of two extra leaves, Fig. 2, providing a top surface 40 x 74 in. Suitable dining chairs for the table can be made by following the plans presented in the following section, which covers the construction of a complete dining-room suite. Actual construction of the table, detailed in Figs. 12, 13 and 14, will be explained later in this chapter.

The pieces of the functional wall ensemble pictured above are coordinated in size to fit together in a number of separate sectional arrangements in addition to the complete grouping shown. For example, the secretary, pictured in use at the bottom of

the opposite page, may be combined with an open-end bookcase at each side. Likewise, the three-shelf unit, with doors at the bottom, may be grouped in the same way. An attractive corner grouping is had by flanking the corner bookcase with end bookcases. Still another arrangement is to place the window unit between two end bookcases. These are but a few of the attractive arrangements that are possible with these sectional pieces. If desired, any one of the three basic units, namely, the secretary, three-drawer chest and two-door chest, may be used individually.

The secretary features a pull-out writing shelf which looks like a drawer when closed. The "drawer" front is hinged with special fixtures and lets down to become part of the writing surface. The secretary, like the others, is made primarily from plywood, with solid stock being used for the drawers, base and edging. The same edging which is characteristic of all the pieces previously presented in our furniture series also is used here to give a hopper-front effect and at the same time to conceal the laminations of the plywood. Figs. 3 and 4

Styled by John Bergen, noted furniture designer

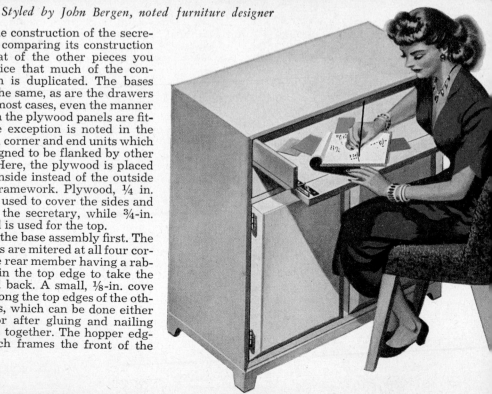

detail the construction of the secretary. In comparing its construction with that of the other pieces you will notice that much of the construction is duplicated. The bases are all the same, as are the drawers and, in most cases, even the manner in which the plywood panels are fitted. The exception is noted in the window, corner and end units which are designed to be flanked by other pieces. Here, the plywood is placed on the inside instead of the outside of the framework. Plywood, ¼ in. thick, is used to cover the sides and back of the secretary, while ¾-in. plywood is used for the top.

Make the base assembly first. The members are mitered at all four corners, the rear member having a rabbet cut in the top edge to take the plywood back. A small, ⅛-in. cove is run along the top edges of the other pieces, which can be done either before or after gluing and nailing the base together. The hopper edging which frames the front of the

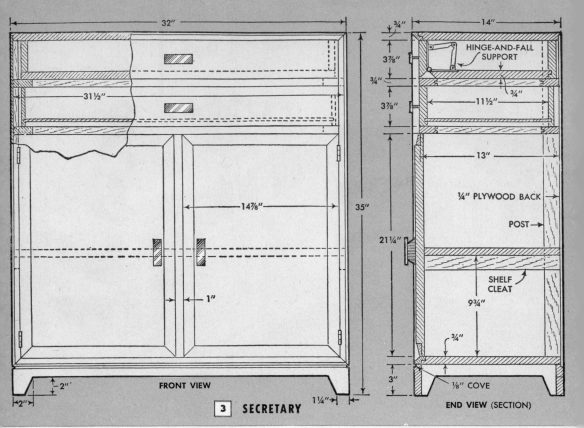

FRONT VIEW

32"
31½"
14⅞"
1"
35"
2"
2"
1¼"
3 SECRETARY

END VIEW (SECTION)

14"
¾"
3⅞"
¾"
HINGE-AND-FALL SUPPORT
11½"
¾"
3⅞"
13"
¼" PLYWOOD BACK
POST →
21¼"
SHELF CLEAT
9¾"
¾"
3"
⅛" COVE

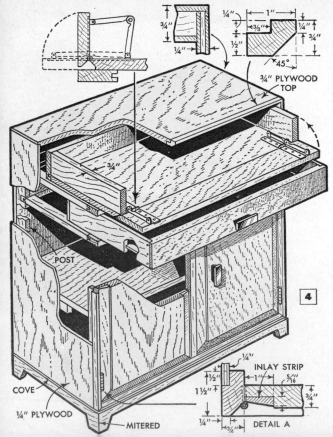

¾"
¼"
¼"
1"
⅜"
¼"
¾"
½"
¼"
45°
¾" PLYWOOD TOP

¾"

POST

4

¼"
INLAY STRIP
1½"
1"
5⁄16"
¾"
¼"
¾"
½"
COVE
¼" PLYWOOD
MITERED
DETAIL A

cabinet is shaped according to the sectional details included with the cutaway drawing, Fig. 4. The center and bottom shelves can be of plywood, or glued up from solid stock. These should be cut 31½ in. long and the front edge of the bottom shelf rabbeted for the hopper edging. Then the bottom shelf is glued and nailed to the base assembly. The ¾-in. top, including the edging, should have the same over-all measurements as the base. This is rabbeted on all four edges. Note at the ends that the rabbets are cut ¼ in. deep and to the thickness of the top ply of the wood. The top is supported at the rear corners by posts and at the front by the hopper edging. Frames for the drawer and writing shelf are typical open frames, being assembled from ¾ x 1¾-in. stock. Inner edges of the front and rear members are grooved to take tenons formed on the ends of the side members. The frames are fitted into notches cut in the rear posts and supported at the front by nailing into them through the edging rabbet. The ¼-in. side panels overlap the edge of the plywood back and are cut to fit accurately in the rabbets of the top and in the edging strips. The writing shelf is made similarly to a drawer except that the front is hinged. Note in the sectional detail, Fig. 4, that the bottom edge of the front piece is beveled to match a similar cut made on the front edge of the shelf. A stop should be fitted in the underside of the top to prevent the shelf from being pulled all the way out, and a bullet friction catch installed to hold the drop front closed. Construction of the drawer is apparent from the drawing. Plywood is best for the two doors, but solid stock can be used. In producing the raised-panel effect in plywood, an inlay strip is used to conceal the plies as indicated in detail A, Fig. 4. The door and drawer handles pictured are made up special from ¼-in. brass. Fig. 11 shows how these are soldered together T-shaped and then drilled and tapped for attaching with machine screws. The edges are rounded slightly with a fine file and then the brass is buffed to a high polish. A thin coat of clear lacquer will keep the handles bright.

The three-drawer chest is

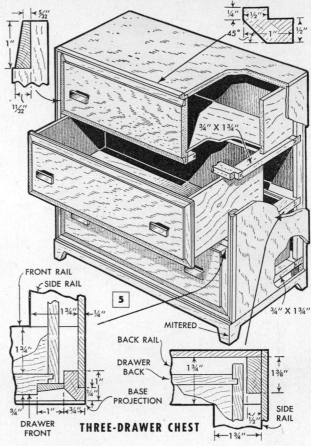

FRONT RAIL
SIDE RAIL
BACK RAIL
DRAWER BACK
BASE PROJECTION
MITERED
SIDE RAIL
DRAWER FRONT

THREE-DRAWER CHEST

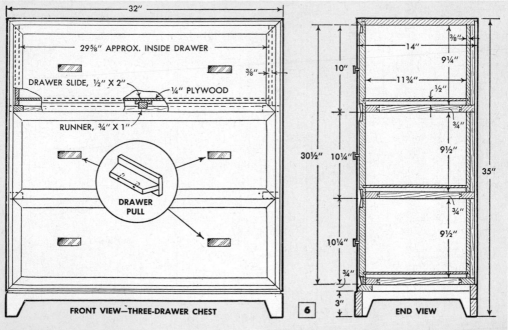

FRONT VIEW—THREE-DRAWER CHEST

6

END VIEW

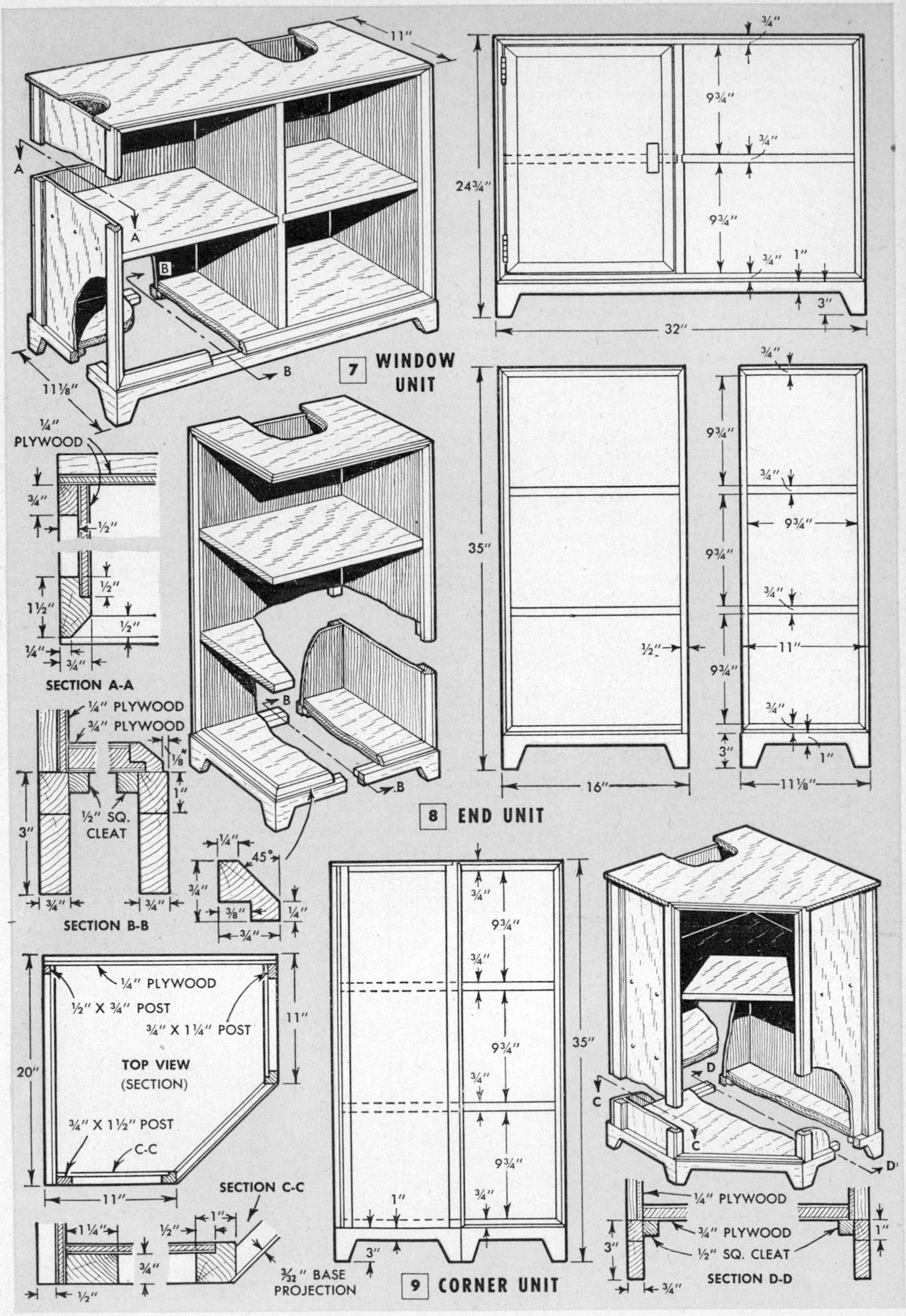

11″
A
A
B
B
11⅛″
7 WINDOW UNIT
¾″
9¾″
¾″
24¾″
9¾″
¾″
1″
3″
32″
¼″ PLYWOOD
¾″
½″
½″
1½″
½″
¼″
¾″
SECTION A-A
B
.B
¾″
9¾″
¾″
9¾″
35″
9¾″
¾″
11″
½″
9¾″
¾″
3″
1″
16″
11⅛″
8 END UNIT
¼″ PLYWOOD
¾″ PLYWOOD
⅛″
1″
3″
½″ SQ. CLEAT
¾″
¾″
SECTION B-B
¼″
45°
¾″
⅜″
¼″
¾″
¾″
9¾″
¾″
9¾″
¾″
9¾″
¾″
1″
3″
35″
9 CORNER UNIT
D
C
C
D
¼″ PLYWOOD
½″ X ¾″ POST
¾″ X 1¼″ POST
20″
11″
TOP VIEW
(SECTION)
¾″ X 1½″ POST
C-C
11″
SECTION C-C
1¼″
½″
1″
¾″
½″
3⁄32″ BASE PROJECTION
¼″ PLYWOOD
¾″ PLYWOOD
½″ SQ. CLEAT
3″
1″
¾″
SECTION D-D

basically of the same construction. The cutaway drawing in Fig. 5 and the front and side views in Fig. 6 give the necessary details. Typical chest construction is employed with frames supporting each drawer. Hopper edging is applied as explained before and the drawer fronts are inlaid around the edges. The front view, Fig. 6, details the drawer runners. The strip nailed to the frame engages a wooden channel which is glued and bradded to the bottom of the drawer. This same type of runner is used for the drawer of the secretary. The lower details, Fig. 5, show plan views of the drawer at the front and rear corners.

Window, end and corner units, Figs. 7, 8 and 9, differ basically in construction in that the plywood side panels are placed on the inside of the cabinets instead of the outside. Whether this should be done on the sides of the corner unit depends upon the grouping arrangement. If placed next to the window unit as pictured on page 19,

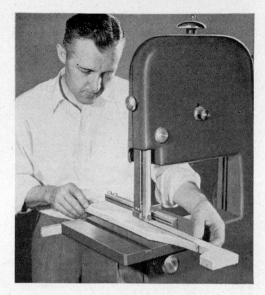

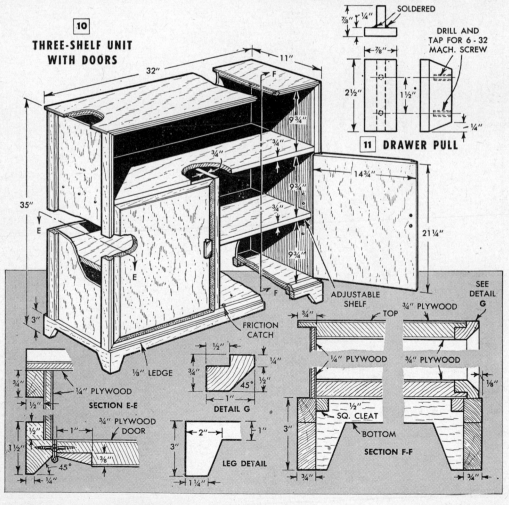

10 THREE-SHELF UNIT WITH DOORS

32″ 11″ 9¾″ ¾″ ¾″ 9¾″ ¾″ 9¾″

35″ E E F F

3″ ⅛″ LEDGE

ADJUSTABLE SHELF

FRICTION CATCH

11 DRAWER PULL

SOLDERED ⅞″ ¼″ DRILL AND TAP FOR 6-32 MACH. SCREW

2½″ ⅞″ 1½″ ¼″

14¾″

21¼″

SEE DETAIL G

¾″ PLYWOOD

¾″ PLYWOOD

¾ ¼″ PLYWOOD ¼″ PLYWOOD

¾″ PLYWOOD

¾″ PLYWOOD ⅛″

TOP

½″ SQ. CLEAT

3″

BOTTOM

SECTION F-F

¾″ ¾″

SECTION E-E

¾″ ¼″ PLYWOOD ½″

½″ ¼″ ½″ 45° 1″

DETAIL G

¾″ PLYWOOD DOOR

½″ 1″

1½″ ⅜″

45°

¼″

2″ 1″

3″

LEG DETAIL

1¼″

23

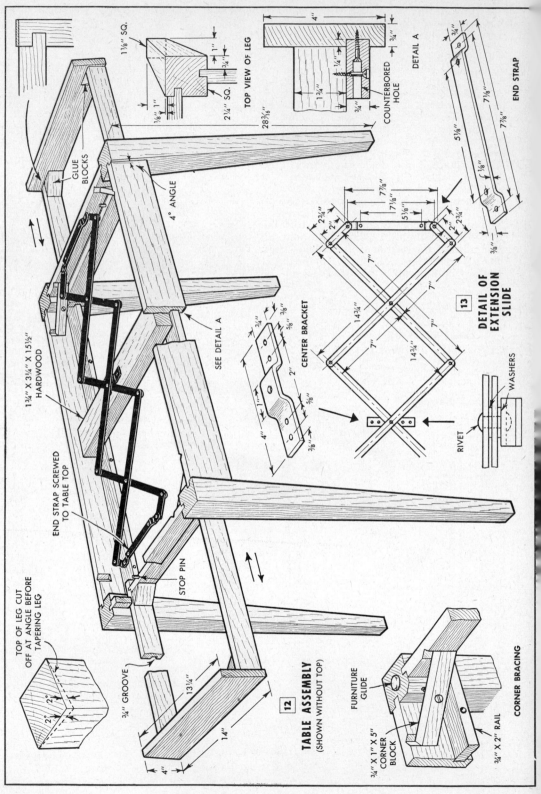

1⅛″ SQ.

1″

¾″

⅛″ 1″

2¼″ SQ.

TOP VIEW OF LEG

4″

¾″

¼″

1¾″

COUNTERBORED HOLE

¾″

DETAIL A

28³⁄₁₆″

¾″

7⅛″

5⅝″

¹⁄₁₆″

7⅞″

END STRAP

⅜″

4° ANGLE

GLUE BLOCKS

1¾″ X 3¼″ X 15½″ HARDWOOD

END STRAP SCREWED TO TABLE TOP

SEE DETAIL A

STOP PIN

7⅞″

5⅝″

1⅞″

2¾″

2″

2″

2¾″

7″

7″

14¾″

14¾″

7″

7″

¾″

⅜″

2″

1″

⅜″

4″

⅜″

5⁄₈″

CENTER BRACKET

13

DETAIL OF EXTENSION SLIDE

WASHERS

RIVET

TOP OF LEG CUT OFF AT ANGLE BEFORE TAPERING LEG

2° 2°

¾″ GROOVE

13¼″

14″

4″

12

TABLE ASSEMBLY
(SHOWN WITHOUT TOP)

FURNITURE GLIDE

¾″ X 1″ X 5″ CORNER BLOCK

¾″ X 2″ RAIL

CORNER BRACING

24

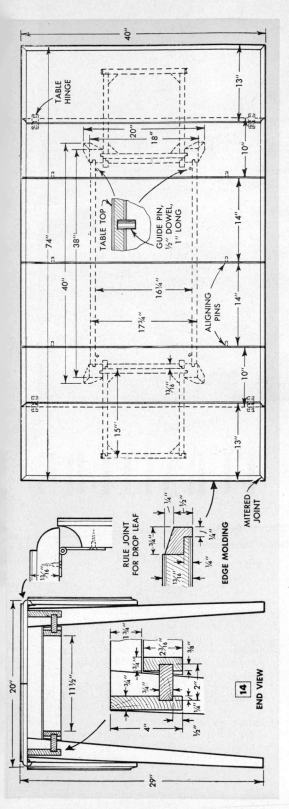

the plywood will have to be applied to the outside. Remember in cutting duplicate parts that the end units will have to be right and left-hand assemblies.

The three-shelf unit, shown fitted with doors in Fig. 10, can be made entirely open, in which case the partition is eliminated and the middle shelf brought out even with the one above it. The sectional details accompanying the cutaway drawing in Fig. 10 show how the ¼-in.-plywood side panels fit in rabbets cut on the inner edge of the hopper edging.

The drop-leaf table, Figs. 12, 13 and 14, has flared, tapered legs which assume the correct slant by making a compound cut at the top and bottom. This is done before tapering the legs in one of two ways: Either set the miter gauge 2 deg. and tilt the saw table 2 deg., or, support the work horizontally on one corner and make the cut with the gauge set at 2 deg. and the table at 90 degs. Only the adjacent inner faces of each leg are tapered, as indicated in the top-view detail, Fig. 12. The leg tapers from a full 2¼-in. square at the top to 1⅛ in. at the bottom. The two side aprons of the table are angle-cut to match the slant of the legs and the ends are rabbeted to fit open mortises cut in the tapered faces of the legs. Note in detail A that the side aprons are grooved along the lower edge to take strips on which the retractable end brackets slide. Half-width aprons are fitted across the ends of the table and then corner blocks are applied in the manner shown in the corner-bracing detail. Notice that a furniture glide is driven into the top of each leg to make the table top pivot easily. The pull-out brackets are made to slide under the end aprons and are corner-blocked for rigidity. A stop pin is provided at each side.

The lazy-tong extension slide is assembled from flat iron and riveted together as indicated in Fig. 13. This is pivoted to a center bracket which in turn is screwed to a hardwood center member installed between the side aprons. Each end of the extension slide is screwed to the underside of the two top leaves of the table. Fig. 14 shows an end view and a plan view of the table top including the two extra leaves. Outer egdes of the plywood top are fitted with a mitered edge molding set in a rabbet, and a rule joint is run on the drop leaves for hinging them with regular drop-leaf hinges. When cutting the rule joints, be sure to allow sufficient clearance between the male and female members so that the joints will not bind after the finish has been applied to the surfaces. Note in the plan view that steel dowel pins forced in blind holes in the underside of the top align and guide the table top when extending it for inserting extra leaves.

HERE'S YOUR
DINING-ROOM FURNITURE

This smart-looking seven-piece dining-room group—one of a special series of fine furniture for the entire house— is our answer to the tremendous response received for more home-built furniture of good, practical design

By Wayne C. Leckey   Part I

W E ASKED if you wanted dining-room furniture and the answer was overwhelmingly yes—so here is a suite for your approval. Designed expressly for the craftsman working with small home-workshop tools, this group features the same simplicity of line and ease of construction characteristic of the living-room and occasional furniture presented in previous sections of this book. The complete ensemble, which is sufficient to furnish a full-size dining room, consists of seven pieces, including an extension table for eight, four chairs, a credenza and a china cabinet. However, if you haven't room for the entire group, you can eliminate the china cabinet

or, in the case of an exceptionally small dinette or dining alcove, the base section of the two-piece china cabinet can be built and used alone as a server to take the place of the large credenza. The table is designed to take an extra leaf which permits serving as many as eight persons, and the seats of the upholstered chairs are spring-filled for real added comfort, a feature not found in all commercial suites.

This, the first of a two-part story, details the construction of the dining-room table and chairs. Part II will cover making the credenza and china cabinet. For the craftsman who prefers to work from plans larger than magazine size, we have prepared a

The beautiful credenza shown above provides abundant storage space. Matching end compartments contain shelf area for glassware, while the center opens to reveal two drawers for silver and shelf space for linens

Most of the work is done on circular saw

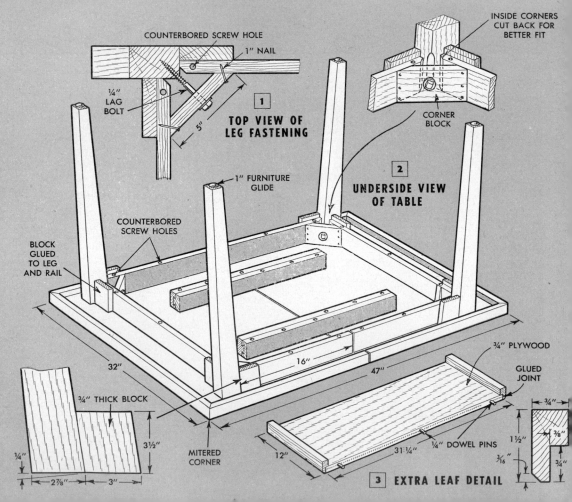

COUNTERBORED SCREW HOLE

1" NAIL

¼" LAG BOLT

5"

1

TOP VIEW OF LEG FASTENING

INSIDE CORNERS CUT BACK FOR BETTER FIT

CORNER BLOCK

2

UNDERSIDE VIEW OF TABLE

1" FURNITURE GLIDE

COUNTERBORED SCREW HOLES

BLOCK GLUED TO LEG AND RAIL

32"

16"

47"

¾" PLYWOOD

GLUED JOINT

¾"

¾" THICK BLOCK

3½"

¾"

2⅞"

3"

MITERED CORNER

12"

31¼"

¼" DOWEL PINS

1½"

⅜"

3/16"

¾"

3 **EXTRA LEAF DETAIL**

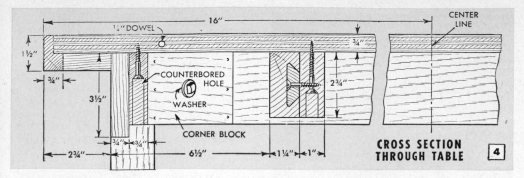

CROSS SECTION THROUGH TABLE

16"
¼" DOWEL
¾"
CENTER LINE
1½"
¾"
3½"
COUNTERBORED HOLE
WASHER
2¾"
CORNER BLOCK
2¾"
¾" ¾"
6½"
1¼" 1"

4

set of large blueprints which can be obtained from our book department.

Construction of the table is detailed in Figs. 1 to 7 inclusive. Like the living-room suite, which incorporated the use of both plywood and solid stock, the table top and extra leaf are cut from ¾-in. plywood to save the work of gluing up solid stock. All the rest of the table is made of solid material. A ¾ x 1½-in. facing or edging strip, mitered at the corners and rabbeted on the back, is glued and nailed to the edge of the plywood to conceal the laminations. The top, of course, consists of two separate sections having the conventional aligning pins and holes in the edges at the joint. The sectional view in Fig. 4 indicates the position of the legs and the slides and also shows how the 3-in. aprons, or rails, are screwed to the underside of the top. The ends of the end aprons are cut off squarely, while the two-piece side ones, which butt together at the joint, are cut at an angle to match the slant of the tapered legs. Locate the side aprons 3½ in. in from the edge of the top and the end ones 6 in. inward. Then glue and screw them securely to the plywood.

The tapered legs, Fig. 7, are cut from 1¾-in. stock. Note in the detail at the left of Fig. 3, that the tops of the legs are cut at a ¼-in. angle. Each leg is placed in the corner formed by the aprons and drawn up rigidly with lag screws. Corner blocks are drilled for the screws and then glued and nailed to the aprons as shown in Fig. 1. The lag screws are the only fastenings the legs require and, if the legs loosen with use, it is easy to make them rigid simply by drawing the lag screws tighter. Additional rigidity is had by the eight overlay blocks which are applied to the face of the aprons at the corners. Note that the blocks at the sides of the table are fitted flush with the face of the legs.

Figs. 4, 5 and 6 show how the dovetail joint is formed in the table slide. The

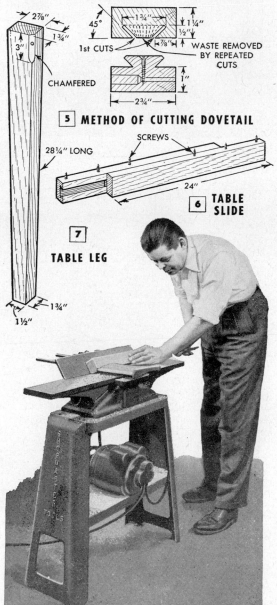

2⅞"
1¾"
3"
CHAMFERED

45°
1¾"
1¼"
½"
⅞"
1st CUTS
WASTE REMOVED BY REPEATED CUTS
1"
2¾"

5 METHOD OF CUTTING DOVETAIL

SCREWS
28¼" LONG
24"
6 TABLE SLIDE

7
TABLE LEG
1¾"
1½"

tenon on the male member of the slide consists of a separate strip shaped as shown and screwed to the face of the piece. This strip engages a matching groove in the female member. The groove can be cut on the circular saw by first making the two 45-deg. outside cuts and then removing the waste portion with repeated cuts, varying the angle of the blade slightly each time. The male members of the slide are glued and screwed to one half of the table and the female members to the other, using three screws in counterbored holes. A coating of wax will make the slides work smoothly.

Chair-frame construction is detailed in Figs. 9 to 12 inclusive. Whether four or more chairs are built, at least one should be made a guest, or host, chair by adding arms as shown in Fig. 8 and increasing the width of the front and back, Fig. 11. The over-all height and depth remain the same. Identical parts can be mass-produced to save time by using stops and jigs on the saw. As the legs are the only part of the

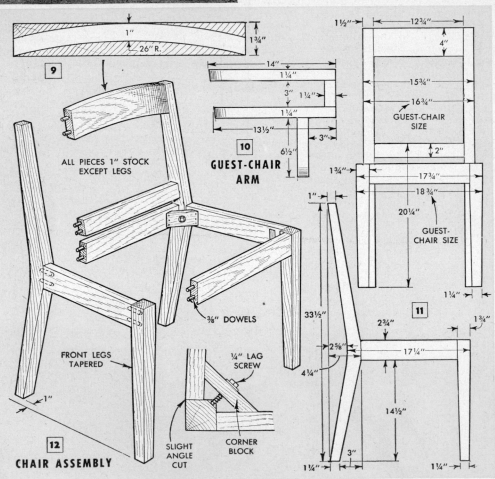

13 WEBBING ENDS DOUBLE-TACKED

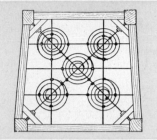

14 SPRINGS CROSSTIED LIKE THIS

15 BURLAP IS TACKED OVER SPRINGS

16 THEN WELT IS TACKED TO EDGE

frame exposed, the rest of the assembly can be rough. Note in Fig. 12 that all members are doweled and each corner of the seat is braced with lag screws the same as the table. The curved back rail is bandsawed from a piece 1¾ x 4 in., Fig. 9, while the front legs are tapered on all four faces from a point 2¾ in. from the top. The exposed part of the legs should be finished before upholstering.

Upholstering the chairs: The first step is to tack furniture webbing to the seat bottom, Fig. 13. Six strips are interlaced and stretched tautly in the manner indicated in the detail to the right of Fig. 16. The ends of the webbing are left about 1 in. long for folding back and double-tacking. Five No. 1 plain-end coil springs are used in the seat. These are placed in position, tack-sewed to the webbing, and then tied and crosstied to the bottom of the seat rails as shown in Fig. 14. The dots in the drawing indicate knots. The springs are compressed so that the center one is about 1½ in. above the top of the seat. The spring twine is brought down through holes punched in the webbing and tacked securely to the underside of the rails. Next, the springs are covered with burlap, Fig. 15. The edges are tacked, folded over and retacked, and then a welt edging is tacked around the outer edge on three sides, Fig. 16. The welt used here is the same as used later on the back, Fig. 25, except that being hidden it can be made up of scrap material wrapped around a length of ¼-in. rope. Hair, tow or moss filling is added next, Fig. 17. This is held in place by tack-sewing it to the burlap. A layer of cotton is applied over the filling so it covers the sides of the seat rails, Fig. 18. After this, the whole job is covered with the finished fabric, and the completed seat should look like Fig. 19. Patterns for the seat covering as well as the rest of the chair are given in Fig. 24. When completed, the underside of the seat is covered with black cambric, the edges being folded under.

Two strips of webbing are tacked to the back, Fig. 20, and then it is covered with burlap, moss and finally cotton. The cotton is brought around the sides and over the top

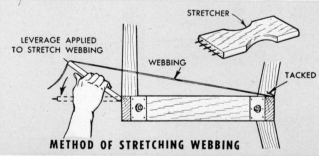

LEVERAGE APPLIED TO STRETCH WEBBING

STRETCHER

WEBBING

TACKED

METHOD OF STRETCHING WEBBING

17 MOSS FILLING COMES NEXT

18 THEN IS COVERED WITH COTTON

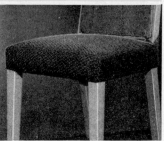

19 AND HERE'S THE COMPLETED SEAT

and the lower edge is folded up under the moss. Note in applying the covering to the front of the back that the fabric is first pulled through and tacked to the face of the rear seat rail, Fig. 25. Before the back covering is applied, a welt made of the finished fabric is tacked to three sides. Then a strip of cardboard, ½-in. wide, is cut to fit across the top between the welt at the sides. The fabric is tacked at the top first, driving the tacks through the cardboard strip as in Fig. 25. With the top tacked, the fabric is brought down over the back, the edges folded under and hand-stitched to the welt. Blued gimp nails are used in tacking the covering where it passes over the exposed surface of the legs. This method is called blind tacking. In addition to concealing the tacks, the cardboard strip provides a firm edge which avoids irregular pleats when the cloth is pulled taut.

20 FIRST, WEBBING IS APPLIED TO THE BACK

21 THEN WEBBING IS COVERED WITH BURLAP

22 LAYER OF MOSS IS TACK-SEWED TO BURLAP

23 COTTON IS ADDED NEXT, THEN THE FABRIC

24 PATTERNS

These fabric patterns were taken from the actual covering on one of the chairs and are somewhat approximate in size. While over-all measurements are ample, the various cuts and folds indicated should be made while fitting to avoid an error

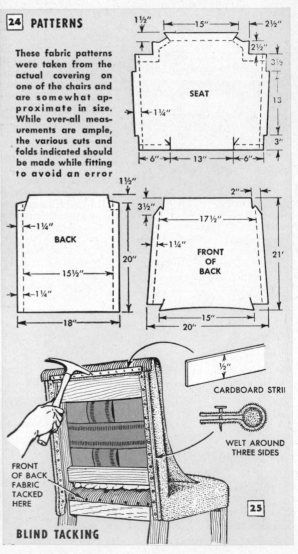

CARDBOARD STRIP

WELT AROUND THREE SIDES

FRONT OF BACK FABRIC TACKED HERE

25

BLIND TACKING

By Benj. Nielsen

Interlocking
WASTEBASKET

Painted in traditional red or black and decorated in gold, this intriguing Chinese wastebasket, with its interlocking corners, makes you wonder how it fits together. It consists of 18 slats, 5/16 in. thick, 14 of which are made 3 in. wide and four 1½ in., all being notched as indicated in the half patterns shown. Note that 10 of the 3-in. slats are beveled on both edges, whereas the others are beveled on just one edge. The basket is built up by fitting a plywood bottom into grooves run on the inside of three of the bottom slats. When all slats are interlocked, the two top half slats are held with brads

BOTTOM
¼" X 8⅞" X 8⅞"

¼"

SECTION AA

1½"

5/16"

¾"

A

A

BOTTOM PIECE
2 REQD.

1½"

5/16"

¾"

5/16"

TOP PIECE
2 REQD.

SLIGHT ANGLE

25°

5"

3"

5/16"

1 7/16"

5/16"

14 REQD.

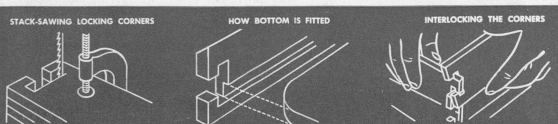

STACK-SAWING LOCKING CORNERS   HOW BOTTOM IS FITTED   INTERLOCKING THE CORNERS

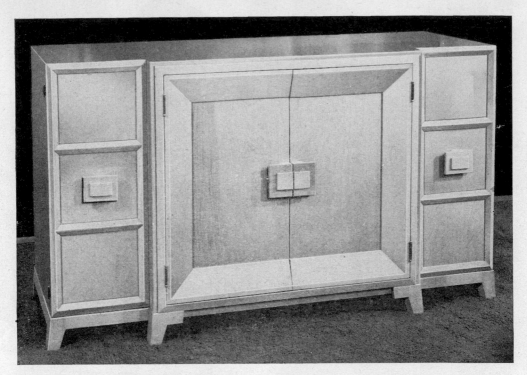

Part II

WITH THE table and chairs completed as detailed in Part I, you should be ready to tackle the more pretentious pieces of the dining-room group — the credenza and the china cabinet. Construction of the credenza is fairly simple as revealed in the cutaway drawing in Fig. 28. Over-all dimensions for this piece are given in Fig. 26, and a view of the interior, Fig. 27, shows how the doors are hinged, where friction catches are installed and how finger pockets in the rails are provided to facilitate

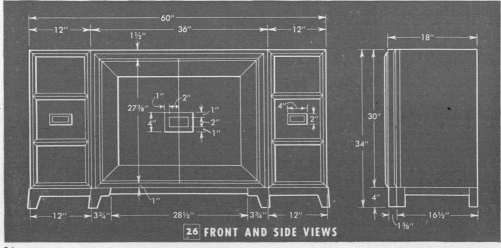

26 FRONT AND SIDE VIEWS

removal of the two silverware drawers.

Start the credenza by making the base framework. Each end is made up exactly the same, right and left hand, and then joined together with front and rear members. Section A-A in Fig. 28 gives the sizes of these members and shows how they are screwed together. Note that the ¾ x 1½-in. strip placed on edge runs the full length of the base and is glued and doweled to the two rear legs. All legs are the same size and shape, six being required, three of which are made for the right side and three for the left. All are doweled to the rails. Note that the outside faces of the end rails are beveled to match the flare of the legs. Section D-D shows how intermediate rails are rabbeted along one edge to receive ¼-in. plywood bottoms. Cleats are fitted on the three other rails to support the plywood. Center legs of the credenza are doweled to the face of the front rails 12 in. in from the corner. Then, the 1 x 1⅛-in. strip is screwed to the projecting ends of the rails and small overlay blocks are used to conceal the screwheads. Section A-A shows how the back rail is built up of two additional pieces, both being the same length and set between the intermediate rails.

Next, the side members of the end compartments are installed. These are cut to size from ¾-in. plywood. The upper ends of the outside panels are mitered 45 deg. while the lower ends are trimmed off squarely and bored for three ¼-in. dowels, which are located in the base to bring the outer panels flush with the rail. The rear edges of the two outer panels are rabbeted for a ¼-in. plywood back. The inner panels of each compartment are made ¾

in. shorter than the outer ones and narrower to permit covering the plies of the wood with a ¾ x 1⅝-in. strip of solid stock as detailed in section B-B. This strip is edge-glued and may be doweled for additional strength. The two panels of each unit are held together at the top with a frame of ¾ x 1½-in. stock. Front and rear pieces of the frame are grooved on the inside edges for tenons on the sidepieces. The frame is screwed in place through the edge so it is even with the bottom of the miter and flush with the top of the inner

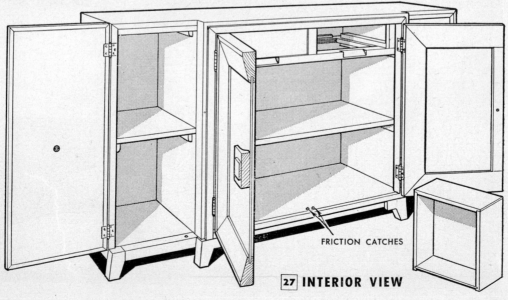

FRICTION CATCHES

27 INTERIOR VIEW

35

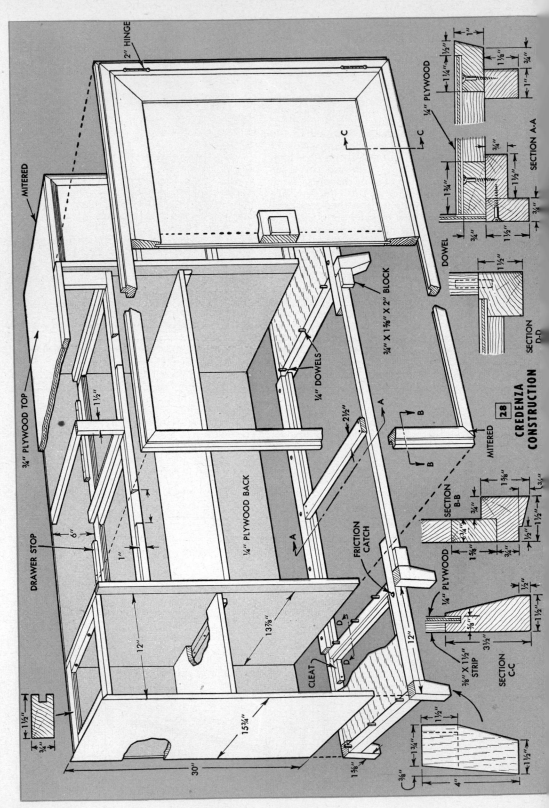

2" HINGE

MITERED

¾" PLYWOOD TOP

DRAWER STOP

¼" PLYWOOD BACK

DRAWER STOP

6"

1½"

1"

1½"

¾"

12"

13⅞"

15¾"

30"

⅝"

1⅝"

1¾"

4"

1½"

1½"

C

C

A

A

B

B

D

D

¾" X 1⅝" X 2" BLOCK

¼" DOWELS

2½"

FRICTION CATCH

CLEAT

¾" X 1½" STRIP

MITERED

12"

SECTION A-A

¼" PLYWOOD

1"

½"

1¼"

1⅛"

¾"

1"

¾"

1¾"

1½"

¾"

¾"

1½"

DOWEL

SECTION D-D

1½"

SECTION B-B

1⅝"

¾"

¾"

1⅝"

¾"

¾"

¼" PLYWOOD

1⅝"

½"

1½"

SECTION C-C

½"

⅝"

3½"

1½"

¼" PLYWOOD

28

CREDENZA CONSTRUCTION

36

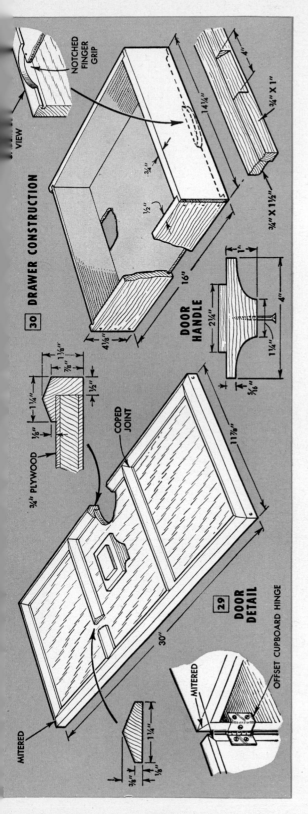

DRAWER CONSTRUCTION

NOTCHED FINGER GRIP

VIEW

30

¾″ X 1″

4″

14¼″

¾″

½″

¾″ X 1½″

16″

4⅛″

DOOR HANDLE

2¼″

4″

1¼″

1¾″

1″

5/16″

¾″ PLYWOOD

1¼″

1⅜″

⅞″

½″

⅛″

COPED JOINT

11⅞″

29

DOOR DETAIL

30″

MITERED

MITERED

1¼″

⅛″

⅜″

OFFSET CUPBOARD HINGE

panel. The plywood back is added next to strengthen the assembly. This is nailed into the rabbets of the outer panels, to the edge of the inner panels and to the framing at the top and bottom.

Next comes the top. This is cut 15¾ in. wide and is mitered at each end to make a perfectly fitting joint with the end panels. As in the case of the inner panels, a ¾ x 1⅝-in. strip of solid stock is edge-glued to the top to build it out flush with the sides. With this done, the center door molding is applied. Sections A-A and B-B give the size of the molding. The side and top members are rabbeted on the outer edge to fit over the edge of the top and inner panels, while the bottom member is rabbeted to take a ¼-in. plywood bottom panel. Facing edges of the molding are beveled according to the sectional views and mitered to fit perfectly at the corners. Note, however, that the center shelf and the drawer frame should be installed before the molding is applied.

The drawer frame is made similarly to the frames at the top of the end units. Drawer runners are installed in the center and at each side after the frame is in place. Note that the front edge of the frame is faced with a hardwood strip which is notched at a 45-deg. angle to provide a finger pocket for each drawer. While the dimension for this is missing in Fig. 28, it is included in Fig. 30. The center doors are built up according to section C-C. They can be made in one piece by framing ¼-in. plywood with a heavy molding grooved to fit over the edge and then sawing in half. A ⅜ x 1½-in. strip is used to reinforce the plywood along each side of the saw cut. Construction of the doors for the end units is detailed in Fig. 29. Plywood is framed with a rabbeted molding to conceal the laminations, and overlay strips, coped at the ends, are surface-glued to the plywood to divide the doors into three equal panels. Regular offset cupboard hinges are used on the end doors, while 3-in., loose-pin hinges are used on the center doors.

The china cabinet consists of two separate units which are held together at the back with a cleat. If space is so limited that you can accommodate neither the large credenza nor the complete china cabinet, just the base of the latter can be built and used as a small server. Fig. 31 shows the general construction of both units of the cabinet. Top, sides, back and dust panels of the lower unit are ¼-in. plywood. Top and bottom frames are joined at the back with ¾ x 1¾-in. posts which are notched for the shelves and two drawer frames. Fig. 32

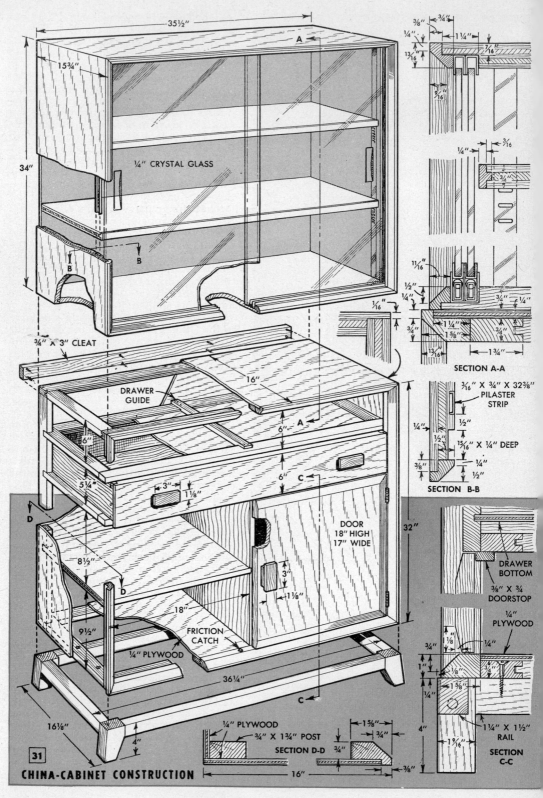

35½"

15¾"

A

¼" CRYSTAL GLASS

34"

B

B

B

¾" X 3" CLEAT

DRAWER GUIDE

16"

6"

A

6"

6"

5¼"

C

3"

1⅛"

D

DOOR 18" HIGH 17" WIDE

32"

D

8½"

3"

9½"

1⅛"

18"

FRICTION CATCH

¼" PLYWOOD

36¼"

C

16⅛"

¼" PLYWOOD

¾" X 1¾" POST

SECTION D-D

4"

1⅝"

¾"

¾"

16"

⅜"

4"

31 CHINA-CABINET CONSTRUCTION

3/8"   3/4"

¼"

1¼"

1/16"

13/16"

9/16"

SECTION A-A

¼"

3/16"

¾"

¼"

11/16"

½"

¼"

1/16"

1¼"

¾"

¾"

¼"

3/4"

1⅝"

13/16"

1¾"

3/16" X ¾" X 32⅜" PILASTER STRIP

¼"

½"

½"

15/16" X ¼" DEEP

⅜"

¼"

½"

SECTION B-B

DRAWER BOTTOM

⅜" X ¾" DOORSTOP

¼" PLYWOOD

¾"

1/8"

¼"

1"

1⅝"

3/4"

¼"

1⅝"

4"

1 9/16"

1¼" X 1½" RAIL

SECTION C-C

shows how the drawer frames are assembled. The top and bottom frames are supported at the front by a rabbeted molding which is mitered and assembled as a picture frame and then glued to the front edges of the frames at top and bottom. Side and top panels fit the rabbeted molding as shown in section D-D. Section C-C shows how the bottom frame is screwed to the base. Note that the top panel is rabbeted at each end to overlap the side panels. Drawers are assembled as in Fig. 30 and made to fit the openings. A grooved runner which rides on the guide is nailed to the underside of each drawer. Fig. 34 shows the simple wooden drawer pull. If desired, a silverware drawer can be included, Fig. 33. A bevel is run around the outer edges of the doors ¼ in. deep and 1⅛ in. wide to give a raised panel effect.

The top unit of the cabinet is made like a box from ¾-in. plywood. Sections A-A and B-B show how the pieces are rabbeted at the front edge to receive a molding which covers the laminations. Note that the rabbets at the top and bottom are made wide enough to house a standard showcase door track (see section A-A) and that rabbets also are made along the sidepieces to provide end grooves for the sliding glass doors. Note in section B-B that a groove is run at the front and back edges of the sidepieces for a standard adjustable shelf pilaster. In ordering glass panels for the doors, notice in section A-A that they must be short enough to permit inserting in the top track and then down into the lower one. Use crystal glass as it is less expensive. Any glass shop can grind the finger grips.

The china cabinet makes the seven-piece group complete. Featuring sliding glass doors, it's designed as two separate units to simplify moving and to permit base alone to be built and used as dinette server

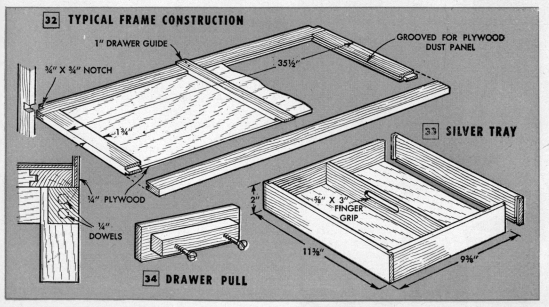

32 **TYPICAL FRAME CONSTRUCTION**

1" DRAWER GUIDE

GROOVED FOR PLYWOOD DUST PANEL

¾" X ¾" NOTCH

35½"

1¾"

33 **SILVER TRAY**

¼" PLYWOOD

¼" DOWELS

2"

⅝" X 3" FINGER GRIP

11⅜"

9⅜"

34 **DRAWER PULL**

Here is a bedroom suite whose beauty lies in modern lines matched by simplified construction appealing to any craftsman

Furniture for

Part I

PICTURE in your home this beautiful bedroom ensemble in honey maple, limed oak or rich walnut and then try to talk your way out of building it. Mom will want it by tomorrow, and if there is a teen-age daughter in your home she will say, "It's simply out of this world." Designed for flexibility the pieces are functional and can be arranged, re-arranged and interchanged to her heart's content.

All pieces are coordinated in size to fit together in sectional groups—chest, night stands and bed are all the same height. The group features a most practical bed which incorporates built-in storage space in the headboard. The front of it opens wide to reveal a spacious compartment for extra bedding and a roomy drawer pulls out at

Your Bedroom

each end of the headboard to provide storage for shoes. The chest-on-chest unit can be stacked to serve as a five-drawer highboy, or a pair of base units can be built and placed end-to-end under a large mirror to obtain the popular Mr. and Mrs. dresser. A novel three-piece vanity consists of two twin end units bridged with a separate top unit which opens to expose a cosmetic compartment and make-up mirror.

A product of a basement shop, the original furniture was built with the power tools shown. Only two tools, a saw and jointer, actually are required as the construction involves just simple,

Right, edges of the plywood are mitered with the saw table tilted at a 45-deg. angle and planed accurately on the jointer to obtain a perfect fit

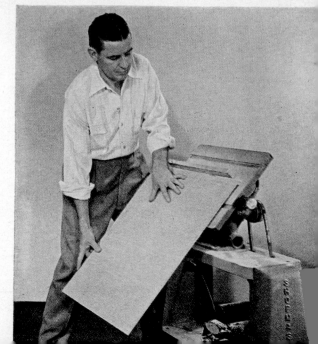

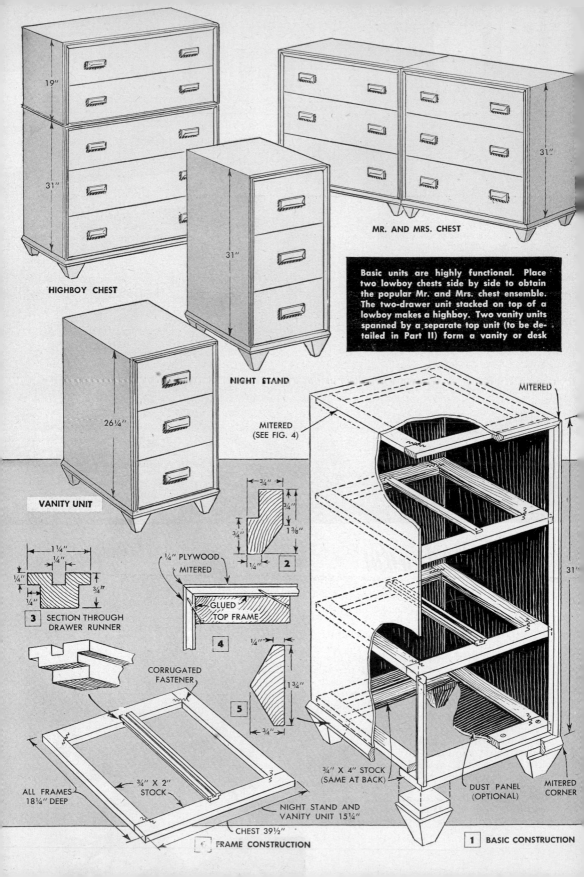

HIGHBOY CHEST

19"

31"

MR. AND MRS. CHEST

31"

31"

NIGHT STAND

Basic units are highly functional. Place two lowboy chests side by side to obtain the popular Mr. and Mrs. chest ensemble. The two-drawer unit stacked on top of a lowboy makes a highboy. Two vanity units spanned by a separate top unit (to be detailed in Part II) form a vanity or desk

VANITY UNIT

26¼"

MITERED
(SEE FIG. 4)

MITERED

¾"
¾"
¾"
1⅜"
¼"
2

¼" PLYWOOD
MITERED

1¼"
¼"
¼"
¾"
¼"

3 SECTION THROUGH DRAWER RUNNER

GLUED
TOP FRAME

4

¼"
1¾"
¾"
5

CORRUGATED
FASTENER

¾" X 2"
STOCK

ALL FRAMES
18¼" DEEP

NIGHT STAND AND
VANITY UNIT 15¼"

CHEST 39½"

FRAME CONSTRUCTION

¾" X 4" STOCK
(SAME AT BACK)

DUST PANEL
(OPTIONAL)

MITERED
CORNER

31"

1 BASIC CONSTRUCTION

straight cuts in dimensional stock and incorporates the use of plywood to simplify the work.

Basic construction of the night stands, chests and vanity units is exactly the same. It's merely a case of increasing the over-all height and width as given for each respective cabinet. Fig. 1 shows the extreme simplicity of construction. Each unit, with the exception of the two-drawer chest, requires three drawer frames and a top frame, four in all, which are made exactly alike as detailed in Fig. 6. Pine or other softwood will do for the frames, although the front rail of each frame can be of hardwood, if you wish. The top frame is of ½-in. stock while the others are ¾-in., and if the bottom frame is to be fitted with a dust panel, a groove is centered in the edge of the members to take a ¼-in. plywood panel. Otherwise, the frame pieces are merely butted, glued and joined together with corrugated fasteners.

The next step is to glue and screw the bottom frame to two ¾ x 4-in. base pieces. These pieces, which are placed across the front and back, are made the same length as the frame. Note that at the front the frame is placed 1⅛ in. in from the edge, while at the back the frame is glued flush with the edge of the base piece. Now, a 1¾-in. molding, Fig. 5, is mitered and glued to the edges of the base pieces so that it is flush with their top surfaces. The molding along the sides is cut ¼ in. longer than the depth of the base to allow for a ¼-in. plywood back. Glue blocks along the sides, plus screws driven at an angle through the edges of the base pieces from the inside, are used to anchor the molding.

The edging which conceals the laminated edges of the plywood at the front is ripped from ¾-in. stock according to Fig. 2. This is mitered and glued together as a separate assembly. The top piece of the edging is cut ½ in. longer than the width of the frame to allow for the side panels. Glue the pieces together on a flat surface and place a temporary brace across the bottom. Next, the top frame is glued to the edging. The frame is kept flush with the rabbeted edge and is fastened with long screws driven through the edge of the frame from the inside. Now, you are ready to attach the edging-and-frame assembly to the base, but first the back panel should be made ready as this is installed at the same time. The plywood back panel is made the same width as the frames and is cut ¼ in. less than the length of the edging. Nail the panel to the back edges of the top and bottom frames and then coat the ends of the edging strips with glue and clamp to the base with bar clamps. After the glue has dried, drill a pilot hole up into the end of each strip and drive a 1½-in. No. 9 flat-headed screw. The re-

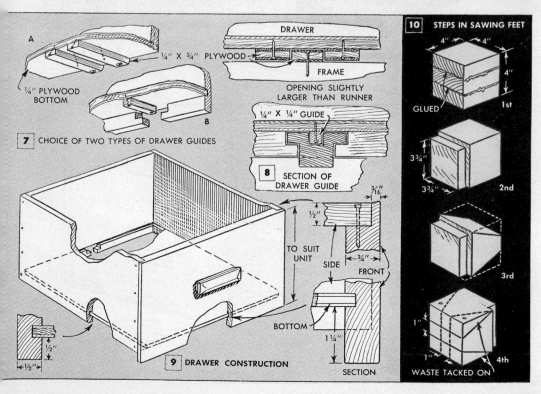

7 CHOICE OF TWO TYPES OF DRAWER GUIDES

A

¼″ X ¾″ PLYWOOD

¼″ PLYWOOD BOTTOM

B

DRAWER

FRAME

OPENING SLIGHTLY LARGER THAN RUNNER

¼″ X ¼″ GUIDE

8 SECTION OF DRAWER GUIDE

TO SUIT UNIT

SIDE

FRONT

BOTTOM

9 DRAWER CONSTRUCTION

SECTION

¾″

½″

¾″

1¼″

3/16″

½″

½″

½″

10 STEPS IN SAWING FEET

4″

4″

4″

GLUED

1st

3¾″

3¾″

2nd

3rd

1″

1″

4th

WASTE TACKED ON

maining two frames are spaced equally between the top and bottom ones. These are fastened to the inside of the edging strips with small screws. Pockets are formed for the screws by drilling and counterboring holes through the frame at an angle.

Now, the framework is ready to be covered with ¼-in. plywood. Fit and install the top piece first. In addition to obtaining a well-fitting mitered joint, it also is important to get a tight fit where the plywood abuts the rabbet of the front edging. Use bar clamps to draw this joint tightly and C-clamps to clamp the plywood firmly to the frame. Brads can be used here, as indicated in Fig. 4, although a good resin-type glue will hold sufficiently. Like the top piece, the sides fit flush with the outer face of the edging and the molding at the bottom. Clamps should be used to draw the mitered joint together. Brads can be used to reinforce the joint and to nail the plywood to the edge of the frames.

Steps in sawing the feet are given in Fig. 10. In most cases, the blocks for these will have to be glued up using three or more pieces. The front feet require a ¼ x 1-in. rabbet on two adjacent edges, while the rear ones need a rabbet only along one side. The feet taper to 1 in. square at the bottom. After sawing two sides, the waste is replaced and held with either brads or cellulose tape so that a flat surface will be had to complete the sawing.

Typical drawer construction is detailed in Fig. 9. The method of fitting the bottom differs somewhat with the type of drawer runner used. Note that the lower edge of each drawer extends to cover the drawer frame. Drawer handles are detailed in Fig. 11. A choice of two types of drawer guides is given. One features a T-shaped runner, Fig. 3, over which the back of the drawer hooks to prevent the drawer from dropping down when all the way open. The runner is grooved for a ¼-in.-square guide, which is nailed to the underside of the drawer bottom as shown in Fig. 7, detail B. Note that the T-slot in the drawer, Fig. 8, is made slightly larger than the cross section of the runner. A more simple guide is pictured in Fig. 7, detail A. This is formed merely by nailing two strips of plywood to the drawer bottom to form a track for a plywood runner nailed to the frame. Fig. 1 shows both types of runners in place.

Construction of the highboy (two-drawer) chest unit, Fig. 12, differs from the other units in one respect; the bottom drawer frame is screwed to a mitered base frame which is beveled to match the edging.

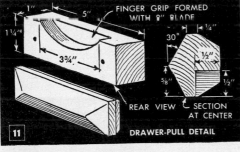

FINGER GRIP FORMED WITH 9" BLADE

1" 5" ¼" 30° ½"

1¼" 3¾" ⅝" ½"

REAR VIEW   SECTION AT CENTER

11   DRAWER-PULL DETAIL

12   CONSTRUCTION OF HIGHBOY-CHEST UNIT

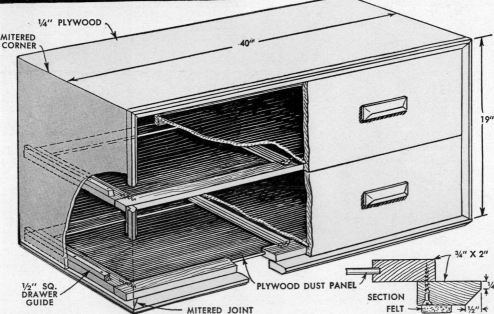

¼" PLYWOOD

MITERED CORNER

40"

19"

½" SQ. DRAWER GUIDE

PLYWOOD DUST PANEL

¾" X 2"

SECTION

FELT

¼"

½"

MITERED JOINT

Furniture for Your Bedroom

W ITH THE night stands, chests and vanity units completed as described in Part I, you can tackle the bed. In addition to its pleasing simplicity, it features a built-in storage compartment in the headboard for bedding and two roomy drawers for shoes. If twin beds are preferred to a full bed, the basic construction is the same. It would be merely a matter of making the bed narrower, installing only one drawer and eliminating the center partition in the storage compartment. Most of the bed is made of ¼-in. plywood. On the original bed, the lid of the storage compartment was a ¾-in.-plywood panel, but to save cost, this too can be of ¼-in. material by gluing it to a half-lapped frame as shown in Figs. 13 and 14.

The bed footboard consists of a ¼-in. plywood panel which is framed on three sides with a ¾ x 2-in. molding. The latter is chamfered and grooved

Right, a jointer plus a bench saw are the only power tools needed. Here, base molding is being run on jointer after being ripped on saw

A roomy drawer opens at each end of the bed headboard to provide storage space for seasonal footwear. Being concealed when the headboard is flanked with night stands, the drawers also provide a safe place for personal papers and jewelry

Another feature of this headboard is a convenient built-in storage compartment for bedding. If you wish, the compartment can be lined with aromatic, red cedar to protect woolen blankets from moths. Open, the lid rests on the bed

⅜ in. deep on its inside face to fit over the edge of the plywood. The panel is faced across the bottom with a ¾ x 1¾-in. molding which matches the molding on the night stands, chests and other pieces. This molding is glued to the plywood so that it overlaps the bottom edge ½ in., sectional detail Fig. 16, and then five rabbeted cleats, 6 in. long, are spaced along the inside and screwed to the molding. Note that the molding is mitered at the ends and returned at the corners for a distance of 4 in., Fig. 16. Note also that the lower ends of the grooved molding, which covers the edges of the plywood, are chamfered on two adjacent outside edges to fit flush with the bottom molding and the upper ends are mitered. The feet are made the same as detailed in Part I, except that here the shoulder must measure 1¼ in. long instead of 1 in. The feet are rabbeted on two adjacent sides and glued into the corners formed by the molding to bring them flush.

The headboard is built around a framework of scrap wood, Fig. 15 Start each end assembly with a ¾ x 4 x 11½-in. base piece and screw a ¾ x 2½ x 15-in. upright piece to it, ¼-in. in from the front edge. Note that the upper end of this piece is notched for a cross member. Another piece, ¾ x 1½ x 30¾ in., is attached vertically to the base piece, ¼ in. in from the rear edge. This piece is joined to the front piece with a cross member located 10 in. up from the top surface of the base, forming the drawer opening. Both end assemblies of the framework are joined together as shown, fitting a ¾ x 1-

13

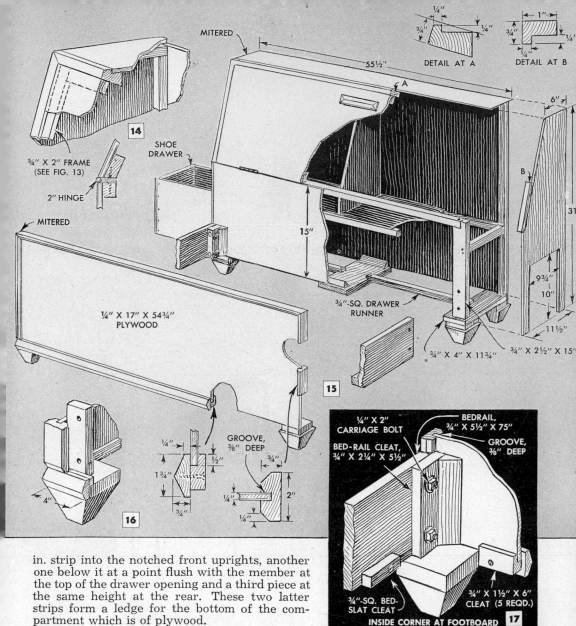

DETAIL AT A

DETAIL AT B

MITERED

55½"

¼"
¾"
¼"

1"
¾"
¼"

A

6"

14

¾" X 2" FRAME
(SEE FIG. 13)

SHOE
DRAWER

B

31'

2" HINGE

MITERED

15"

9¾"

10"

¼" X 17" X 54¾"
PLYWOOD

¾"-SQ. DRAWER
RUNNER

11½"

15

¾" X 4" X 11¾"

¾" X 2½" X 15"

GROOVE,
⅜" DEEP

¼"
½"
¾"

1¾"
¾"
2"
¼"
¼"

4"

16

BEDRAIL,
¾" X 5½" X 75"

¼" X 2"
CARRIAGE BOLT

GROOVE,
⅜" DEEP

BED-RAIL CLEAT,
¾" X 2¼" X 5½"

¾"-SQ. BED-
SLAT CLEAT

¾" X 1½" X 6"
CLEAT (5 REQD.)

INSIDE CORNER AT FOOTBOARD   17

BED RAIL

½"

1¼"

4½"

GLUE
BLOCK

¼" X 4"
CARRIAGE BOLTS

18

INSIDE CORNER AT HEADBOARD

in. strip into the notched front uprights, another
one below it at a point flush with the member at
the top of the drawer opening and a third piece at
the same height at the rear. These two latter
strips form a ledge for the bottom of the compartment which is of plywood.

Now, cover the back of the framework. This
requires a fir-plywood panel, ¼ x 30¾ x 55 in.,
which is nailed and glued so that the edges are
flush with the framework. Next, fit the front
panel, cutting it 15 x 55 in. The plywood pieces
covering the ends of the headboard taper to 6 in.
at the top from a point 15 in. up from the bottom.
These are made right and left hand, selecting the
best face of the plywood for the outside, and mitered at the top. After the ends are glued in
place, the drawer-runner assembly is installed.
The runners are simply ¾-in.-square strips,
notched at each end to hook over the base pieces
and a center piece fastened to the plywood with
glue blocks.

Fit the panel forming the bottom of the bedding

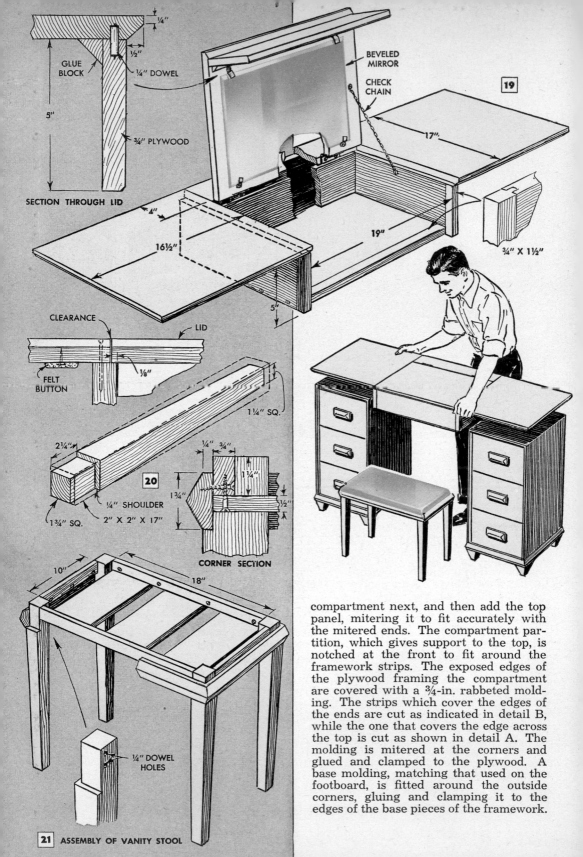

SECTION THROUGH LID

¼"

½"

¼" DOWEL

GLUE BLOCK

5"

¾" PLYWOOD

BEVELED MIRROR

CHECK CHAIN

19

17"

4"

16½"

19"

5"

¾" X 1½"

CLEARANCE

LID

FELT BUTTON

⅛"

1¼" SQ.

2¼"

20

¼" SHOULDER

1¾" SQ.

2" X 2" X 17"

¼" ¾"

1¼"

1¾"

½"

CORNER SECTION

10"

18"

¼" DOWEL HOLES

21 ASSEMBLY OF VANITY STOOL

compartment next, and then add the top panel, mitering it to fit accurately with the mitered ends. The compartment partition, which gives support to the top, is notched at the front to fit around the framework strips. The exposed edges of the plywood framing the compartment are covered with a ¾-in. rabbeted molding. The strips which cover the edges of the ends are cut as indicated in detail B, while the one that covers the edge across the top is cut as shown in detail A. The molding is mitered at the corners and glued and clamped to the plywood. A base molding, matching that used on the footboard, is fitted around the outside corners, gluing and clamping it to the edges of the base pieces of the framework.

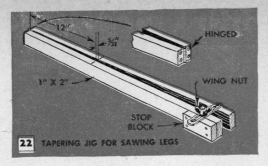

22 TAPERING JIG FOR SAWING LEGS

The compartment lid is hinged as shown in the sectional detail, Fig. 14, and drawers and handles are made as described in Part I. Bedrails are attached to the head and footboard as detailed in Figs. 17 and 18.

The separate top, Fig. 19, which merely rests on two base units to form a vanity, is made of ¾-in. plywood and solid stock. The top requires a panel 17 x 52½ in. Three edges are chamfered on the underside and then the panel is cut into four pieces. The cosmetic compartment is made like a box. The sides and back are screwed to a plywood bottom and a fourth piece is installed to support the narrow fill-in piece to which the lid is hinged. Note how end grain of the side and bottom members of the compartment is concealed with edging strips, tongued and grooved. The outboard panels are nailed and glued to the top edges of the compartment ⅛ in. in from the inner faces to provide a shoulder for the lid. This is shown in the detail above Fig. 20. The front apron is attached to the lid with dowels and a triangular glue block is placed on the inside. The lid can be leaned against the wall when opened or a check chain can be used to hold it at the right angle.

Assembly of the vanity stool is detailed in Fig. 21. First make the legs by cutting a ¼ x 2¼-in. rabbet on two adjacent faces of each one. The legs taper from 2 in. square at the shoulder to 1¼ in. square at the bottom, Fig. 20. Before tapering the legs, bore holes in adjacent inner faces as shown for doweling ¾ x 1¼-in. rails flush with the face of the rabbets. A jig like the one shown in Fig. 22 may be used to rip the taper on each face, after which the cut is dressed smooth on a jointer. The corner-section detail at the right of Fig. 20 shows how a mitered face molding is attached to the rails with screws from the inside. A choice of two methods for upholstering the stool is given in Fig. 23. If tow or hair is used, the seat is supported by three ½-in. pieces spaced as in Fig. 21. If foam rubber is used, the bottom of the stool is covered with a piece of ¼-in. plywood held by cleats screwed to the rails.

(Methods of finishing will be described in Part 3)

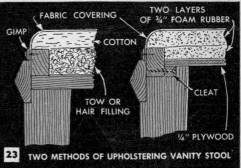

23 TWO METHODS OF UPHOLSTERING VANITY STOOL

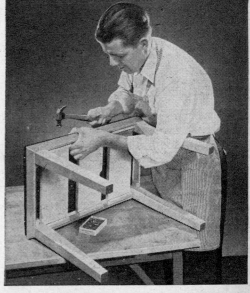

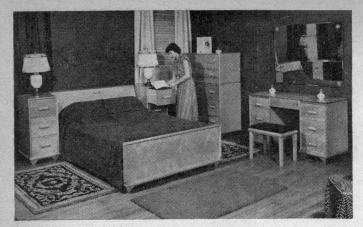

When building new furniture or restoring old pieces, each step of the finishing process, from bleaching and filling to varnishing or lacquering, is of the utmost importance. Perfection, of course, comes only with practice, but the following information will get you off to a good start

Part III

Furniture for

Filling, Staining

AFTER COMPLETING the bedroom furniture described in the previous two parts, it's time for the all-important job of finishing it, because right here you can either flatter or ruin the appearance of the furniture.

No doubt, you have built the furniture of a wood suitable to take the particular finish desired, whether it be harvest wheat or heather mahogany, ambered walnut or limed oak. Naturally, the kind of wood used is a determining factor as, for instance, one cannot expect to obtain a limed-oak finish on birch. The finishing schedules presented below give a condensed procedure to follow in producing

a number of the popular, modern finishes, but, if the final results are to compare with finishes seen on store furniture, the finishing operation demands the same careful attention that you put into the cabinet work. Brushes and materials, as well as the room where the work is done, must be clean. Finishing should not be attempted in a cold room and the materials should not be cold. These precautions are important.

Sanding: Perhaps the most important

FINISHING SCHEDULES

FINISH	APPLICATION
Ambered walnut	Bleach. Stain with amber stain. Apply sealer coat of thin lacquer. Fill with natural filler. Finish with clear lacquer.
Old-World walnut	Bleach. Seal. Fill with natural filler lightly tinted with burnt umber. Seal. Shade with brown wiping stain. Finish with clear lacquer.
Honeytone maple or birch	Tone with blond toner, using 1 part white lacquer to 4 parts clear, flat lacquer. Finish with water-white lacquer.
Pickled pine	Bleach. Stain with gray stain for pine. Finish with water-white lacquer or clear varnish.
Limed oak	Bleach. Seal. Fill pores with white paste wood filler. Finish with water-white lacquer.
Harvest-wheat mahogany	Bleaching will give required wheat color. Fill with natural filler lightly tinted with raw-sienna color in oil. Finish with lacquer.
Tweed mahogany	Bleach. Seal. Fill pores with red paste wood filler. Finish with water-white lacquer or clear varnish.
Heather mahogany	Bleach. Seal. Fill pores with white paste wood filler. Finish with water-white lacquer or clear varnish.

step in producing a beautiful, flawless finish is the sanding of the wood. Application of any number of finishing coats will not compensate for a careless job of sanding, but only tends to emphasize defects. Power sanders of the oscillating or belt types take the work out of sanding; however, if these are not available, you can do a satisfactory job of sanding by hand, wrapping the paper around a flat, felt-covered block and working with progressively finer grades of garnet paper from medium down to 5-0 grade.

Bleaching: Practically all of the

Your Bedroom
and Varnishing

so-called blond finishes are produced by first bleaching the wood to remove its natural color. This is done to obtain such popular mahogany finishes as harvest wheat, heather and tweed, and limed oak, and ambered walnut. Mahogany, when bleached and filled with white filler, is known as heather mahogany. When filled with red filler (natural filler with red oil

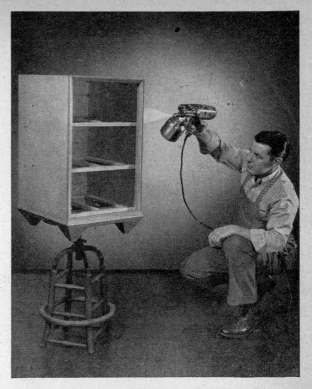

Above, a piano or draftsman's stool provides an excellent turntable when spraying lacquer on the smaller units. Below, a power sander makes play of sanding the broad, flat surfaces, but care must be used to avoid cutting through the top veneer

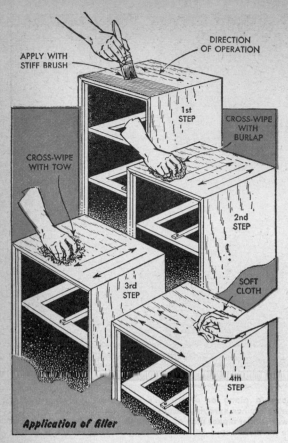

APPLY WITH STIFF BRUSH

DIRECTION OF OPERATION

1st STEP

CROSS-WIPE WITH BURLAP

CROSS-WIPE WITH TOW

2nd STEP

3rd STEP

SOFT CLOTH

4th STEP

Application of filler

the filler is applied liberally in the direction of the grain, preferably with a short-bristled brush. Do not cover more than 6 or 8 sq. ft. of surface at one time or you will get ahead of the wiping and cleaning-up operations that follow. As soon as the filler flattens, it is wiped off. This is done by wiping across the grain with a coarse cloth such as burlap, or excelsior, using a circular motion.

This is followed by cross-wiping with a fine material called tow, commonly used for upholstering purposes. This second wiping across the grain cuts the surplus filler flush with the surface of the wood.

A third cross-wiping with a soft cloth wrapped around a felt block is excellent practice. A second application of filler, somewhat thinner than the first, is sometimes required when filling mahogany or other wood having a very open grain. This is determined by noting whether the pores are completely filled.

Finally, the work is wiped lightly with the grain, using a soft cloth. This serves to remove any traces of filler missed in the towing-off operation. The filler should be allowed to dry 24 to 48 hrs. and then sanded very lightly with 5-0 waterproof garnet paper.

Toning: Toning is not successful on dark wood such as walnut, but very much so on naturally light-colored woods such as birch and maple. Toning, to some extent, takes the place of the bleaching process and is accomplished by spraying the bare wood with a semitransparent undercoat to further lighten the wood.

Toning is recommended for all extremely light finishes, as it does not obscure the grain, being almost as clear as water. Toner is made by adding white lacquer, 1 part, to clear flat lacquer, 4 or 5 parts. In the case of oak and mahogany, the toner should be made with tan-colored lacquer instead of white.

Sealing: Whether or not the bleached wood has been toned or stained, the surface must be sealed with a wash coat of shellac or lacquer before the work is filled. The wash sealer is made by cutting 1 part of clear shellac or lacquer with 6 parts of thinner. This coat is sanded lightly when dry, and then, after the grain is filled, a second sealer coat is applied. This is likewise sanded when dry, and followed with a coat of varnish or lacquer sealer. The latter coat, which fills any tiny open pores remaining, also is sanded. From here on, varnish or lacquer coats are applied, using a rubbed-effect or full-gloss type.

color added), it is called tweed, because of its pleasing pink tone. Bleached and filled with natural filler, it's called harvest-wheat mahogany. After bleaching, almost any color desired can be had by giving the wood a coat of diluted stain.

Bleaching is done with a commercial chemical solution consisting of two separate solutions which are mixed together and used immediately. As all bleaching solutions are highly corrosive, they should be handled carefully. You should wear rubber gloves. Use a sponge to swab the solution on the wood and see that you wet the entire surface evenly.

One application of bleach is usually sufficient although, in any case, it is good practice to make a test on a wood sample. Let the bleach stand and dry for at least 48 hrs.

Filling: Open-grained woods, such as oak, walnut, mahogany, etc., must be filled, that is, the pores of the surface and end grain must be packed level with a prepared paste filler. Fillers are available for either lacquer or varnish finishes and require cutting with benzine or turpentine to the consistency of thick cream before applying, so that they will sink into the pores.

COFFEE TABLE

Diagonal slice from hardwood log produces beautiful grain effect to give this graceful coffee table a distinctive and exclusive touch. Legs are half-lapped and interlock

By W. J. LaFleur

IF IT'S the unusual you crave in occasional furniture, this coffee table should really intrigue you. Its novel construction calls for a top sliced diagonally from a log. Cut in this manner, the top assumes the natural contour of the log and the grain is enhanced by the annual-growth rings which take on a beautiful pattern.

The original table top was cut from an 18-in. cherry log, 4 ft. long. The log should be fairly round, thoroughly seasoned and the bark should be removed. To mark the log for cutting, make a wooden frame from stock 1⅜ in. wide, measuring 18 by 29⅛ in., inside measurement. The frame is placed over the log as in Fig. 3 and is tacked temporarily in place. Then a pencil is run around both sides of the frame to mark the log and the space between the lines is chalked. Fig. 1 shows how the log can be supported at an angle with a ladder and braced for sawing. Work carefully with a crosscut saw and try to make both cuts parallel. The saw will produce a rough surface which must be planed flat on the side selected for the underside of the top. Then ³⁄₁₆-in. grooves are run on

1

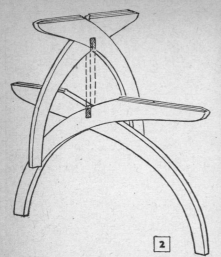

2

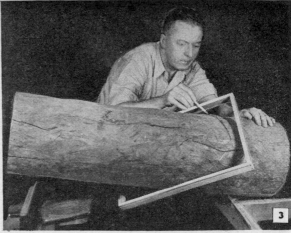

3

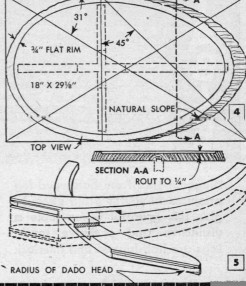

4

the underside for the leg tenons, locating them according to Fig. 4. Each groove can be cut on a bench saw by cutting a wooden strip to slide in one of the saw-table grooves and tacking it to the underside of the work parallel with the line of cut. A ¾-in. rim is marked around the top surface and the area inside the rim is routed ¼ in. deep. This can be done with a router bit in a drill press, or with a portable router. After sanding smooth, a sealer should be applied to both sides of the top to seal the end grain and to retard checking. Fig. 6 details the leg patterns. Although the point of half lap is indicated by dotted lines, it is best to determine this by placing one corresponding leg on top of the other, as in Fig. 5, and marking directly. The assembled pairs of legs are notched to fit together as in Fig. 2 and then the top is glued to the leg tenons.

31°

45°

¾" FLAT RIM

18" X 29⅛"

NATURAL SLOPE

TOP VIEW

A

A

SECTION A-A

ROUT TO ¼"

RADIUS OF DADO HEAD

5

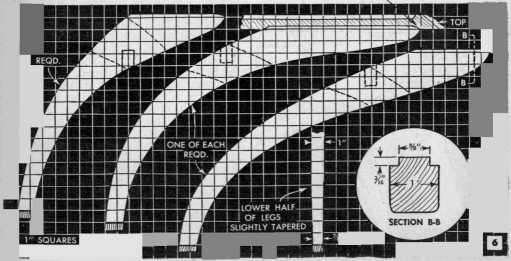

TOP

B

B

REQD.

ONE OF EACH REQD.

1"

LOWER HALF OF LEGS SLIGHTLY TAPERED

⅝"

3/16"

1"

SECTION B-B

1" SQUARES

6

Breakfast Set Folds into Wall

By William H. Freeman

THIS FOLD-AWAY breakfast set has been designed especially to solve the problem of space in small kitchens. It seats four persons comfortably and when not in use the whole unit folds into the wall behind doors that close flush, leaving the wall and floor space clear. Note in the details below that the width of the table is given as 25 in. and the width of the wall recess as 30 in. The latter dimension is the approximate width of the wall opening before installing the header, false studs and jambs. Locating the breakfast set on an outside wall provides maximum depth for the opening and, if the unit must be installed in exceptionally limited space, some changes in dimensions may be necessary. Finish the wall opening and hang the doors first, then make the table and benches from ¾-in. plywood. Assemble the hinged parts with the special hinge fittings shown in the details. In the original design, the rear end of the table is guided by steel pins sliding in stopped grooves cut at an angle in the jambs. This construction can be simplified by using two hardwood strips nailed to each jamb and spaced to allow the pins to slide freely. Provide stop blocks at the lower ends of the guides.

When not in use, benches and table fold into wall behind doors that close flush, leaving wall space clear

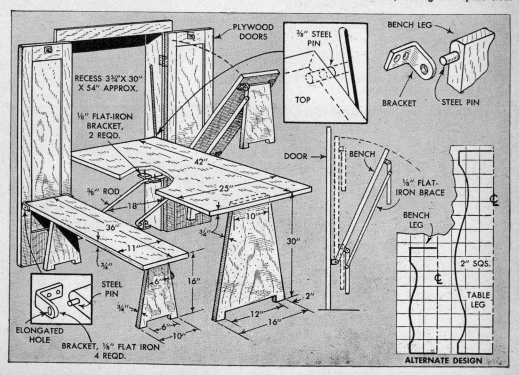

PLYWOOD DOORS

RECESS 3¾"X 30" X 54" APPROX.

⅛" FLAT-IRON BRACKET, 2 REQD.

⅜" STEEL PIN

TOP

BENCH LEG

BRACKET   STEEL PIN

42"

⅜" ROD

18"

25"

36"

11"

¾"

¾"

STEEL PIN

¾"

6"

16"

12"

16"

2"

6"

10"

ELONGATED HOLE

BRACKET, ⅛" FLAT IRON 4 REQD.

DOOR   BENCH

⅛" FLAT-IRON BRACE

BENCH LEG

30"

10"

¾"

2"

2" SQS.

TABLE LEG

ALTERNATE DESIGN

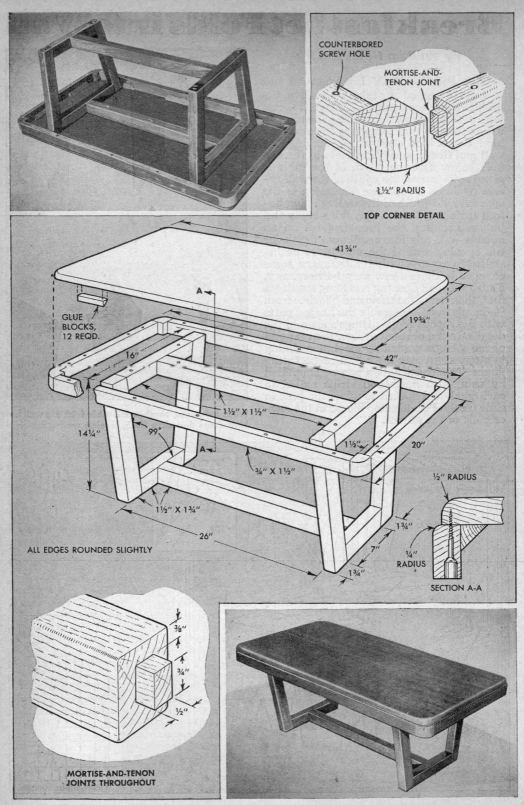

COUNTERBORED
SCREW HOLE

MORTISE-AND-
TENON JOINT

1½" RADIUS

TOP CORNER DETAIL

41¾"

A

19¾"

GLUE
BLOCKS,
12 REQD.

16"

42"

1½" X 1½"

14¼"

99°

1½"

20"

A

¾" X 1½"

½" RADIUS

1½" X 1¾"

1¾"

26"

7"

RADIUS

1¾"

¼"
RADIUS

SECTION A-A

ALL EDGES ROUNDED SLIGHTLY

⅜"

¾"

½"

**MORTISE-AND-TENON
JOINTS THROUGHOUT**

COFFEE TABLE *in Mahogany*

By Richard A. Buell

SIMPLE modern styling, which features an offset top rail and a subdued combination of straight and curved lines, individualizes the design of this smart-looking coffee table. Although the table shown was made of mahogany, other woods can be used when it is desirable to match the finish of other furnishings in both color and graining. White mahogany (primavera) is a popular choice as it finishes light colored with an attractive ribbon grain. The top is built up to the required width by gluing together a number of narrow strips of ¾-in. stock. Use five ⅜-in. dowels equally spaced in each joint. After the glue is dry, sand the top smooth, trim it to the finish dimensions given on the opposite page and round the edges to a ½-in. radius.

The top rail is built up as a frame, the side and end members being mortised into rounded corner blocks. Note also that the corners of the top are rounded to the same radius as the blocks. The top corners of the rails and blocks are rounded to a ¼-in. radius as in section A-A of the assembly details. The completed rail is then attached to the top with screws and 12 triangular glue blocks spaced as shown. The legs are assembled as units, each consisting of two posts joined to a top and bottom rail with mortise-and-tenon joints. These units then are joined to top and bottom stretchers with mortise-and-tenon joints as in the assembly detail. Tenons on the top and bottom rails of the leg units are ¾ in. long and must be shouldered at an angle to give the posts the proper slant. Width of the top shoulder is given in the lower detail.

Duncan Phyfe Lyre Table

By Norbert Engels

BUILT of solid mahogany with a matched grain, veneered top, this attractive occasional table is fashioned from an original designed by a famous craftsman. Distinctive features are the oval design of the top with offsets and the adaptation of the lyre as a basis for the pedestal construction.

Figs. 1, 2 and 4 detail the top. Because of the exposed edges, solid mahogany is used as a core under the four-way matched veneer. Edge-glue flat stock to produce a panel having a width and length slightly greater than the finished size. Then cut four pieces of mahogany veneer, preferably of the quality known as "ribbon" grained, and plane the edges true by clamping the pieces between two strips of waste stock. Make a trial fit of the four pieces to be sure the joints are tight, then join the four pieces with tape so that the grain matches in a diamond pattern. Finally glue the veneer to the mahogany core. After the glue is thoroughly dry, bandsaw the top to the pattern in Fig. 4 and run the molding on a shaper. Next build up the apron as in Fig. 2, shaping the edges as in the sectional view, Fig. 4. Note that the top overhangs the apron slightly as in Figs. 2 and 4, and that it is bandsawed to the same pattern and glued and screwed to the underside of the top. Finish the top in the regular way by sanding smooth and applying stain, filler, sealer and several coats of varnish rubbed down with rottenstone and rubbing oil.

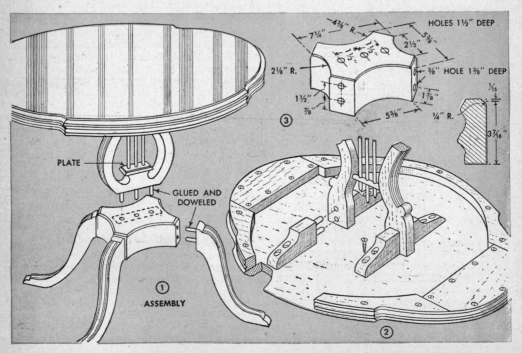

HOLES 1½" DEEP

4⅜" R.

7¼"

5⅜"

2½"

2⅛" R.

1½"

⅜" HOLE 1⅜" DEEP

1½"

1⅞"

1½"

⅞"

5⅜"

¼" R.

1/16

3 7/16"

③

PLATE

GLUED AND DOWELED

① ASSEMBLY

②

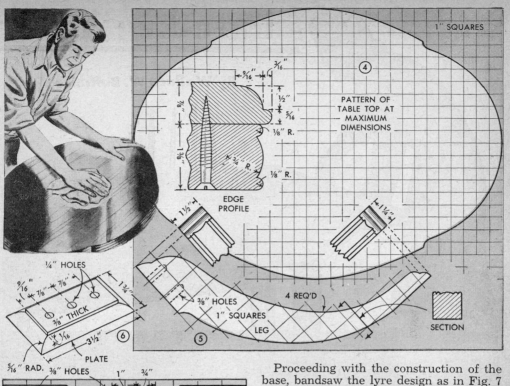

1″ SQUARES

PATTERN OF TABLE TOP AT MAXIMUM DIMENSIONS

④

³⁄₁₆″
⁹⁄₁₆″
½″
⁵⁄₁₆″
⅛″ R.
¾″ R.
⅛″ R.
⅜″
⅜″
¾″

EDGE PROFILE

1½″
1¼″

SECTION

4 REQ'D
⅜″ HOLES
1″ SQUARES
LEG
⑤

¼″ HOLES
⁹⁄₁₆″ ⅞″ ⅞″
1¾″
⅜″ THICK
¼₆″
3½″
⑥
PLATE

⁵⁄₁₆″ RAD. ⅜″ HOLES 1″ ¾″

¾″
1″
2″
⅜″
4 REQ'D
⅜″
1¼″
⅛″

COUNTERBORED FOR SCREWS

½″ **DOWEL**

1″ SQUARES

1¼″ THICK

SECTION

¼″ **DOWELS**

PLATE

½″ DRILL 1½″ 1½″
⑦

Proceeding with the construction of the base, bandsaw the lyre design as in Fig. 7 and the legs and lyre base as in Figs. 3, 5 and 6. Shape and finish-sand the legs and join to the base with dowels and glue as indicated. Note particularly the position of the dowel-and-plate assembly that simulates the strings of the lyre, Figs. 6 and 7, and fit and assemble these parts before doweling to the base. It's important that all parts be sanded smooth so that they will take a finish to match the top. For the final assembly, lay the top face down on a soft pad to prevent marring the finished surface and attach the upper ends of the lyre to the underside of the top as in Fig. 2. To assure a rigid assembly very close fitting is necessary here. Make sure that the lyre is exactly centered and that it stands perpendicular to the top. Finally, finish the base to match, using stain, filler, sealer and two or more coats of varnish. In staining, the base may be high lighted by wiping the stain before it dries on the outer exposed edges.

Paint Preserved for Future Use

Prevent paint from hardening in the can after exposure to the air by pouring a thin layer of turpentine over the surface. Put a bit of the paint in the groove in the friction top of the can also, and then drive the cover down tightly. This seals the can and the paint will not skin over as so often happens if the can is not well sealed.

Gate-Leg Table

By Wallace W. Buffmire

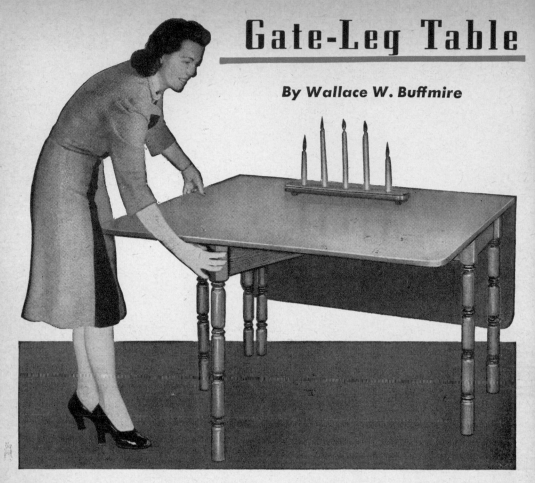

Popular item for the combination living-dining room and small apartment. Takes little space when folded, yet opens to big-table size, seating twelve

HERE'S a dining table that really makes use of limited space. Folded and tucked away against a wall, Fig. 7, it requires only 20 in. of space, but when brought out into the open and fitted with two extra leaves its large top (40 x 84 in.) will accommodate a family gathering of 12 or more. It's a practical answer to the problem of space in the small home or apartment.

The original table was made of American black walnut, the top being walnut burl veneered to a core of poplar. This was done to cut cost, but the whole table, with the exception of the extension-slide assembly, can be made of solid stock. Turn the legs first. These are made from 2-in. turning squares, dressed on four sides. Note that each leg is left square for a distance at the top and the rest is turned to the largest diameter possible. This calls for accurate centering of the turning square in the lathe to assure that all legs have very nearly the same diameter. After the leg is in the round, so to speak, spot the beads with dividers and finish with a roundnose chisel. Although 1-in. stock was used for the rails, ¾-in. material will do. The rails are mortised into the legs as in Fig. 4, the tenons being glued and crosspinned to lock them in place. If you do not have a mortising attachment for the drill press, the leg mortises can be cut by drilling a series of overlapping holes and then cleaning and squaring up the mortise by hand with a chisel. Locate the mortises so that the rails set in about ³⁄₁₆ in. from the face of the legs. Draw up each assembly with a bar clamp before nailing through the tenons.

The extension slides for the top are made from 1¼-in. hardwood as in Fig. 3. The members slide on a dovetail. Note that the female part of the dovetail has a ⅛-in. groove cut in the bottom, which is stopped about 1 in. from the end of the slide, is for a stop pin which prevents

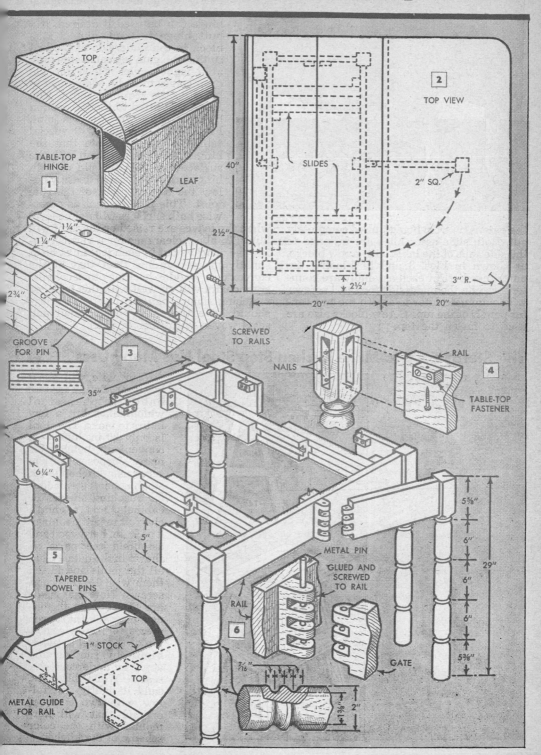

TOP

TABLE-TOP
HINGE

LEAF

1

2

TOP VIEW

40"

SLIDES

2" SQ.

2½"

2¾"

1¼"
1¼"

GROOVE
FOR PIN

SCREWED
TO RAILS

3

2½"

3" R.

20"

20"

NAILS

RAIL

4

TABLE-TOP
FASTENER

35"

6¼"

5"

METAL PIN

GLUED AND
SCREWED
TO RAIL

5⅝"

6"

29"

6"

5

TAPERED
DOWEL PINS

6

RAIL

6"

5⅜"

1" STOCK

TOP

GATE

METAL GUIDE
FOR RAIL

7⁄16"

2"
1⅜"

Fig. 2 shows how the gate legs nest against the side rails of the table. The wooden hinge detailed in Fig. 6 was used on the original table, although a regular butt hinge can be used if desired. If a butt hinge is used, glue a stop block to the underside of the leaf so that the gate leg can swing only at a right angle. Stock for the drop leaves must be edge-glued to build up the required width. The leaves are fitted to the top section by what is known as a rule joint, Fig. 1, and are hinged with special table-top hinges. Note that the hinges are mortised flush with the surface and that the pin of both hinges must be located directly below the shoulder cut of the rule joint. This is important as otherwise both surfaces will not be level when the leaves are raised or the joint will bind. To allow clearance for a varnish finish, the concave cut in each leaf must be of slightly greater radius than that of the convex cut. Ladder-back or other colonial style chairs will go well with this table, or matching chairs can be built. The legs should have the same spool design and seats woven with fiber or rush.

the extension from being pulled completely out. Both slide assemblies are fastened to the side rails of the table with screw blocks, as shown in Figs. 3 and 5. Finally, the outer members of each assembly are counterbored on the underside for short screws, which are used later to attach the two center panels of the top. Screw blocks also are used to fasten the top.

This Sturdy Easy-to-Make Kitchen Step Stool Has Many Uses

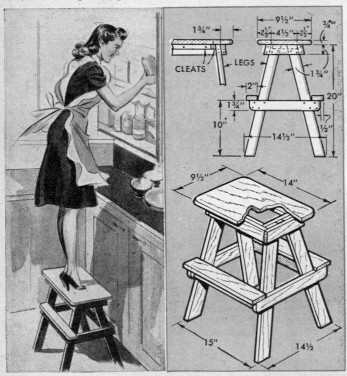

Your wife will show her appreciation for this handy kitchen stool which takes but a few hours to make. The stool is only 20 in. high — a convenient height for many purposes. It can serve as a kitchen work stool, a small stepladder for reaching shelves or cabinets, and a child's chair at mealtime. Make it of ¾-in. hardwood and assemble the parts as shown in the detail. Glue all the joints and fasten them with 1½-in. wood screws. Note that cleats are attached to the inner faces of the apron pieces for screwing the top of the stool in place. Finish by sanding and apply an undercoater or sealer. When this dries, sand it lightly and follow with two coats of enamel that will harmonize with the color scheme of the kitchen.

Kitchen Desk and Breakfast Table

By Charles E. Troutt

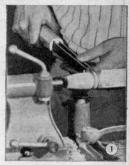

FINISHED in enamel or lacquer with brightly colored handles, this table adds a note of cheer to a room, and offers the utmost in utility and space saving. When used as a breakfast table it will seat four persons comfortably with ample space for coffee percolator, waffle iron, etc. By dropping the back leaf it becomes a kitchen desk, Fig. 7, and thereby folds to less than half its former size. The five drawers provide storage for kitchen linens and utensils. Fine cabinet woods are unnecessary, although the posts should be made of wood that can be turned satisfactorily.

Making the legs: Only the three front legs have feet turned on the lower ends.

The back legs are square. Care should be taken to center exactly the legs that are to be turned, otherwise you will not be able to turn them to the dimensions given. Fig. 1 shows the bead being cut with a shaper cutter in a homemade holder. All legs are grooved 1/4 by 5/16 in. to receive the panels. The cuts should be stopped before reaching the turned feet and the ends of the grooves squared with a chisel. Also, all legs must be notched to receive the drawer

frames, including the frames above the top drawers. The notches can be cut with a router as in Fig. 2, or with a hand chisel. The legs are fluted on a shaper, using a ¼-in. round-nose cutter. Note that the flutes on the inside surface of the legs next to the kneehole section stop before reaching the drawer. The single front rail at the bottom of the drawer section should have two flutes as shown in Fig. 6. It is necessary for the top back rails to be 4¾ in. wide to cover the back opening of the kneehole drawer. With the exception of the two back rails of the kneehole section, all rails are grooved on one side for ¼-in. panels.

The drawer frames: These are of open mortise-and-tenon construction, ¼ by ½-in. tenons being used. Before the frames are assembled, cut a notch ½ in. deep and ¾ in. wide in the center edge of each front and back rail to receive the drawer guide. Accurate centering of the notch is necessary as any discrepancy would be multiplied if the rail ends were reversed in assembling. The molded shape on the edge of the front rail also is cut before assembly.

After the drawer frames are assembled and before the guides are glued in, notch each corner as indicated in the circular de-

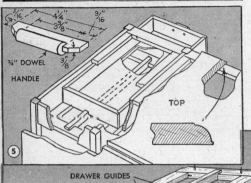

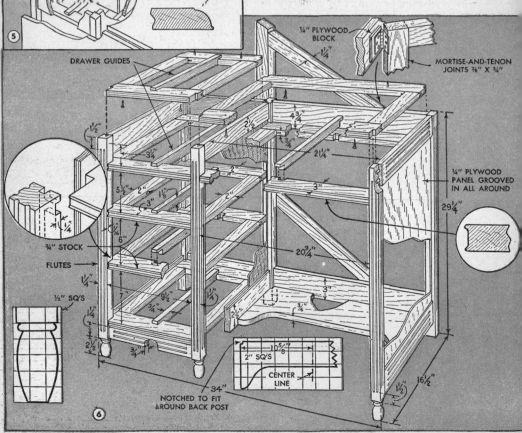

tail of Fig. 6. The drawer guides also will serve as drawer stops if they are notched to come within ⅞ in. of the front edge of the front rail. Detail for the bottom kneehole brace is given in the plan. The back corners are notched to fit around the legs.

The drop leaf and support: In making the support, note that the top rail is mortised into the outside stile ½ in. down from the top, but that it is flush with the top of the inside stile, Figs. 4 and 8. These mortises are best cut with a hollow chisel on a drill press. In joining stock for the top, warping can be minimized by using pieces not over 4 in. wide and reversing the end grain in alternate pieces. To assure a close butt joint between the drop leaf and the desk top when the leaf is raised, it is necessary to cut a shallow recess for the hinge pin in both pieces. Mold all edges except those where the top and drop leaf are butted together.

Drawers and pulls: No exact dimensions are given for the drawers as the pieces vary with the type of joint used. Dovetail joints are preferred, although a simple rabbeted joint will serve the purpose. Regardless of the type of joint, the drawer bottoms should set up ½ in. from the bottom edge, and there should be a notch 1¾₁₆ in. wide by ½ in. deep cut in the bottom edge of the drawer back to fit over the guide. Fig. 5 shows how this notch fits over the drawer guide. Details for a simple and attractive drawer pull also are given. Holes for attachment screws should be drilled in the base before the pull is assembled. The top part of the pull is a ¾-in. dowel grooved to fit over the base. After cutting the four panels you are ready for final assembly. Note that one panel must be sound on both sides. In the event plywood is not available, hard-pressed board can be substituted.

Final assembly: Sand as many of the pieces as possible before assembly. All rails are doweled to the legs. It is advisable to improvise a jig to hold the rails rigidly up-

right while drilling the dowel holes in the end grain.

Glue the two side panels and the center panel first, Fig. 3. The panel that is good on both sides goes between the right-hand legs. The drop-leaf support and the drawer frames should be glued at this time. Be sure to drill the dowel holes for the back rails, as well as the dowel holes for the bottom kneehole-section brace, before this gluing operation. Since the top is screwed in place, the holes should be drilled and countersunk on the bottom side of the top drawer frames. These two frames are doweled to the side rails for extra strength.

The drop-leaf support is hinged to the back rails, and filler blocks must be used under the hinges to align the support with the posts. Attach the top, leaving a ¾-in. overhang on the front and sides. A block should be screwed to the underside of the drop leaf to stop the support when it swings out to the center of the leaf. Sufficient sanding with the proper grit of paper is necessary for a good finish. Use a very fine grit for the final sanding and slightly round the corners of the legs. Follow with a sealer to prevent the grain from raising and showing through the finishing coats. Apply lacquer or enamel as it comes from the can and be careful that it does not sag on the vertical surfaces. Use a quick-drying enamel.

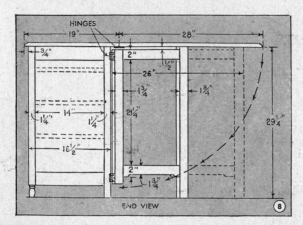

HINGES

END VIEW

Drop-Leaf PHONE STAND

By Norbert Engels

TWO small drawers in this attractive telephone stand provide ample space for storing directories, memo pads and similar items, which often are stacked on the stand or on the floor near by. The stand has space for a lamp and a bowl of flowers as well as the telephone and, used with one or both of the end wings or leaves raised, it will serve as an emergency occasional table in any room in the house.

The stand looks most attractive when done in walnut, mahogany or maple. If desired, its construction can be brought entirely within the scope of hand tools by substituting tapered, square legs for the turned ones. All other work, except the knobs, which may be purchased, can be done with hand tools alone, including the shaped edges of the top piece and leaves as indicated in Fig. 1.

In shaping these edges, preliminary saw cuts remove much of the waste stock and provide a straight rabbeted edge for the joint at the same time, as indicated by the two lower details, which show views of one leaf and table top. The material remaining on the edge of the top is rounded off with a sharp chisel or plane, and excess stock on the leaf is gouged out on the underside of the edges as indicated by the dotted lines. Note that only one edge of each leaf is so treated, but both edges of the top are shaped. If the job is laid out carefully as shown in the circular detail of Fig. 1, a neat, free-working joint will result. How-

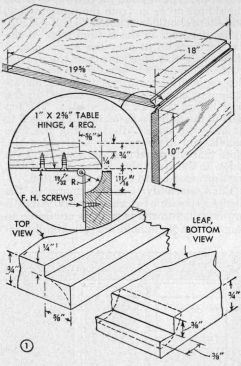

ever, if you have access to a power shaper, much tedious work can be avoided by cutting the joint on it, using a set of cutters designed especially for this kind of construction. The same type of shaper cutters designed for use on a bench saw also are

ward the outside of the piece. Cut the mortises and tenons carefully to get snug fits, and then glue them into place. It is best to run the mortises in the legs before shaping them. When this has been done turn the legs to the size and shape indicated in Fig. 4, and assemble as in Fig. 2. The outside edge of the square portion of each leg may be beaded if desired, but it should be at least slightly rounded. On top of each side panel a 1-in. strip is pivoted to serve as a supporting arm when the leaves are raised to a horizontal position. They bear against the underside of both the leaf and table top and afford a very secure surface.

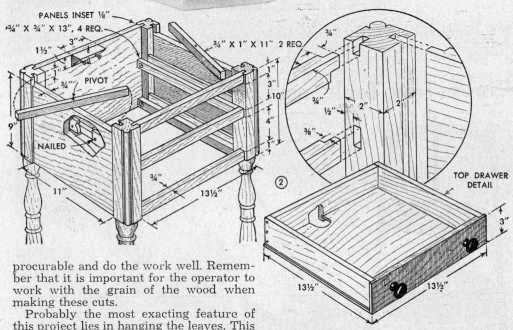

procurable and do the work well. Remember that it is important for the operator to work with the grain of the wood when making these cuts.

Probably the most exacting feature of this project lies in hanging the leaves. This is done with the top piece turned upside down and the leaves in place. Set the four table hinges in position about 4 in. in from both front and back edges, pressing the parts together so that the joint works tightly, and then sand the contacting edges until it works freely. Careful attention to this detail will result in perfect positioning of the leaves, whether in the raised position, or hanging as in Fig. 1.

Full length mortises and tenons join the back and both side panels to the legs, Fig. 2, the mortises running ⅛ in. from the outside surface of the legs. Mortises can be cut with a rabbet plane or circular saw. The three parting strips that space the drawers are similarly mortised and tenoned. In all these joints the shoulder of the tenon faces to-

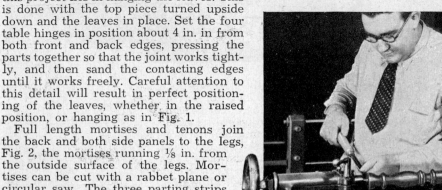

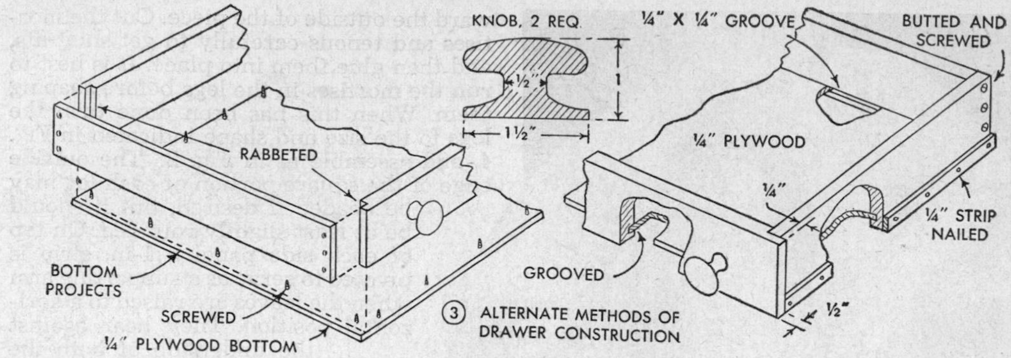
KNOB, 2 REQ.
1/2"
1
1 1/2"
1/4" X 1/4" GROOVE
BUTTED AND SCREWED
1/4" PLYWOOD
1/4"
1/4" STRIP NAILED
RABBETED
BOTTOM PROJECTS
SCREWED
1/4" PLYWOOD BOTTOM
GROOVED
1/2"
(3) ALTERNATE METHODS OF DRAWER CONSTRUCTION

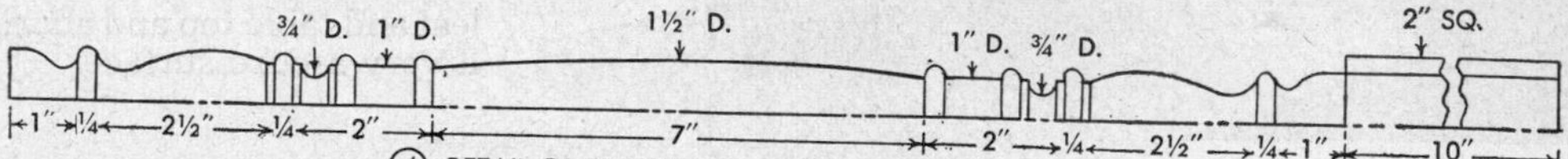
3/4" D.
1" D.
1 1/2" D.
1" D.
3/4" D.
2" SQ.
1"
1/4
2 1/2"
1/4
2"
7"
2"
1/4
2 1/2"
1/4
1"
10"
(4) DETAIL OF TURNED LEG, 4 REQUIRED

The drawer runners should be assembled before they are screwed in place. A side strip is nailed to the back of each runner, and acts as a guide for the drawer. Spacer strips nailed to the sides work against the runner guide strips.

Three-Tray Table on Casters Has Many Uses

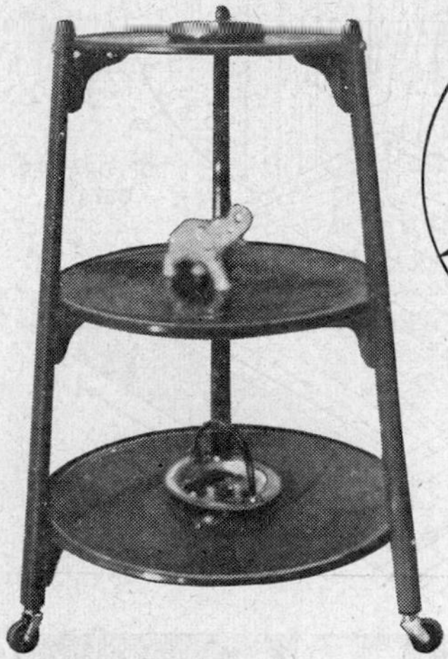

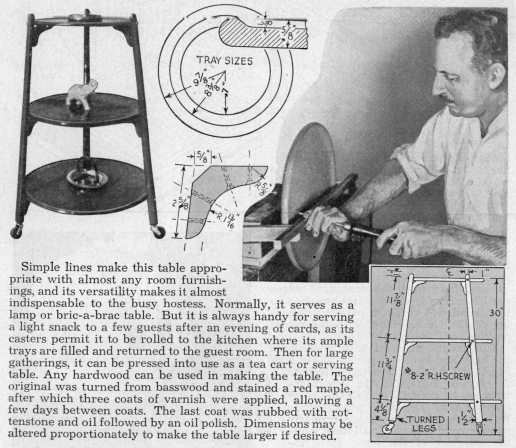

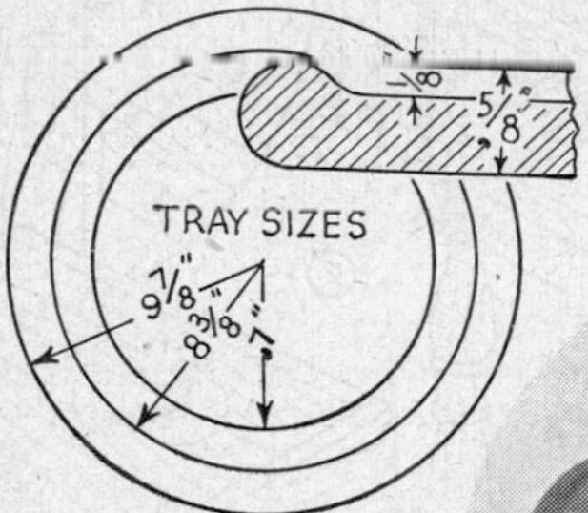
1/8
5/8"
TRAY SIZES
9 7/8"
8 3/8"
7"

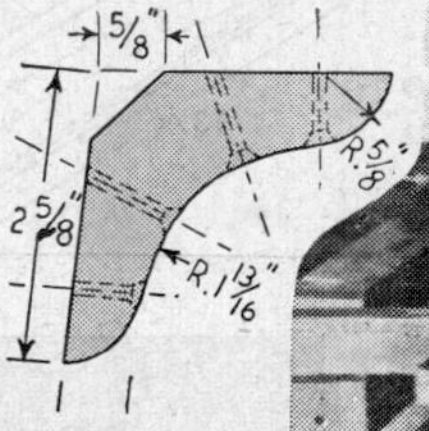
5/8"
R. 5/8"
2 5/8"
R. 1 13/16"

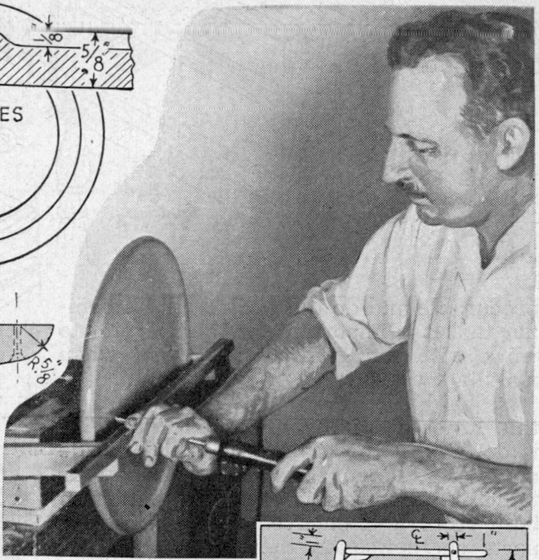

Simple lines make this table appropriate with almost any room furnishings, and its versatility makes it almost indispensable to the busy hostess. Normally, it serves as a lamp or bric-a-brac table. But it is always handy for serving a light snack to a few guests after an evening of cards, as its casters permit it to be rolled to the kitchen where its ample trays are filled and returned to the guest room. Then for large gatherings, it can be pressed into use as a tea cart or serving table. Any hardwood can be used in making the table. The original was turned from basswood and stained a red maple, after which three coats of varnish were applied, allowing a few days between coats. The last coat was rubbed with rottenstone and oil followed by an oil polish. Dimensions may be altered proportionately to make the table larger if desired.

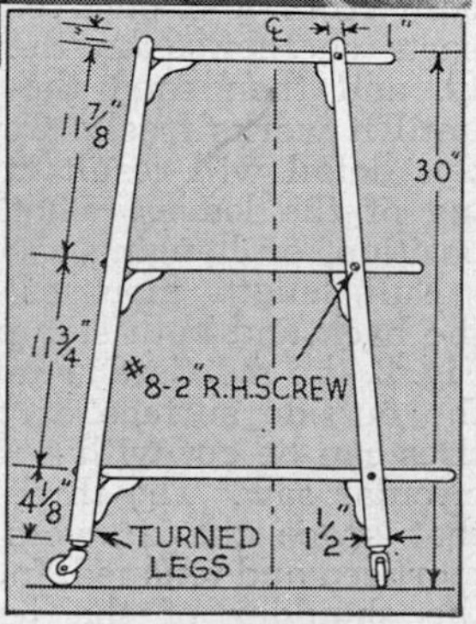
℄
1"
11 7/8"
30"
11 3/4"
#8-2" R.H.SCREW
4 1/8"
TURNED LEGS
1 1/2"

EACH TABLE IS A COMPLETE UNIT

PYRAMIDED FOR CORNER WHATNOT

THERE is a place in almost every home for three multi-purpose tables which, in addition to the arrangements shown, can be hung on walls individually as whatnot shelves. Each table has two closed sides at right angles to each other and an open front, rounded at an 18-in. radius. As the curved edges must be flush when the tables are nested, the tables are of different sizes as shown in the lower detail. The arcs for the three sets of curved edges are struck from pivot points located on the diagonal center line, 4, 5 and 6 in. from either straight edge of the largest table top.

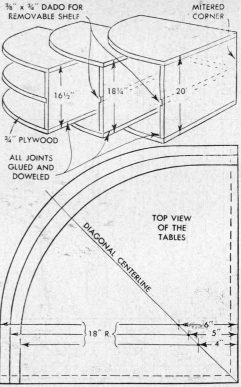

3/8" x 3/4" DADO FOR REMOVABLE SHELF

MITERED CORNER

16 1/2"   18 1/4"   20"

3/4" PLYWOOD

ALL JOINTS GLUED AND DOWELED

TOP VIEW OF THE TABLES

DIAGONAL CENTERLINE

18" R

6"
5"
4"

ALL THREE TABLES NESTED AS ONE

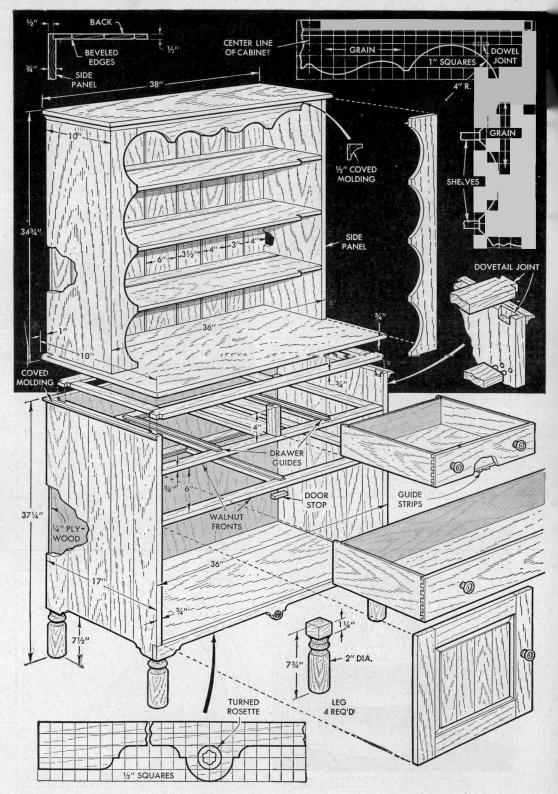

BACK

BEVELED EDGES

SIDE PANEL

CENTER LINE OF CABINET

GRAIN

1" SQUARES

DOWEL JOINT

4" R.

GRAIN

SHELVES

½" COVED MOLDING

SIDE PANEL

38"

10"

34¾"

6" 3½" 4" 3" 4"

36"

¾"

1"

10"

COVED MOLDING

DOVETAIL JOINT

DRAWER GUIDES

4"

¾" 6"

WALNUT FRONTS

DOOR STOP

GUIDE STRIPS

37¼"

¼" PLY-WOOD

17"

¾"

36"

7½"

1¼"

7¾"

2" DIA.

TURNED ROSETTE

LEG 4 REQ'D

½" SQUARES

A fine, rugged piece of Early American furniture to lend authentic setting to your pewter or silver collection. Cabinet base provides storage galore for silverware, linen and china. Its plainness makes it simple to duplicate with ordinary tools

By W. W. Buffmire

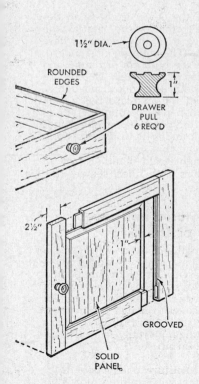

1½" DIA.

ROUNDED EDGES

DRAWER PULL
6 REQ'D

1"

2½"

1"

GROOVED

SOLID PANEL

Reproduce this
WELSH DRESSER
for your best china

To be traditionally authentic this quaint old piece should be reproduced in American black walnut, although it can be copied in maple or birch and finished to match other Early American pieces that you may have. A study of the pull-apart view on the opposite page will acquaint you with the way the whole job goes together. Start by gluing edgewise two or more ¾-in. pieces to build up wide panels for the top and ends of the lower unit. Except for the plywood panel covering the back of the cabinet, solid stock is used throughout, although the bottom could be of plywood, too, as the front edge of it is faced with a scrolled apron. The bottom is set 1¼ in. up from the lower edge of the ends and the turned legs are glued and screwed in the corners formed by the apron across the front. The bottom, however, is not assembled until the three drawer frames are made ready, then the whole unit is clamped together at one time. Note in the detail that the top frame is fitted to the ends in dovetail mortises, while the other two are simply doweled and glued in blind holes.

The ½-in. shelves of the upper unit can be doweled or set in grooves cut in the sides. The scrollwork around the face of the unit fits flush in the notched shelves and the back of the unit is paneled vertically with ½-in. pieces of varying widths. Drawers and doors are assembled as shown, the latter being held shut with spring-type friction catches.

All-Wood Smoking Stand—

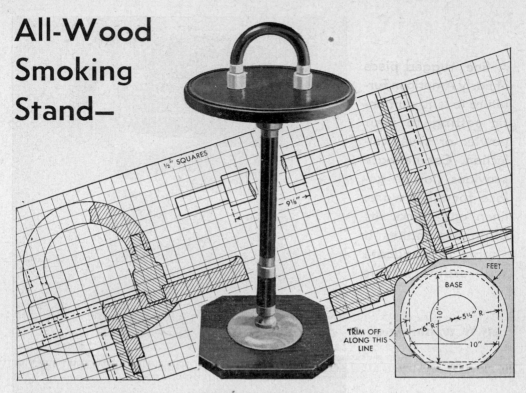

THE light color of maple contrasting with the dark color of walnut or mahogany gives this all-wood smoking stand an unusually attractive appearance. The base and top or tray are 12-in. disks turned from 1-in. stock. The top surface of the tray is turned out to form a narrow rim around the edge, and a recess is turned in the underside surface to take a supporting disk of maple, which is set in as in the lower left-hand detail.

The base also is turned on the underside to form a ½-in. rim, and the upper surface is recessed for a maple disk similar to the tray. Then the base is trimmed at the edges as indicated in the lower right-hand detail. Trimming removes the rim at the sides, but leaves it at the corners where it serves as feet. The column, or standard, and the handle are built up of maple and walnut assembled as indicated. Note in the left-hand detail that the walnut portion at the upper end of the standard has a long tenon over which the maple portion is slipped, this latter piece being glued into a hole in the disk under the tray. Assembly to the base is somewhat similar, as you will notice in the right-hand detail. Finish in the natural colors with filler, sealer, varnish and, finally, a paste wax.

Child's Toys Stored in Drawer Under Chest or Dresser

Living in a small apartment where space was restricted, one father added an extra drawer to a dresser in which his small child could store its toys. Slides were provided between the dresser legs as shown, and the drawer was finished to match the dresser, thus providing the extra drawer space without detracting materially from the appearance of the furniture.

❡Since warm furniture polish penetrates wood pores faster, you can do a more efficient polishing job by first warming the bottle of polish in hot water.

PENNSYLVANIA DUTCH CUPBOARD

By NORBERT ENGELS

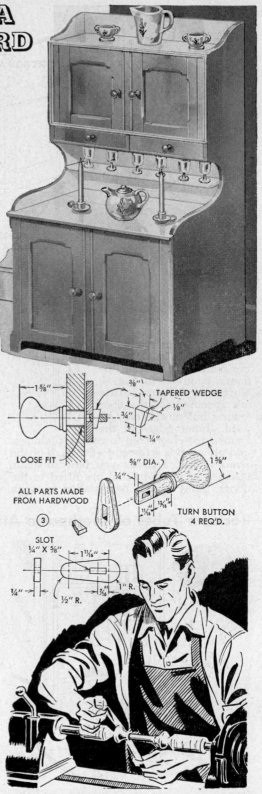

IF your taste in furniture leans toward the plain and simple lines of colonial days, here's a charming old cupboard that typifies the simplicity of early American craftsmanship. It's the type of furniture that challenges the skill of the craftsman who works with hand tools mainly and who takes special pride in producing an expert job of finishing.

Begin by building up two panels of solid stock for the sides of the cupboard. This is done by jointing four or five narrow boards, using either tongue-and-groove joints or plain butt joints doweled and glued. A saving in stock may be had by running only two of the boards the full length and using shorter lengths for the lower half. In arranging the pieces keep in mind that right and left-hand side members are required. You may find it more convenient to cut the rabbet for the plywood back if it is done before the boards are glued together. The scroll cuts likewise may be roughed out beforehand and later dressed down with a spokeshave or file, although they can be done afterward with a keyhole saw. Except for one shelf, which is set in a dado as shown in Fig. 2, the eight shelves simply are butted against the side members and glueblocked. Note that the ½-in. shelves, Fig. 1, are cut out along the front edge, and that the desk shelf, Fig. 4, is notched at the front corners to project 1¼ in. and fit flush with the surface of the sides. The plywood back will add rigidity to the whole assembly, and it's a good idea when attaching it to do so while the framework is still clamped.

Next, the facing strips to which the lower doors are hinged are fitted to the front corners of the assembly. These are chamfered on the outer edge and are cut out at the bottom to form a part of the leg. Finally, the opening is divided equally with a beaded upright, which is fastened at the top to a nailing block and at the bottom by driving nails up through the lower shelf. The upper compartment is fitted the same way except that the pieces are set in flush with the sides and the shelves. A small molding like the one shown in the sectional detail A-A in Fig. 4 is mitered at the corners and glued and bradded to the facing edges of the opening. The two-drawer

1 5⁄8″

3⁄8″   TAPERED WEDGE
                1⁄8″
           3⁄4″
LOOSE FIT   1⁄4″

ALL PARTS MADE FROM HARDWOOD

5⁄8″ DIA.   1 5⁄8″
1⁄4″
     1 1⁄16″ 13⁄16″
TURN BUTTON 4 REQ'D.

③

SLOT
1⁄4″ X 5⁄8″   1 11⁄16″
                      1″ R.
1⁄4″   7⁄16″
    1⁄2″ R.

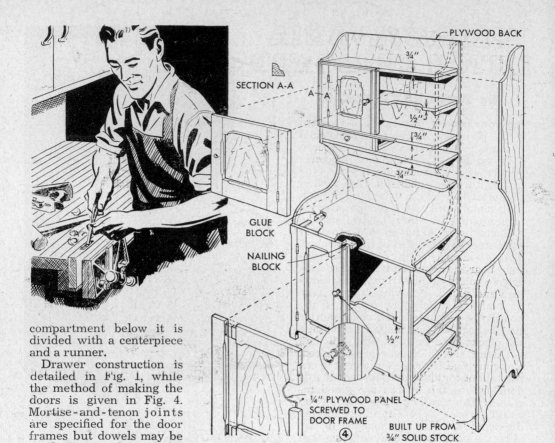

SECTION A-A

A — A

GLUE BLOCK

NAILING BLOCK

PLYWOOD BACK

3/4"

1/2"

3/4"

3/4"

1/2"

1/4" PLYWOOD PANEL SCREWED TO DOOR FRAME ④

BUILT UP FROM 3/4" SOLID STOCK

compartment below it is divided with a centerpiece and a runner.

Drawer construction is detailed in Fig. 1, while the method of making the doors is given in Fig. 4. Mortise-and-tenon joints are specified for the door frames but dowels may be used. Inner edges of the frames are chamfered to relieve plainness and plywood is screwed to the back of the frames. Fig. 3 shows you how to make wooden turnbuttons that are fitted to the doors. They should be installed to work freely and latch against the back of the beaded uprights. A natural or a varnish finish is applied to the exterior of the cupboard, but the interior may be painted a pastel shade of bluish-green.

Rack for Tubes of Toothpaste Attached to Cabinet Shelf

If you wish to keep toothpaste tubes and other similar containers out of sight, a simple holder like the one shown may be screwed to the underside of one of the shelves in the bathroom cabinet. Any piece of non-rusting sheet metal will do for the holder and it can be made any size desired, depending on the number of tubes to be kept in the rack.

Repairs for Desk Drawers

If the joints of a drawer have become loose, it will be difficult to open and close it. In such a case, the remedy is to renail and glue the drawer so that it will slide easily. If swelling or warping is the cause of the trouble, the high spots should be sanded and waxed. It may be necessary to plane high spots lightly before the drawer will work smoothly.

Sheraton NIGHT STAND in cherry

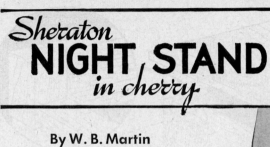

By W. B. Martin

COPIED from an early nineteenth century Sheraton design, this night stand, or side table, Fig. 1, was made of cherry, but it would look well in either mahogany or maple, depending on the furnishings of your bedroom.

Begin construction by turning the legs to the shape and dimensions given in Fig. 3. Take particular care in turning the portion of each leg that is to be reeded so that the thickness and taper will be uniform on all four of them. The reeding may be omitted but as it gives the legs a slender, graceful appearance, the additional work is well worth while. The job of reeding can best be done with a shaper, but if you do not have one available, the work can be done in a drill press, or even a lathe. Fig. 2 shows a portable shaper clamped in a drill-press spindle and used for the job, but similar results can be had by using the shaper cutter on the drill-press spindle with an adapter.

A jig having two nail centers and an improvised indexing head is needed to hold a leg while reeding it. A strip clamped to the drill-press table serves as a fence to guide the jig as it is moved along to cut the grooves. The left-hand block of the jig in which the center is driven is slotted for horizontal adjustment. It is held by a bolt and wing nut so that it can be pivoted

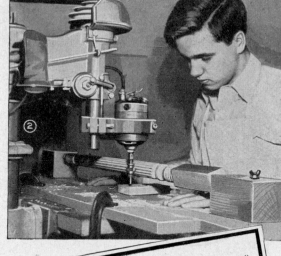

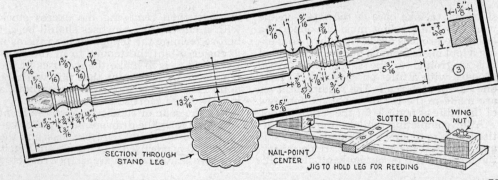

SECTION THROUGH STAND LEG

NAIL-POINT CENTER

SLOTTED BLOCK

WING NUT

JIG TO HOLD LEG FOR REEDING

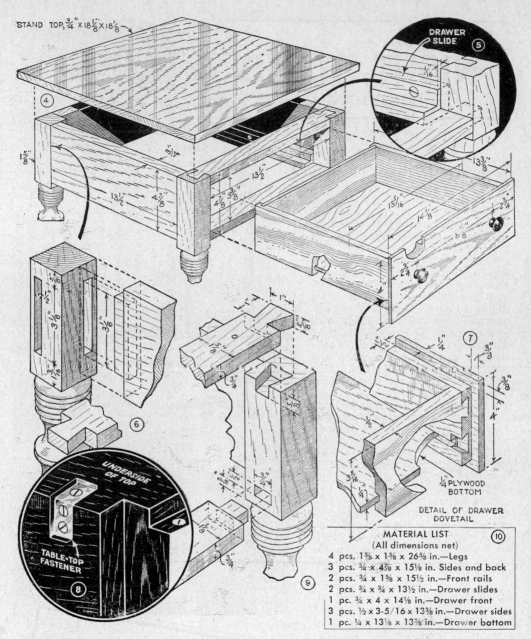

STAND TOP, ¾" X 18⅛ X 18⅛

DRAWER SLIDE ⑤

DETAIL OF DRAWER DOVETAIL

UNDERSIDE OF TOP

TABLE-TOP FASTENER ⑧

¼ PLYWOOD BOTTOM

MATERIAL LIST ⑩
(All dimensions net)
4 pcs. 1⅝ x 1⅝ x 26⅝ in.—Legs
3 pcs. ¾ x 4⅞ x 15⅛ in. Sides and back
2 pcs. ¾ x 1⅝ x 15½ in.—Front rails
2 pcs. ¾ x ¾ x 13½ in.—Drawer slides
1 pc. ¾ x 4 x 14⅛ in.—Drawer front
3 pcs. ½ x 3-5/16 x 13⅜ in.—Drawer sides
1 pc. ¼ x 13⅛ x 13⅜ in.—Drawer bottom

sideways to take care of the taper on the work. If the reeding must be done in a lathe, the grooves are scraped by hand, using a tool made from an old file. The end of this is ground to the shape of the reed grooves with a fillet on each side to form one half of each reed. The reeding grooves are made in the leg by using the tool rest of the lathe as a guide for the scraping tool.

After completing the legs, they are mortised to take tenons on the ends of the side and rear rail pieces, Fig. 6. If necessary, the mortises can be cut by hand, first drill-

ing and then removing the excess stock with a chisel. The mortises should be cut before forming the tenons on the rails as it is easier to cut the tenons to fit the mortises than it is to make the mortises fit the tenons. It is important that this work be done carefully as glue will never hold a loosely fitted mortise-and-tenon joint.

For the sake of rigidity, one of the front rails that form the drawer opening is dovetailed into the top of the front legs, and the other rail is mortised into them as in Fig. 9. The two drawer slides are simply rabbeted strips screwed to the side rails, Fig. 5, the screw heads being countersunk. Notice that the slides project slightly above the lower rail so that the drawer does not rub on it. Construction of the drawer is not difficult. The front piece is dovetailed to the sides, and the back piece fits in grooves cut in the front and sides. Time and labor can be saved here if the work has to be done with hand tools by making the dovetails extra large and using only two on each side. The drawer bottom is set in grooves cut in the front and sides, but not the back of the drawer, as in Fig. 7. Pulls for the drawer can be turned on a lathe or purchased as desired. A list of materials required is given in Fig. 10.

The stand top, Fig. 4, is made by gluing two or more pieces together. Use only the best glue for this work, and clamp the work securely until the glue dries. If this is not done, the joints may open and ruin your stand. The top is attached to the rails by means of table-top fasteners, Fig. 8. These are nothing more than iron angles drilled for the use of screws.

Finishing the table, Fig. 11, is a matter of preference. Waxing was very much in vogue at the time the original was made, and as it continually improves with age, it should prove very satisfactory, and it is

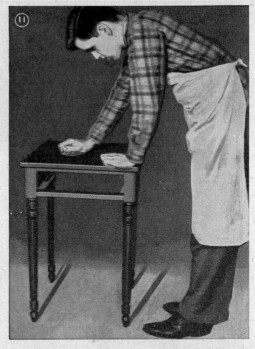

not difficult to apply. For a glossier finish, follow any of the methods described in the section beginning on page 50.

Gaily Colored Wastepaper Basket of Linoleum

Strong and attractive wastepaper baskets of colorful linoleum to match or complement the decorative scheme of any room can be made in various sizes. All you have to do is band or scroll-saw an oval or circular bottom from a piece of ½ or ¾-in. wood and attach to this two vertical pieces as shown in the details. Note how screws and dowels provide rigidity at the joints, and that the rounded upper ends of the pieces are bored to form finger holes to facilitate carrying the basket. Before attaching the linoleum, lay it in the sun or in a heated room until it is warmed thoroughly so that it will not crack when shaped around the basket bottom. Apply the linoleum so that the seam comes directly over one of the vertical pieces.

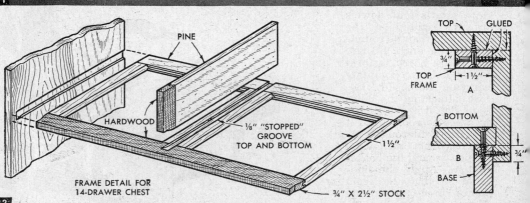

PINE

TOP   GLUED

¾"

TOP
FRAME
⌐ 1½" ⌐

A

HARDWOOD

⅛" "STOPPED"
GROOVE
TOP AND BOTTOM

1½"

BOTTOM

B

¾"

BASE

FRAME DETAIL FOR
14-DRAWER CHEST

¾" X 2½" STOCK

HER OWN CHEST OF DRAWERS

By Wallace W. Buffmire

FOR the little girl in your home—or the small boy, for that matter —chests of drawers, such as the two shown here, will do much to improve the appearance of the bedroom and also serve as an incentive for the youngster to keep her clothes and possessions in a neat and orderly manner. Either chest may complement and serve to expand a suite that you have already. There is ample space in both for all your youngster's linen with possibly a drawer or so left over for a collection of childish treasures. The chest with two doors, Fig. 1, has a top drawer that is shallower and a bottom drawer that is deeper than the other five. All extend the full width of the chest. If you want to store blankets and bulky clothing, drawers like these are best. The other chest, Fig. 5, has fourteen drawers of equal size. Where many individual compartments are required, this chest would be the better choice. Selection of the one you prefer to build may be governed by these factors. The chests look best when made of hardwoods, such as walnut or maple, and stained. Or they can be made of the semi-hardwoods such as poplar or gum and then painted. The originals were made of maple and given a blond or bleached finish.

Construction of the closed chest is given in Fig. 3. The doors are glued up from solid stock and splined top and bottom as in Fig. 4 to prevent warping. Drawer construction is of the usual type. However, in this case narrow strips were nailed to the sides near the lower edge. The strips help avoid binding by preventing the entire side from coming in contact with the chest. Notice that the chest top overhangs an amount equal to the thickness of the doors so they are flush. If available, use long piano hinges to hang the doors. These will help prevent warping also. Friction catches are used in the top edge to hold the doors closed.

The sides, top and bottom are made of built-up sections joined as shown in Fig. 3. The back is plywood rabbeted to the sides. Blind grooves are cut in the sides for the frames which are

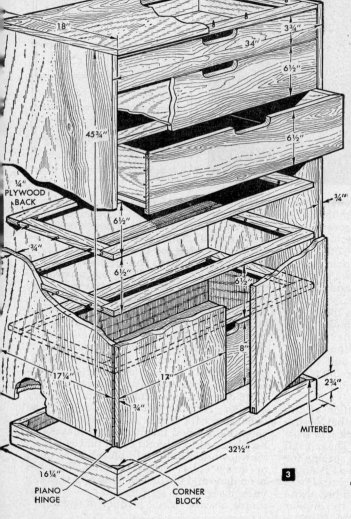

18"
34"
3¾"
6½"
6½"
45¾"
6½"
¼" PLYWOOD BACK
¾"
6½"
6½"
6½"
¾"
8"
17¼"
12"
2¾"
MITERED
¾"
32½"
16¼"
PIANO HINGE
CORNER BLOCK

3

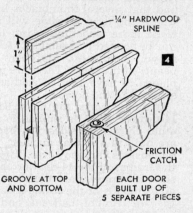

¼" HARDWOOD SPLINE
1"

4

GROOVE AT TOP AND BOTTOM
FRICTION CATCH
EACH DOOR BUILT UP OF 5 SEPARATE PIECES

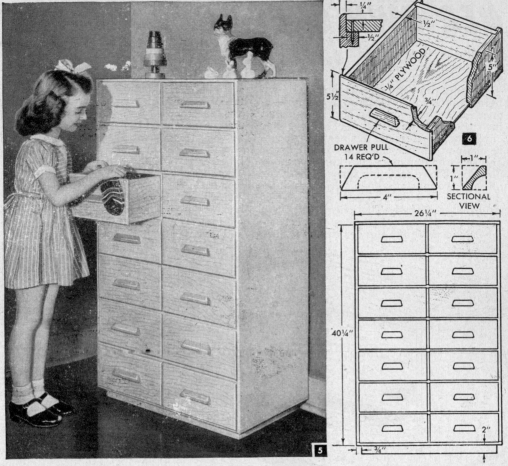

DRAWER PULL
14 REQ'D

SECTIONAL
VIEW

cut at the front corners to fit. Tongue-and-groove joints are used in assembling the frames. These are glued and screwed in place. The base has mitered joints reinforced with corner blocks and sets inside the cabinet. It is attached as indicated in detail B of Fig. 2. Detail A shows how the top is fastened to the sides and frame. After the cabinet is assembled, you may find that several thumbtacks in the frame where the drawers slide will make them work more smoothly. Also, the runners can be waxed occasionally. Although not shown, handles for the doors add to the beauty of the chest. These are round pieces planed to have one flat side and they are screwed to the doors.

In many ways, the construction of the 14-drawer chest is similar to that of the other chest. The sides, top, back and base are built in a similar manner. The overall dimensions vary, however. The spacing for the frames of the 14-drawer chest is equal since all drawers are the same size. Fig. 2 gives details of the frame assembly. Note that the front of the frame and the divider

can be hardwood while the remainder is pine or some other less expensive wood. This will reduce the cost of construction to some extent. The same type of construction can be used for the door chest. Fig. 6 gives the dimensions and method of assembly for the drawers. Plywood is used for the bottom, and the sides, front and back are made from solid stock. The front overlaps the frame on all sides. The drawer pulls are cut from 1-in.-square stock. In this chest the top is flush with the sides and does not overlap as in the previous case.

Many effects may be obtained in finishing the chests. If they are made of a semi-soft wood, spraying with a bone-white lacquer gives an excellent finish that is very popular. As a further touch, they may be decorated with decals. If hardwood is used, some light-toned finish is best. Maple can be bleached to a blond color that is almost white, while walnut will bleach to a russet or straw color. After the bleaching has been done and the bleach neutralized, spray with clear gloss lacquer. If the wood is maple a water-white lacquer is used.

CHILD'S BED HAS ROPE SPRINGS

Inexpensive and easy to build, this Hollywood-type youth bed is just the thing for baby when he begins to outgrow his crib. Except for a headboard panel of ¼-in. plywood, the bed is made entirely of solid stock. Over-all dimensions of the bed and the length of the guard rails are not given in the detail as these are determined by the size of the mattress, the guard rails being approximately half the length of the bed. Note that the bed rails are fastened permanently to the headboard and the footboard by mitering the ends and gluing and nailing them into mortises in the tapered legs. After the bed is assembled, a rope spring (clothesline will do) is laced through notched strips of 1 x 1-in. stock screwed to the sides of the bed rails as well as to the headboard and the footboard. After all nails are set and puttied over, the bed is enameled, using either a two-tone effect or a color to harmonize with the bedroom.

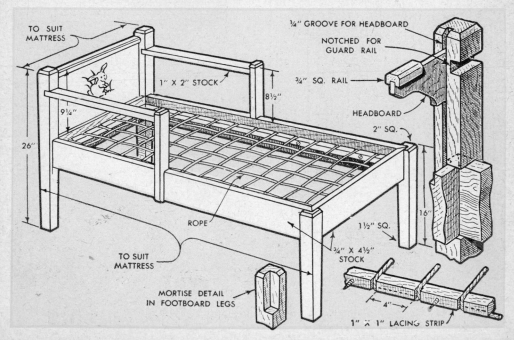

TO SUIT MATTRESS

1" X 2" STOCK

8½"

9¼"

26"

ROPE

TO SUIT MATTRESS

MORTISE DETAIL IN FOOTBOARD LEGS

¾" GROOVE FOR HEADBOARD

NOTCHED FOR GUARD RAIL

¾" SQ. RAIL

HEADBOARD

2" SQ.

16"

1½" SQ.

¾" X 4½" STOCK

4"

1" X 1" LACING STRIP

Easy-To-Make

It's actually a 5-gal. paint pail fitted with a padded seat and tailored inside and out with a gay-colored slip cover. Seat lifts off for storing shoes inside

By Peter R. Ruppe

UTILIZING a common 5-gal. pail for its framework, this vanity stool is both light-weight and sturdy, simple to make and provides a convenient storage compartment for shoes, hats, etc. Select a pail having straight sides—one in which paint comes will do—remove the handle if it has one, and clean the inside thoroughly by scraping or burning out the old paint.

A tacking strip or ring is fitted inside the pail about 2 in. down from the top and is fastened with flathead screws from the outside as in Fig. 2. The ring need not be in one piece—it can be of several segments

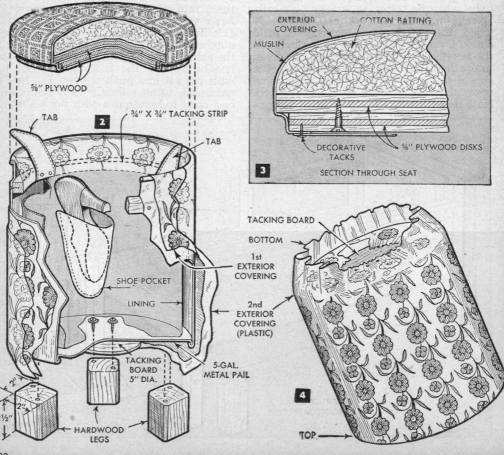

⅝" PLYWOOD

TAB

2

¾" X ¾" TACKING STRIP

TAB

EXTERIOR COVERING

COTTON BATTING

MUSLIN

DECORATIVE TACKS

⅝" PLYWOOD DISKS

3 SECTION THROUGH SEAT

SHOE POCKET

LINING

1st EXTERIOR COVERING

2nd EXTERIOR COVERING (PLASTIC)

5-GAL. METAL PAIL

TACKING BOARD 5" DIA.

2"
2"
2½"
HARDWOOD LEGS

TACKING BOARD

BOTTOM

4

TOP

VANITY STOOL

as it is hidden from view. Next, the bottom of the pail is drilled for screws to attach the three stub legs. These can be made of fancy hardwood and varnished, or cut from pine and painted. Two 1-in. screws are used to attach each leg. Holes are drilled in the bottom also for fastening a ⅜ by 5-in. wood disk to serve as a tacking surface for the outer covering. This is located in the center of the pail. The rabbeted edge of the seat board is formed by two ⅝-in.-plywood disks screwed together, one being the same diameter as the pail and the other about ¼ in. smaller, Fig. 3.

You're now ready to tackle the upholstering. The inside lining is applied first. This can be of a material contrasting with that used on the outside. Make a tubular shaped bag of it to fit the inside diameter of the tacking ring. If the stool is to be used for shoe storage, pockets should be sewed to the lining before it is tacked in place at the top. The outside covering is likewise sewed in a tubular shape to be pulled snugly over the pail. Fold the upper edge of it under and tack it neatly to the wood ring, forming small pleats where necessary to eliminate wrinkles. After the top edge is tacked, the fabric is pulled down smoothly and tacked to the wood disk at the bottom. Although optional, the outside covering of the stool can be protected from soiling by covering it with any of the transparent plastic materials, tacking it the same as before. See Fig. 4. Finally, two strong tabs of cloth are tacked to opposite sides of the wood ring to provide handles for carrying

the stool. These should be long enough to extend out from under the seat as shown in Fig. 1. This leaves the seat to be padded as indicated in the cross-sectional view in Fig. 3. Cotton batting is first applied generously and is held in place with a muslin cover. Several thicknesses of foam rubber, available in sheet form, could be used in place of the cotton. The outer covering is brought around and tacked neatly to the under edge and finished with a circular piece. Where the material covers the rabbeted edge it should be tacked to the underside of the top disk.

Fireplace Rails of Brass Pipe Assembled With Door-Hinge Parts

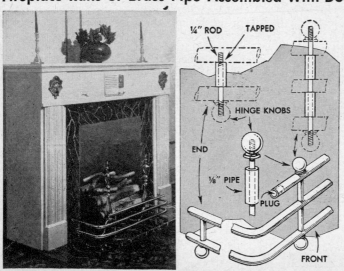

¼" ROD   TAPPED
HINGE KNOBS
END
⅛" PIPE
PLUG
FRONT

Add a bright touch to your fireplace by setting modernistic brass rails in front of the andirons. The rails, cut and bent from lengths of ½-in. brass pipe, are held together with several ball tips taken from loose-pin door hinges. Spacers of ⅛-in. brass pipe are placed between the rails and the tips, after being tapped, are screwed onto the threaded ends of ¼-in. rod. To give the appearance of rod stock, the open ends of the short top rail are plugged with pieces of brass stock, pressed in place and filed flush.

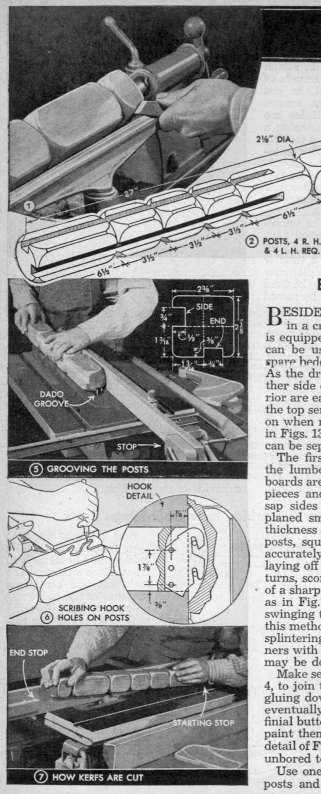

BUNKS and

GAUGE STICK

STOP

2⅛" DIA.

2⅜"

③ MARKING BEAD DIVISION

1" DIA.

2.7"

3½"

6½"

3½"   3½"   3½"

6½"

② POSTS, 4 R. H. & 4 L. H. REQ.

1⅜"   11"   1⅜"

④ SEPARATOR

SIDE

END

¾"

1 3/16"

2⅜"

2⅜"

½"   ⅜"

¾"

DADO GROOVE

STOP

⑤ GROOVING THE POSTS

HOOK DETAIL

⅞"

1⅞"

⅜"

SCRIBING HOOK
⑥ HOLES ON POSTS

END STOP

STARTING STOP

⑦ HOW KERFS ARE CUT

By Edwin M. Love

BESIDES saving considerable floor space in a crowded room, this bunk-bed unit is equipped with a mammoth drawer that can be used for storage, whether this is spare bedding or a fleet of model airplanes. As the drawer can be pulled out from either side of the bunk all parts of the interior are easily accessible. A plank fitted to the top serves as a handy platform to stand on when making the upper bed, as shown in Figs. 13, 15 and 16. The beds, however, can be separated and used as twin beds.

The first step in construction is to cut the lumber roughly to size. If the wide boards are warped, rip them into narrower pieces and glue together with heart and sap sides alternating. They then can be planed smooth without too much loss of thickness and will remain flat. To turn the posts, square the pieces and center them accurately. Use a gauge stick, Fig. 3, for laying off the bead divisions. As the work turns, score these divisions with the point of a sharp skew chisel held on the tool rest as in Fig. 1, and shape the bead ends by swinging the tool to the right and left. By this method the bead ends are cut without splintering the corners. Chamfer the corners with a light cut on the jointer, or this may be done by hand.

Make separator blocks as detailed in Fig. 4, to join the upper and lower bunk posts, gluing dowels in their ends. If the bunks eventually are to be used as twin beds, turn finial buttons to go into the post holes, and paint them to match the beds. See upper detail of Fig. 10. Disks are sufficient for the unbored tops of the upper bunk posts.

Use one blade of a dado saw to slit the posts and bed-rail ends to take the rail

STORAGE SPACE *in One Unit*

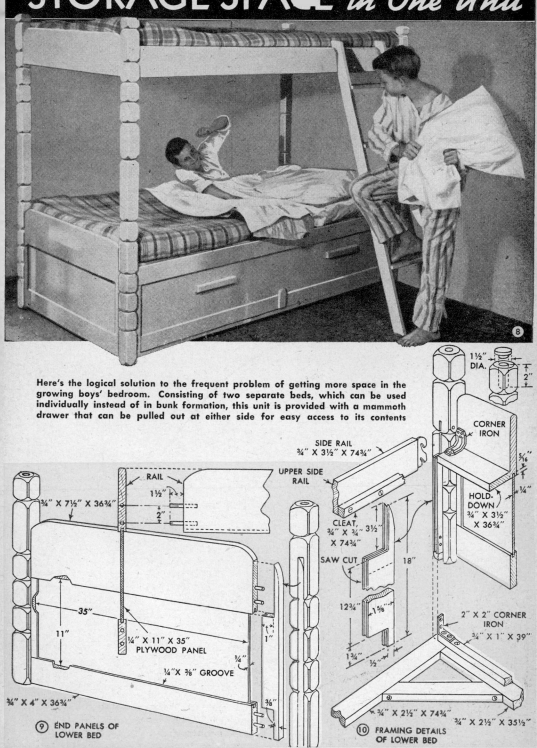

Here's the logical solution to the frequent problem of getting more space in the growing boys' bedroom. Consisting of two separate beds, which can be used individually instead of in bunk formation, this unit is provided with a mammoth drawer that can be pulled out at either side for easy access to its contents

1½" DIA.
2"

CORNER IRON

5/16"
¼"

HOLD-DOWN
¾" X 3½" X 36¾"

SIDE RAIL
¾" X 3½" X 74¾"

UPPER SIDE RAIL

CLEAT,
¾" X ¾" X 3½"
X 74¾"

SAW CUT

18"

12¾"   1⅝"

13¾"
½"

2" X 2" CORNER IRON
¾" X 1" X 39"

RAIL

1½"
2"

¾" X 7½" X 36¾"

35"

11"

¼" X 11" X 35" PLYWOOD PANEL

¼"

¼" X ⅜" GROOVE

1"

3/8"

¾" X 4" X 36¾"

⑨ END PANELS OF LOWER BED

¾" X 2½" X 74¾"   ¾" X 2½" X 35½"

⑩ FRAMING DETAILS OF LOWER BED

hooks. Install the hooks in the rails and secure the pins with wooden wedges to prevent them from dropping out. Use one rail end fitted with a hook as a template for scribing the pin locations on a post as in Fig. 6, taking a pattern from this for the rest. Center the pins where the hooks will bear against them and draw the rail ends tight when the rail is ⅛ in. above level. The joints will be rigid when the rails are driven down to position. Then determine the length of the saw kerfs in the posts, and set start and stop blocks on the circular saw to correspond, as shown in Fig. 7.

Next mount a ¾-in. dado head and groove the posts ½ in. deep to receive the panel stiles as shown in Figs. 2 and 5. Make the stiles, rounding the ends to fit the grooves or chiseling the groove ends square, as preferred. The exact position of the grooves is shown in the detail of Fig. 5. Kerf the ends of the drawer stiles to receive the ends of the hooks that project below the rails.

Bore dowel holes in the end rails and use them as patterns for locating the post dowel holes. As-

⑪ DRILLING HOLES FOR SPRING TIES

⑫ SPRING

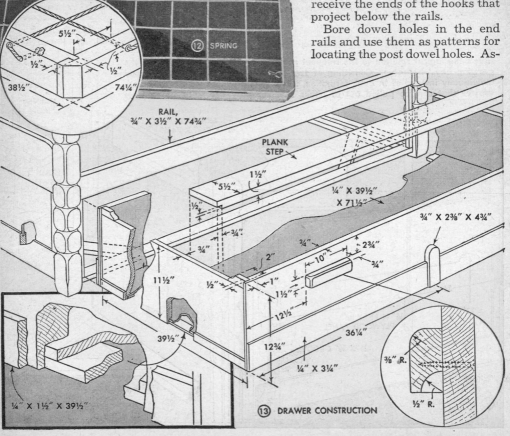

RAIL,
¾" X 3½" X 74¾"

PLANK STEP

⑬ DRAWER CONSTRUCTION

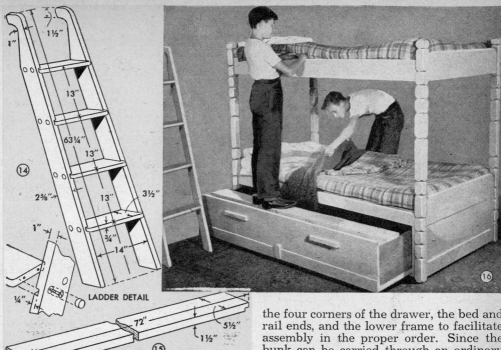

LADDER DETAIL

PLANK STEP

semble the rails and stiles with the end panels and when the glue is dry assemble with the posts as in Fig. 9. Clean up the ends and attach the side rails. Build the lower frame to fit, screwing in the corner braces as in Fig. 10 and reinforcing all joints with corrugated fasteners driven into the underside. Wax the upper side of the frame. To support the frame make six blocks of suitable thickness, nailing one under each corner, set well back, and one at the center of each drawer rail. Add the drawer guides, which are flush with the sides of the drawer, since this can be pulled from either side. The four corner irons screwed to the guides and inner surfaces of the drawer stiles prevent the frame from dropping if the bunk is lifted. The corner irons are not intended to take the weight of the drawer, for which purpose the blocks, already mentioned, are provided.

Build the drawer with the sides rabbeted into the fronts and the bottom rabbeted into the front and sides as in Fig. 13. Hardwood strips nailed to the ends and across the center take the wear and provide clearance for easy sliding of the drawer. Use plywood to make overlays for the drawer fronts. A wooden overlay shaped to match the post turning is placed at the center. Both sides are made exactly alike.

Before taking the bunk apart, number the four corners of the drawer, the bed and rail ends, and the lower frame to facilitate assembly in the proper order. Since the bunk can be carried through an ordinary doorway, the ends and rails may be assembled by means of dowels, making a rigid housing for the drawer and eliminating the bother of fitting rail hooks. The upper bunk ends are assembled with two posts and a wide rail, and are put together with the rails like any ordinary bed.

Glue and screw cleats inside the rails near the lower edges to carry the springs. Rope springs, Fig. 12, are quite satisfactory, although they tend to sag like hammocks when the ropes stretch, and the ropes cannot be drawn too tightly or the sides bow in unduly. If tight and flat springs are desired, stiffen the sides by nailing a 1 by 6-in. board lengthwise under each edge, setting it in ¾ in. to allow for the rail cleats. Then rope is laced through holes drilled in the spring frames as shown in Fig. 11, the ends of the rope being knotted. Details of frame corner construction and sizes are given in the circular insert of Fig. 12.

A simple four-step ladder is shown in Figs. 8 and 14. Gain the ends of the steps into the sides of the ladder and secure them with screws having heads sunk in counterbored holes. Glue plugs into the holes and dress them flush when dry.

Monks' Cloth Reclaims Table Top

If the top of one of your tables is marred beyond the point of refinishing, you can still reclaim it by covering it with monks' cloth. Draw the cloth tightly over the top, tacking underneath, and then varnish.

A House All

By A. T. Eyman

YOU won't have to coax your children to hang up their clothes if they have a wardrobe house like this one. Complete with cedar-shingled roof and lapped siding, it can be placed anywhere against a wall. Besides the space inside the house for hanging clothes there's an "attic" for storing blankets and other extras. Drawers fitted into the side of the house take the place of a dresser or chest for slippers, sweaters and other small garments. Notice that the house is floored. This detail can be omitted and a threshold substituted for the doorstep if the house is made as an extension to an already existing closet. A small mirror attached to the outside surface of the door will give the entrance a realistic appearance as well as reflect the little owner's features. Or you can hang a mirror on the inside of the door, reserving the outside for a miniature knocker, house number or name plate. A toggle switch that controls interior lighting occupies the place of a bell button beside the door.

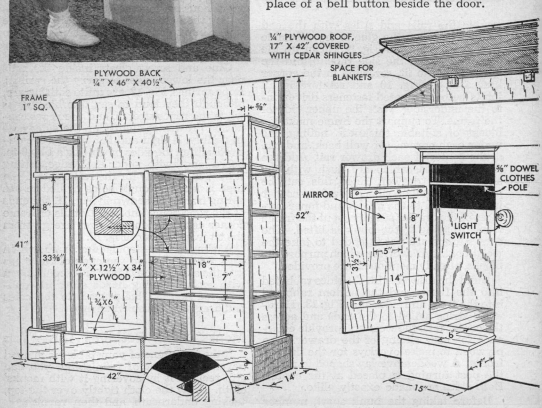

¼" PLYWOOD ROOF, 17" X 42" COVERED WITH CEDAR SHINGLES

SPACE FOR BLANKETS

PLYWOOD BACK ¼" X 46" X 40½"

FRAME 1" SQ.

⅝"

8"

41"

33⅜"

¼" X 12½" X 34" PLYWOOD

¾" X 6"

18"

7"

52"

42"

14"

MIRROR

8"

5"

3½"

14"

⅝" DOWEL CLOTHES POLE

LIGHT SWITCH

6"

7"

15"

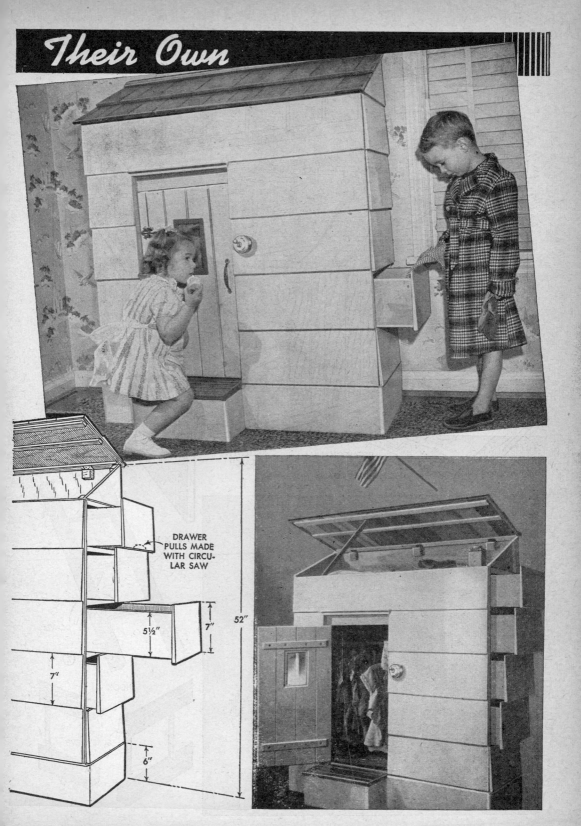

DRAWER
PULLS MADE
WITH CIRCU-
LAR SAW

52"

7"

5½"

7"

6"

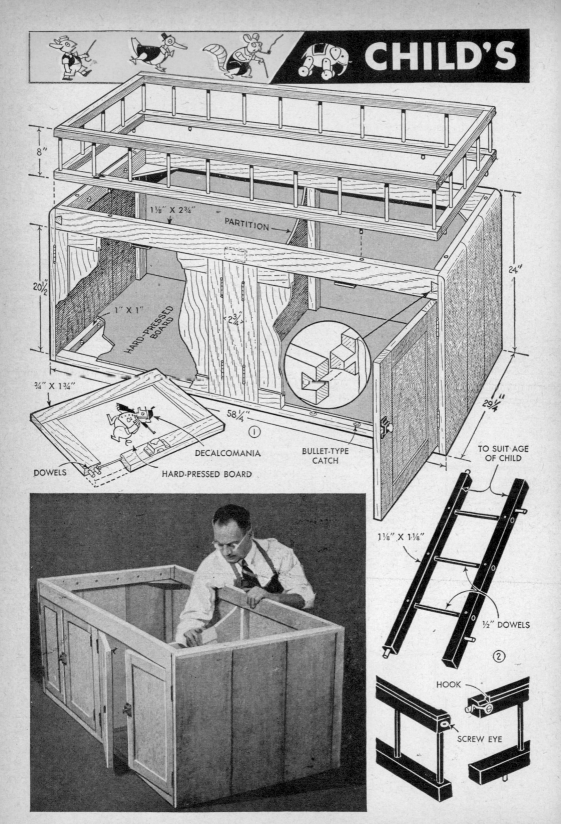

8"

1⅛" X 2¾"

PARTITION

20½"

1" X 1"

HARD-PRESSED BOARD

2¾"

24"

29¼"

¾" X 1¾"

DECALCOMANIA

58¼"

①

DOWELS

HARD-PRESSED BOARD

BULLET-TYPE CATCH

TO SUIT AGE OF CHILD

1⅛" X 1⅛"

½" DOWELS

②

HOOK

SCREW EYE

CHEST-BED

IN SMALL homes and apartments where it is impossible to furnish a room for the child, this combination bed and chest will be of real value, as it serves as a comfortable bed at night and provides storage space for extra blankets, toys and other household items. In daytime, removing the railings and covering the chest with an appropriate drapery converts it into a useful couch. If made higher than shown in Fig. 1, the railings can be removed and set up separately to form a child's play pen. When used in this way, however, a floor for the pen must be assembled and drilled for pegs to keep the railings in place.

Before assembling the frame, have the springs at hand so they can be measured, as the exact size of the chest depends upon these dimensions. Corners of the frame are dovetailed and glued, with triangular blocks glued and screwed to the underside of the top members at each corner to support the springs. Note that the ends of the chest are built up of tongue-and-groove stock, glued and screwed to the frame. To improve the appearance, the outer edges of these boards are rounded at the top.

Note that the chest is fitted with a partition which is curved at the top to prevent the springs hitting it when they are pressed down by weight of a person sitting or lying on them. Railings are assembled quickly by clamping the upper and lower members together and drilling them both at the same time. The holes should be just large enough to provide a sliding fit for the dowels, these being held in place by glue and small finishing nails driven in from the sides. To prevent shifting of the railings, tapered pegs are fitted in the lower members to correspond with holes drilled at the top of the chest frame as shown in Fig. 2. End railings are also fitted with pegs which slip into holes drilled in the side railings. Hooks and screw eyes lock the railings together.

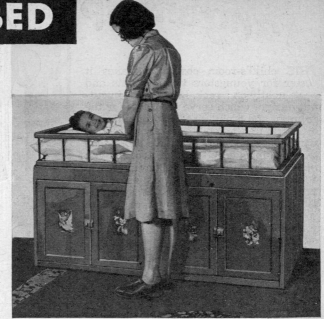

Doors are hung with hinges having removable pins for convenience in detaching them, in case the edges need planing to make them fit accurately. A stop block at the top and bullet-type catches in the bottom rail hold the doors shut. Or, you can fit them with elbow catches and cabinet latches, if desired. Although the bed is somewhat higher than cribs in general, this gives the advantages of adding to the storage space, Fig. 3, and facilitating making the bed with a minimum of stooping for the housewife. Low railings are also a convenience where the bed is made without removing them. Decalcomania transfers are applied in the center of each door.

Hang 'em up

THIS child's-room costumer makes it easier for youngsters to hang hats and coats neatly on a rack. Pony heads in cut-out design, which serve as braces for the column, and a pint-sized Scotty sitting at attention on the top effectively match the usual decorations of a child's room. The whole thing's easy to make, too. All you need are hand tools and a few pieces of suitable hardwood. Birch is especially recommended because it is so easy to finish with either colored enamels or varnish to match the other furnishings. Parts are joined with screws and all edges are sanded smooth before finishing.

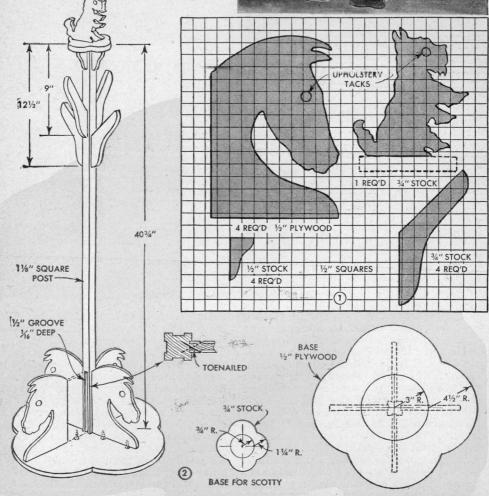

9"

12½"

40¾"

1⅛" SQUARE POST

½" GROOVE ¹⁄₁₆" DEEP

TOENAILED

UPHOLSTERY TACKS

1 REQ'D ¾" STOCK

4 REQ'D ½" PLYWOOD

½" STOCK 4 REQ'D

½" SQUARES

¾" STOCK 4 REQ'D

①

BASE ½" PLYWOOD

3" R.

4½" R.

¾" STOCK

¾" R.

1¼" R.

②

BASE FOR SCOTTY

Chinese-Modern
"FIRE SCREEN"

FROM a decorative standpoint, the blackened interior of an unused fireplace is an eyesore, especially during spring and summer months when color is necessary to give a new lift to old surroundings. That's when you need this attractive trellis "fire screen" to camouflage the opening. Chinese in motif both in color and design, the screen, when augmented with a growing or artificial vine, provides a smart summer treatment for an uninviting fireplace. The outer framework of the trellis is mortised at the corners. Then the diamond shape in the center is fastened with long screws and the remaining parts with corrugated fasteners. The back of the trellis is covered with hardware cloth which is painted black to contrast with a Chinese-red framework. The base and shelf of the screen are cut from plywood, and the wooden flower box, mitered and splined at the corners, is fitted with a copper lining. The flower box and shelf are painted black to set off the red.

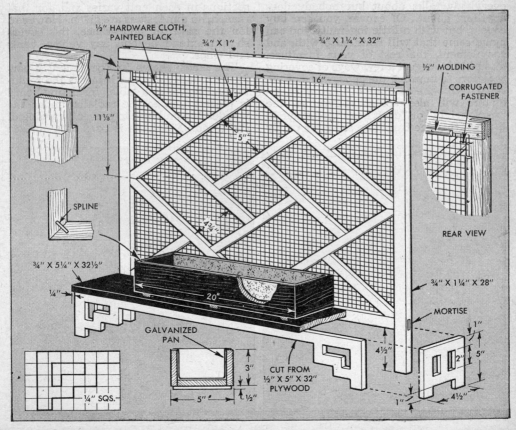

½" HARDWARE CLOTH, PAINTED BLACK
¾" X 1"
¾" X 1¼" X 32"
½" MOLDING
CORRUGATED FASTENER
16"
5"
11⅛"
REAR VIEW
SPLINE
¾" X 5¼" X 32½"
4¾"
¾" X 1¼" X 28"
¼"
20"
MORTISE
GALVANIZED PAN
CUT FROM ½" X 5" X 32" PLYWOOD
4½"
1"
5"
2"
3"
5"
½"
1"
4½"
¼" SQS.

AN acknowledged eyesore around the home, uncovered radiators are one of those things that everybody talks about but nobody does anything about. Of course, you can buy covers, but with a little ingenuity you can make some that will harmonize with, and complement, the rest of your furniture. The photos suggest a few ways of covering radiators to improve the appearance of the room. With the addition of the covers, radiators will also act as convectors, the "stack height" or "draft head" being due to the fact that the front and sides are partly

By John F. Shrock

covered. Although the height, width and depth of radiator sections are standardized, the number of sections in each unit varies and, for that reason, no dimensions are given. However, for the sake of appearance, the covers should extend beyond any valves, vents and traps.

The cover shown in Figs. 1 and 2 performs a dual function: it masks the radiator and serves as a table. Insulating board is placed next to the radiator under the wooden top and face to prevent warping of the wood. Linoleum is used as a surface

Cover 'em up!

Photos courtesy U. S. Gypsum Co.

for the table and top of the cover. Note that instead of using legs to support the table in the raised position, two brackets fold out to support it. Circulation of air is through the open ends. Fig. 4 is the "before" and Fig. 3 the "after" view of a living-room radiator that is covered with pressed board bent to shape and lined with insulating board. Reinforcement at the ends increases the strength of the cabinet. Perforations are drilled in the top to increase the circulation of air. Sheet metal could have been used instead of wood in this case.

Horizontal lines are emphasized in the design of another type of living-room cover shown in Fig. 5. It is constructed of wood and insulating board and lined with grass cloth, the latter being porous enough to permit free circulation of air. In Figs. 6 and 7 are shown the before and after views of a bedroom radiator. Like the one in Fig. 3, it is formed of pressed board and lined with insulation. The top of this one also has perforations. All units are finished with a high-gloss enamel.

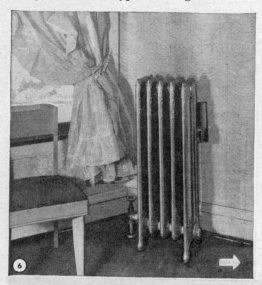

WOOD CHEST and BELLOWS

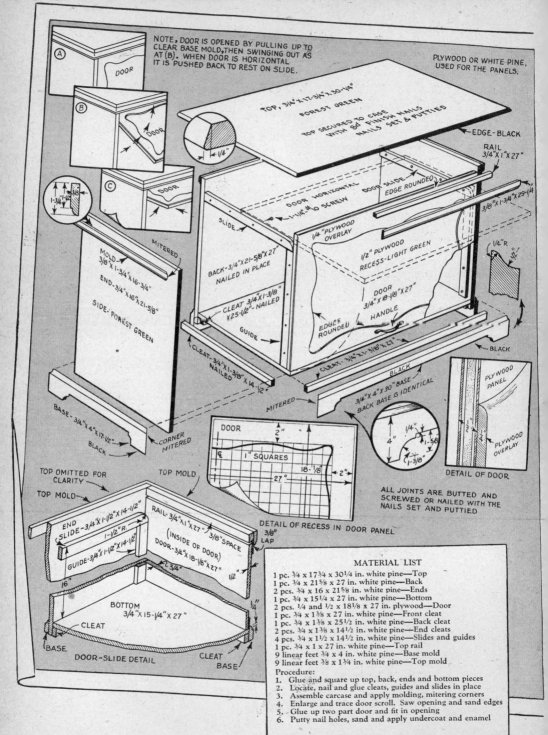

NOTE, DOOR IS OPENED BY PULLING UP TO CLEAR BASE MOLD, THEN SWINGING OUT AS AT (B). WHEN DOOR IS HORIZONTAL IT IS PUSHED BACK TO REST ON SLIDE.

PLYWOOD OR WHITE PINE, USED FOR THE PANELS.

Ⓐ DOOR

Ⓑ DOOR

Ⓒ DOOR

1/4"

1-3/4" 3/8

TOP, 3/4" X 17-3/4" X 30-1/4"
FOREST GREEN
TOP SECURED TO CASE WITH 8d FINISH NAILS NAILS SET & PUTTIED

EDGE - BLACK

RAIL 3/4" X 1" X 27"

DOOR HORIZONTAL 1-1/4" #10 SCREW

DOOR SLIDE

EDGE ROUNDED

3/8" X 1-3/4" X 29-1/4"

MITERED

MOLD 3/8" X 1-3/4" X 16-3/4"

END - 3/4" X 16" X 21-5/8"

SIDE - FOREST GREEN

SLIDE

BACK - 3/4" X 21-5/8" X 27" NAILED IN PLACE

1/4 "PLYWOOD OVERLAY

1/2" PLYWOOD RECESS - LIGHT GREEN

1/4"R 1/2"

CLEAT 3/4" X 1-3/8" X 25-1/2" NAILED

GUIDE

DOOR 3/4" X 18-1/8" X 27"

HANDLE

EDGES ROUNDED

CLEAT - 3/4" X 1-3/8" X 14-1/2" NAILED

CLEAT - 3/4" X 1-3/8" X 21"

BLACK

BASE - 3/4" X 4" X 17-1/2"

CORNER MITERED

BLACK

MITERED

3/4" X 4" X 30" BASE BACK BASE IS IDENTICAL

BLACK

DOOR
2"
1" SQUARES
18-1/8
27"

1/4"
4"
1-5/8
1-3/8

PLYWOOD PANEL

PLYWOOD OVERLAY

DETAIL OF DOOR

DETAIL OF RECESS IN DOOR PANEL

ALL JOINTS ARE BUTTED AND SCREWED OR NAILED WITH THE NAILS SET AND PUTTIED

TOP OMITTED FOR CLARITY

TOP MOLD

TOP MOLD

END
SLIDE - 3/4" X 1-1/2" X 14-1/2"
1-1/2"R.

GUIDE - 3/4" X 1-1/2" X 14-1/2"

16"

RAIL- 3/4" X 1" X 27"
(INSIDE OF DOOR)
DOOR - 3/4" X 18-1/8" X 27"

3/8" SPACE

2-3/4"

1/2"

3/8" LAP

1/4"

BOTTOM 3/4" X 15-1/4" X 27"

CLEAT

BASE

DOOR-SLIDE DETAIL

CLEAT

BASE

MATERIAL LIST

1 pc. 3/4 x 17-3/4 x 30-1/4 in. white pine—Top
1 pc. 3/4 x 21-5/8 x 27 in. white pine—Back
2 pcs. 3/4 x 16 x 21-5/8 in. white pine—Ends
1 pc. 3/4 x 15-1/4 x 27 in. white pine—Bottom
2 pcs. 1/4 and 1/2 x 18-1/8 x 27 in. plywood—Door
1 pc. 3/4 x 1-3/8 x 27 in. white pine—Front cleat
1 pc. 3/4 x 1-3/8 x 25-1/2 in. white pine—Back cleat
2 pcs. 3/4 x 1-3/8 x 14-1/2 in. white pine—End cleats
4 pcs. 3/4 x 1-1/2 x 14-1/2 in. white pine—Slides and guides
1 pc. 3/4 x 1 x 27 in. white pine—Top rail
9 linear feet 3/4 x 4 in. white pine—Base mold
9 linear feet 3/8 x 1-3/4 in. white pine—Top mold

Procedure:
1. Glue and square up top, back, ends and bottom pieces
2. Locate, nail and glue cleats, guides and slides in place
3. Assemble carcase and apply molding, mitering corners
4. Enlarge and trace door scroll. Saw opening and sand edges
5. Glue up two part door and fit in opening
6. Putty nail holes, sand and apply undercoat and enamel

for Your Fireplace

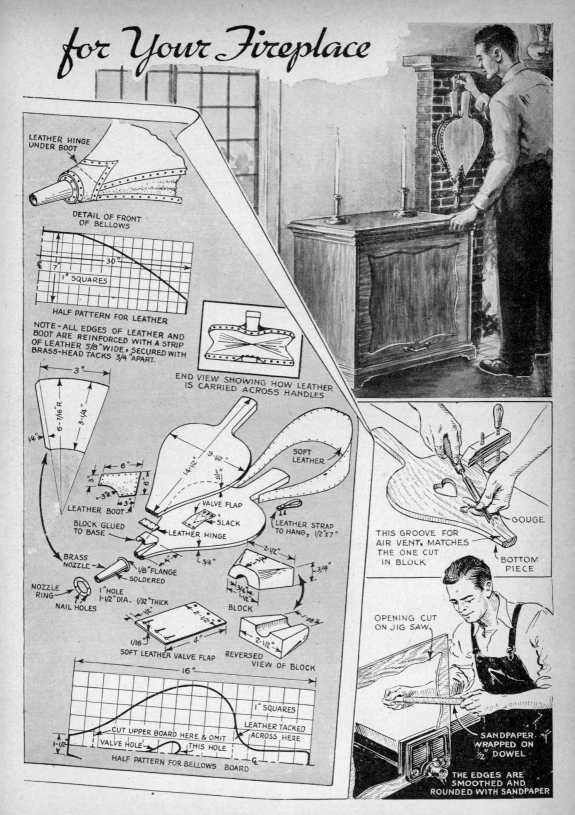

LEATHER HINGE UNDER BOOT

DETAIL OF FRONT OF BELLOWS

½" — 7" — 30" — 1" SQUARES

HALF PATTERN FOR LEATHER

NOTE - ALL EDGES OF LEATHER AND BOOT ARE REINFORCED WITH A STRIP OF LEATHER 5/8" WIDE, SECURED WITH BRASS-HEAD TACKS ¾" APART.

END VIEW SHOWING HOW LEATHER IS CARRIED ACROSS HANDLES

3" — 6-7/16" R — 3-¼" — ¼"

6" — 3" — 3" R — 3"

LEATHER BOOT

BLOCK GLUED TO BASE

BRASS NOZZLE

NOZZLE RING

NAIL HOLES

1/8" FLANGE SOLDERED

1" HOLE 1-½" DIA. 1/32" THICK

14-½" — 9-½" — ¾"

SOFT LEATHER

VALVE FLAP

SLACK

LEATHER HINGE

LEATHER STRAP TO HANG, ½"X7"

¾"

2-½" — ¾" — ¾" — 1-½"

BLOCK

2-½" — 2-½"

REVERSED VIEW OF BLOCK

½" — 2-½" — 4" — 1/16

SOFT LEATHER VALVE FLAP

16" — 1" SQUARES

CUT UPPER BOARD HERE & OMIT THIS HOLE

LEATHER TACKED ACROSS HERE

VALVE HOLE — 1-½"

HALF PATTERN FOR BELLOWS BOARD

THIS GROOVE FOR AIR VENT, MATCHES THE ONE CUT IN BLOCK

GOUGE

BOTTOM PIECE

OPENING CUT ON JIG SAW

SANDPAPER WRAPPED ON ½" DOWEL

THE EDGES ARE SMOOTHED AND ROUNDED WITH SANDPAPER

ALL-WOOD FIREPLACE, BOOKCASE

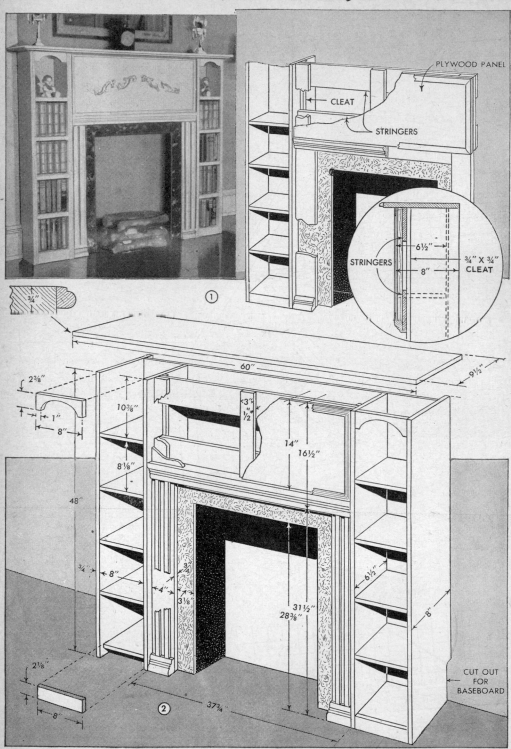

PLYWOOD PANEL

CLEAT

STRINGERS

STRINGERS

6½"

¾" X ¾" CLEAT

8"

①

¾"

2⅜"

1"

8"

10⅜"

3"
½"

60"

9½"

14"

16½"

8⅛"

48"

¾"   8"

3"
4

4"

3⅛"

6½

8"

31½"
28⅜"

CUT OUT
FOR
BASEBOARD

2⅛"

8"

②

37¾"

AND MANTEL

By Carl F. Baries

BLACK marbleized linoleum contrasting with a white or ivory finish gives this unit a pleasing appearance in almost any surroundings. Construction is simple as the unit is nothing more than two pier cabinets or bookcases joined by stringers faced with plywood in which an opening is cut. If the unit is to be painted, almost any wood will do, but hardwood is better if you intend to use a stain-and-varnish finish. In this case, plywood to match the cabinets should be used for the mantel and front panels.

The cabinets are made as shown in Fig. 2, the rear edges of the side pieces being cut to fit over the baseboard. To accommodate books of varying heights, the top shelf is 10½ in. and the others 8½ in. Strips of wood are placed across the bottoms of the cabinets for aprons, and arched lintels are used across the tops. These serve not only as trim, but as a support to which the top may be nailed. Cleats are attached along the inside surfaces of the sides for stringers that hold the cases together, Fig. 1. Over the stringers three lengths of wood are nailed to support the panel and space it so that it extends flush with the edge of the molding as shown in the circular detail of Fig. 1. The mantel is a plywood panel that extends over the front and sides of the cabinets, and a strip of molding is bradded along the edges, as diagrammed in the upper left-hand detail of Fig. 2.

For the fireplace, a three-sided back is made of plywood, Fig. 3. This is placed loose between the cabinets or it can be nailed to the sides, in which case the dimensions shown will have to be increased. Sides of the back are hidden by an inverted U-shaped frame on which marbleized linoleum is pasted. The frame is held in place by two wood strips attached to the cabinet sides, and molding is added to the strips for trim. The back should be painted brick red so that when a light is placed behind a stack of logs in the "fireplace," the reflection will suggest the glow of a real fire. Molding is applied to the edge of the sides and shelves of the cabinets, Fig. 4, and an ornament is glued on the front panel.

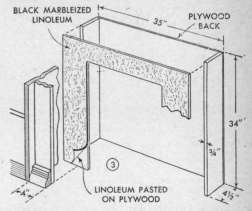

BLACK MARBLEIZED LINOLEUM — PLYWOOD BACK
35"
34"
¾"
4"
4½"
③
LINOLEUM PASTED ON PLYWOOD

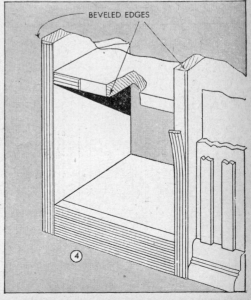

BEVELED EDGES
④

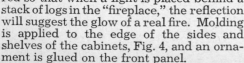

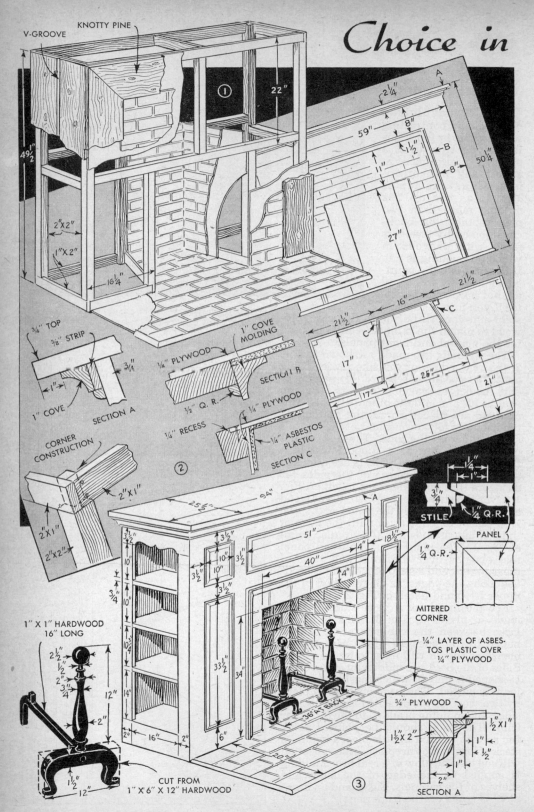

V-GROOVE
KNOTTY PINE

Choice in

49½"

① 22"

2"X2"
1"X2"
16¼"

2¼"
59"
8"
1½"
11"
8"
B
27"
50¼"
A

¾" TOP
3⁄8" STRIP
3⁄4"
1"
1" COVE
SECTION A

1" COVE MOLDING
¼" PLYWOOD
SECTION B
½" Q. R.

¼" PLYWOOD
¼" RECESS
¼" ASBESTOS PLASTIC
SECTION C

CORNER CONSTRUCTION
2"X1"
2"X1"
2"X2"

②

2½"
C
2½"
16"
C
17"
26"
21"
17"

¼"
1"
¾"
¼" Q.R.
STILE
PANEL
¼" Q.R.
MITERED CORNER

1" X 1" HARDWOOD
16" LONG
2½"
2½"
½"
2"
2¾"
12"
12"
2"
1½"
12"
CUT FROM
1" X 6" X 12" HARDWOOD

9½"
25½"
51"
40"
A
18½"
4"
4"
3½"
3½"
3½"
3½"
10"
10"
10"
10"
10¾"
¾"
33½"
34"
14"
16"
2"
2"
6"
36" AT BACK
20"
¼" LAYER OF ASBESTOS PLASTIC OVER ¼" PLYWOOD

③

¾" PLYWOOD
1½" X 2"
½" X 1"
1"
1½"
1"
2"
SECTION A

Imitation FIREPLACES

Four practical designs incorporating built-in book shelves and storage space. Plastic coating is applied and molded to imitate brick and stone

By Carl W. Bertsch

SO REALISTIC looking are these imitation fireplaces, you'll find it difficult to distinguish them from the real thing, especially when they are fitted with homemade wooden andirons and a "glowing" log. Among the four designs given there is one to suit practically any setting, from a modern living room to a den of knotty pine. The hearth of each is a separate unit from the rest of the fireplace for easy handling when moving.

Construction is basically the same for all, that is, a rough framework similar to the one shown in Fig. 1, is made first, which is covered with plywood before adding the finished trim and the imitation brick or stone. Slight variation of this procedure will be noted in the construction of the modern fireplace detailed in Figs. 4 and 5, as no inner plywood covering is necessary here. In case you are unable to obtain ¼-in. plywood, some of the bet-

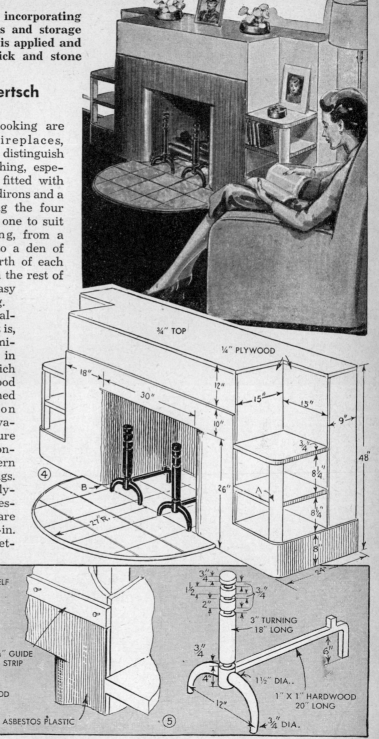

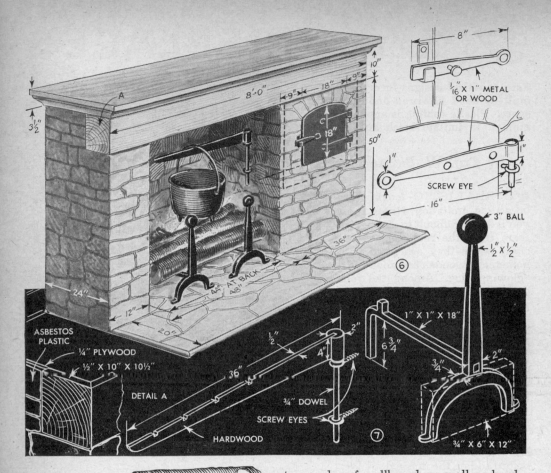

8'-0"

9" 18" 9"

10"

3½"

A

50"

18"

C

SCREW EYE

8"

¹⁄₁₆" X 1" METAL
OR WOOD

1"

16"

3" BALL

½" X ½"

6

24"

12"

20"

36"

44" AT BACK
48"

ASBESTOS
PLASTIC

¼" PLYWOOD

½" X 10" X 10½"

36"

DETAIL A

HARDWOOD

SCREW EYES

¾" DOWEL

½"

4"

2"

1" X 1" X 18"

6¾"

¾"

2"

¾"

¾" X 6" X 12"

7

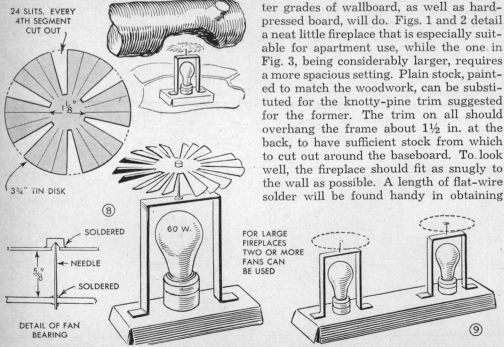

24 SLITS. EVERY
4TH SEGMENT
CUT OUT

1⅛"

3¾" TIN DISK

8

SOLDERED

NEEDLE

SOLDERED

⅝"

DETAIL OF FAN
BEARING

60 W.

FOR LARGE
FIREPLACES
TWO OR MORE
FANS CAN
BE USED

9

ter grades of wallboard, as well as hard-pressed board, will do. Figs. 1 and 2 detail a neat little fireplace that is especially suitable for apartment use, while the one in Fig. 3, being considerably larger, requires a more spacious setting. Plain stock, painted to match the woodwork, can be substituted for the knotty-pine trim suggested for the former. The trim on all should overhang the frame about 1½ in. at the back, to have sufficient stock from which to cut out around the baseboard. To look well, the fireplace should fit as snugly to the wall as possible. A length of flat-wire solder will be found handy in obtaining the shape of the baseboard for transferring to the end boards. Areas to be covered with plastic should have ¼-in. wire mesh tacked to them to make it adhere. However, if you are unable to obtain this material, another way to key the plastic is to groove the plywood deeply with a sharp tool, undercutting the grooves thus made, then size the wood with a coat of shellac.

Now to mix and apply the plastic: The ingredients of this are listed in the formula given in Fig. 13. Weigh and measure these carefully, and when adding the asbestos-whiting mixture, stir constantly and finally knead with the hands. Be careful not to add more water than is specified. A pail is a good container in which to mix and store the plastic. It can be kept for as long as a

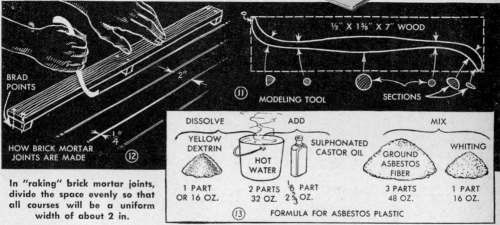

BRAD POINTS

2"

¼"

HOW BRICK MORTAR JOINTS ARE MADE ⑫

½" X 1⅝" X 7" WOOD

⑪ MODELING TOOL

SECTIONS

In "raking" brick mortar joints, divide the space evenly so that all courses will be a uniform width of about 2 in.

DISSOLVE		ADD		MIX	
YELLOW DEXTRIN	HOT WATER	SULPHONATED CASTOR OIL	GROUND ASBESTOS FIBER	WHITING
1 PART OR 16 OZ.	2 PARTS 32 OZ.	⅙ PART 2⅔ OZ.	3 PARTS 48 OZ.	1 PART 16 OZ.

⑬ FORMULA FOR ASBESTOS PLASTIC

month if covered with wet cloths to prevent it from drying out. Apply the plastic with the fingers or putty knife, pressing it into the wire-covered surface, and build up a layer about ¼ in. thick. Then smooth it lightly with a trowel dipped in water frequently. Avoid troweling the plastic too smoothly in order to have the texture resemble that of brickwork. To simulate stone as is used on the colonial fireplace detailed in Figs. 6 and 7, a wooden modeling tool like the one in Fig. 11 is needed to form the "mortar joints." This is used freehand as in Fig. 10 to produce irregular joints, but it is run along a straightedge as shown in Fig. 12 for producing brickwork effects. Where a rough stone effect is wanted, build up the thickness of the plastic by adding a second layer. The plastic dries hard in 48 hrs., the same color as cement.

Artists' oil colors, thinned with turpen-tine, are best to tint the plastic. Burnt sienna, Indian red or Venetian red, with or without lampblack added, will give practically any brick shade wanted. Apply a wash coat of this, leaving the mortar joints unpainted. Then tone individual bricks here and there a little darker than others. The back and sides of the fire pit should be given a coat of lampblack to make it look smoked. Stone surfaces require more care in coloring. Experiment with yellow, blue, green or orange colors mixed with sepia or raw umber to obtain the stone effect.

A log charred on the underside by applying a blowtorch or other flame to it, and placed over a hidden colored bulb as shown in Figs. 8 and 9, will give a flickering glow to further add realism. Also, by "peening" the wooden andirons and giving them a coat of flat-black paint, it will be hard to tell them from iron.

TWO CABINETS *Hold Your*

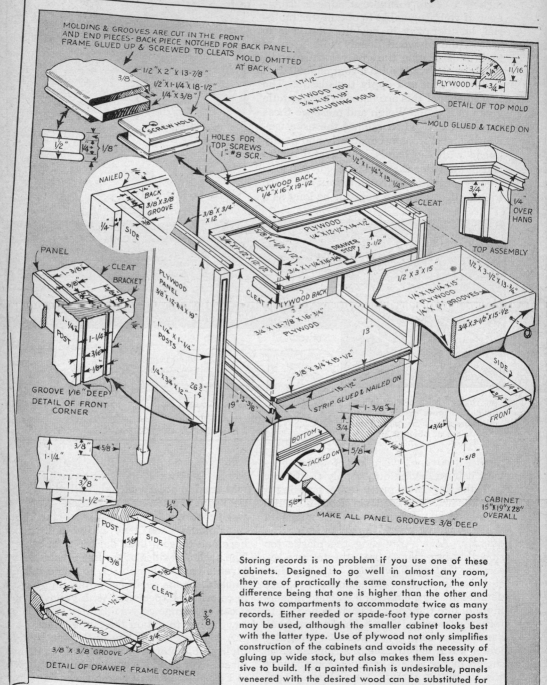

MOLDING & GROOVES ARE CUT IN THE FRONT AND END PIECES. BACK PIECE NOTCHED FOR BACK PANEL. FRAME GLUED UP & SCREWED TO CLEATS

MOLD OMITTED AT BACK

3/8"
1/2" X 2" X 13-7/8"
1/2" X 1-1/4 X 18-1/2"
1/4" X 3/8"

SCREW HOLE

1/2" 1/4" 1/8"

DETAIL OF TOP MOLD
PLYWOOD
3/8 1/16"
3/4

17-1/2"

PLYWOOD TOP 3/4"X 15"X19" INCLUDING MOLD
1-1/4"

MOLD GLUED & TACKED ON

NAILED
BACK 3/8"X 3/8" GROOVE
1/4" SIDE 3/8"

HOLES FOR TOP SCREWS 1- #8 SCR.

1/2" X 1-1/4 X 15-1/4"
PLYWOOD BACK 1/4"X 16"X 19-1/2"
CLEAT

3/8" X 3/4" X 12"

PLYWOOD 1/4"X12-1/2"X14-1/2"

DRAWER STOP

3-1/2"

3/4 3/4
OVER HANG
TOP ASSEMBLY

PANEL
CLEAT
1-3/8
5/8
BRACKET

PLYWOOD PANEL 3/8"X 12-3/4 X 19"

3/8"X 1-1/2"X 9"
3/4"X 1-1/4"X 16-3/4"
CLEAT
PLYWOOD BACK

1/2" X 3" X 15"
1/2" X 3-1/2 X 13-3/4"
1/4"X 13-1/4"X 15" PLYWOOD
1/4" X 5/16" GROOVES
3/4"X3-1/2"X15-1/2"

POST 1-1/4 1-1/4 3/16 1/8

1-1/4"X 1-1/4" POSTS
1/4" X 3/4 X 12"

3/4"X 13-7/8"X16-3/4" PLYWOOD

13"

SIDE 1/4 3/4 FRONT

GROOVE 1/16" DEEP DETAIL OF FRONT CORNER

26 3/4

3/8"X 3/4"X15-1/2"

15-1/2"
STRIP GLUED & NAILED ON

19" 13-3/8" 1-3/8"

1" 4"

3/8" 5/8"
1-1/4"
3/8"
1-1/2"

BOTTOM
TACKED ON
5/8" 3/4
5/8"

3/4 3/4
1-5/8"
3/4

CABINET 15"X19"X28" OVERALL

POST SIDE 3/8"
CLEAT 5/8
1-1/2"
1/4 PLYWOOD
3/4
3/8" X 3/8" GROOVE
3/8"

DETAIL OF DRAWER FRAME CORNER

MAKE ALL PANEL GROOVES 3/8" DEEP

Storing records is no problem if you use one of these cabinets. Designed to go well in almost any room, they are of practically the same construction, the only difference being that one is higher than the other and has two compartments to accommodate twice as many records. Either reeded or spade-foot type corner posts may be used, although the smaller cabinet looks best with the latter type. Use of plywood not only simplifies construction of the cabinets and avoids the necessity of gluing up wide stock, but also makes them less expensive to build. If a painted finish is undesirable, panels veneered with the desired wood can be substituted for the plywood and finished to match other furniture, still making the cabinet less expensive than if solid stock were used in the construction

PHONOGRAPH RECORDS

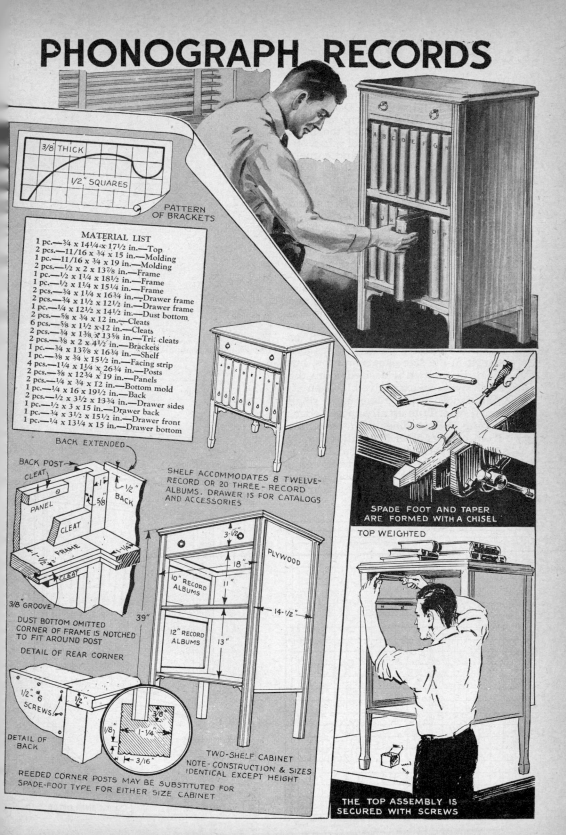

PATTERN OF BRACKETS

3/8 THICK
1/2" SQUARES

MATERIAL LIST

1 pc.—¾ x 14¼ x 17½ in.—Top
2 pcs.—11/16 x ¾ x 15 in.—Molding
1 pc.—11/16 x ¾ x 19 in.—Molding
2 pcs.—½ x 2 x 13⅞ in.—Frame
1 pc.—½ x 1¼ x 18½ in.—Frame
1 pc.—½ x 1¼ x 15¼ in.—Frame
2 pcs.—¾ x 1¼ x 16¾ in.—Drawer frame
2 pcs.—¾ x 1½ x 12½ in.—Drawer frame
1 pc.—¼ x 12½ x 14½ in.—Dust bottom
2 pcs.—⅝ x ¾ x 12 in.—Cleats
6 pcs.—⅝ x 1½ x 12 in.—Cleats
2 pcs.—¾ x 1⅜ x 13⅝ in.—Tri. cleats
2 pcs.—⅜ x 2 x 4½ in.—Brackets
1 pc.—¾ x 13⅞ x 16¾ in.—Shelf
1 pc.—⅜ x ¾ x 15½ in.—Facing strip
4 pcs.—1¼ x 1¼ x 26¾ in.—Posts
2 pcs.—⅜ x 12¾ x 19 in.—Panels
2 pcs.—¼ x ¾ x 12 in.—Bottom mold
1 pc.—¼ x 16 x 19½ in.—Back
2 pcs.—½ x 3½ x 13¾ in.—Drawer sides
1 pc.—½ x 3 x 15 in.—Drawer back
1 pc.—¾ x 3½ x 15½ in.—Drawer front
1 pc.—¼ x 13¼ x 15 in.—Drawer bottom

BACK EXTENDED

BACK POST
CLEAT
PANEL
CLEAT
FRAME
CLEAT
3/8 GROOVE

1"
5/8
1/2"
BACK
1-1/4

SHELF ACCOMMODATES 8 TWELVE-RECORD OR 20 THREE-RECORD ALBUMS. DRAWER IS FOR CATALOGS AND ACCESSORIES

1-1/2

DUST BOTTOM OMITTED
CORNER OF FRAME IS NOTCHED TO FIT AROUND POST

DETAIL OF REAR CORNER

1/2"—6 SCREWS
1/2"

DETAIL OF BACK

3/8
1/8
1-1/4
3/16

39"

3-1/2"
18"
10" RECORD ALBUMS
11"
PLYWOOD
14-1/2"
12" RECORD ALBUMS
13"

TWO-SHELF CABINET
NOTE—CONSTRUCTION & SIZES IDENTICAL EXCEPT HEIGHT

REEDED CORNER POSTS MAY BE SUBSTITUTED FOR SPADE-FOOT TYPE FOR EITHER SIZE CABINET

SPADE FOOT AND TAPER ARE FORMED WITH A CHISEL

TOP WEIGHTED

THE TOP ASSEMBLY IS SECURED WITH SCREWS

CLOTHES HAMPER

THIS hamper was designed with the simplest possible construction in mind and it is as easy to build as a box. Design features are a novel floral pattern, made by boring holes of varying size in the front and sides, and a recessed panel effect obtained by finishing the edges and corners with half-round molding, detail A. If an enamel finish is desired use birch plywood, ½ in. thick for the back and hinged top, and ⅛ or ¼ in. thick for the front and sides. Cut the back and bottom panels to size and join with screws and glue. Then make the frame, using ½ by ⅝-in. strips for the horizontal members and 1 by 1-in. strips for the corner uprights. Plane these latter members to a triangular shape as indicated in the sectional detail C, and assemble the frame members with nails and glue, or use screws. Next, cut the side and front panels to size and locate and bore the holes forming the floral design as shown on the squared pattern. Holes also are shown in the side panels and top, but these can be omitted if desired. Bore the large holes with an expansive bit. Then attach the panels to the frame using small brads and glue. True up all exposed edges by planing and sanding, then bevel the two front corners as in the sectional view C. Install the partition, using small triangular strips to hold it in place as in detail B. Sand the edges of the plywood top and hinge to the back panel. Finally attach the half-round moldings.

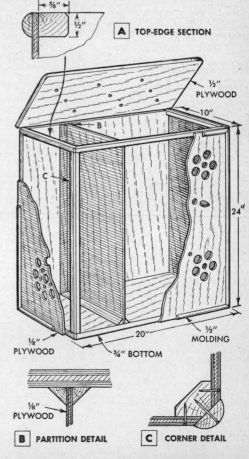

A TOP-EDGE SECTION

⅝" ½"

½" PLYWOOD

10"

24"

B

C

⅛" PLYWOOD

20"

¾" BOTTOM

½" MOLDING

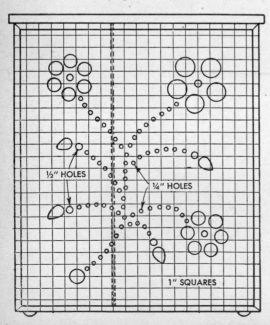

½" HOLES

¼" HOLES

1" SQUARES

⅛" PLYWOOD

B PARTITION DETAIL

C CORNER DETAIL

All-Purpose KNEEHOLE DESK

By Willard Allphin

HERE is the desk you've been waiting for—a big roomy one, good looking, with built-in typewriter slide, and designed to harmonize with both modern and traditional furniture. What's more, it is very easy to make. Ends, front and top are plywood, hardwood faced, which can be had in oak, birch, walnut, mahogany, etc. The rest of the desk is made of solid hardwood stock with inner shelves, partitions and other unexposed parts being made of soft and less expensive wood. Both end compartments of the desk are assembled as separate units. Cut out the three corner posts of each unit first.

Finished in limed oak, bleached mahogany, blond or rich walnut, this stunning desk will harmonize with most furniture. Featuring a built-in typewriter slide and the latest "island" base, the desk has four roomy drawers and a 24 by 48-in. working surface. Clean lines make construction easy

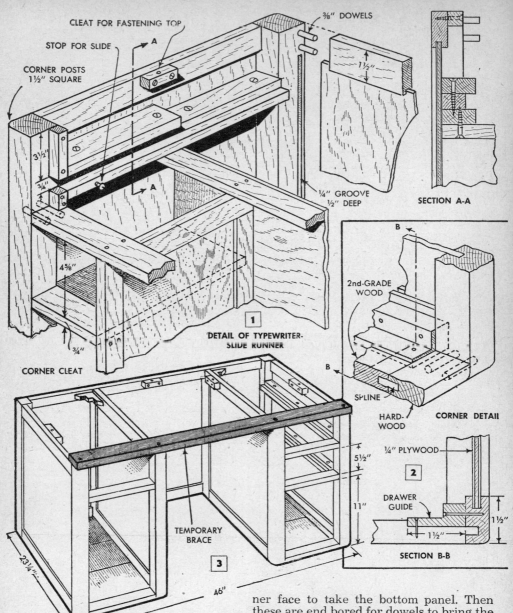

CLEAT FOR FASTENING TOP

STOP FOR SLIDE

CORNER POSTS 1½" SQUARE

⅜" DOWELS

3½"

¾"

4⅝"

¾"

CORNER CLEAT

¼" GROOVE ½" DEEP

SECTION A-A

1

DETAIL OF TYPEWRITER-SLIDE RUNNER

2nd-GRADE WOOD

SPLINE

HARD-WOOD

CORNER DETAIL

¼" PLYWOOD

2

DRAWER GUIDE

5½"

11"

1½"

1½"

SECTION B-B

TEMPORARY BRACE

23¼"

46"

3

These are 1½-in. square stock and are grooved lengthwise for ¼-in. plywood. Note that the grooves are run ¼ in. in from the outside edge and that they are stopped 1 in. from each end for dowel joints. The rear posts of each unit are grooved on one face only, whereas the others are grooved on two adjacent faces. All end rails are edge-grooved for the plywood panels, the lower ones also being grooved on the in-

ner face to take the bottom panel. Then these are end bored for dowels to bring the rails flush with the outer face of the corner posts. The bottom panel of each unit is made up of soft wood and the front edge is faced with a hardwood rail. The bottom panel of the right-hand unit differs from the other in that a shallow groove is run along each edge for an L-shaped drawer guide, as detailed in Fig. 2. The outer corners of all posts and the lower edge of all bottom rails are rounded ½ in. The panels of the kneehole are made the same size as the end panels, except that the edge which butts against the front panel is edged with

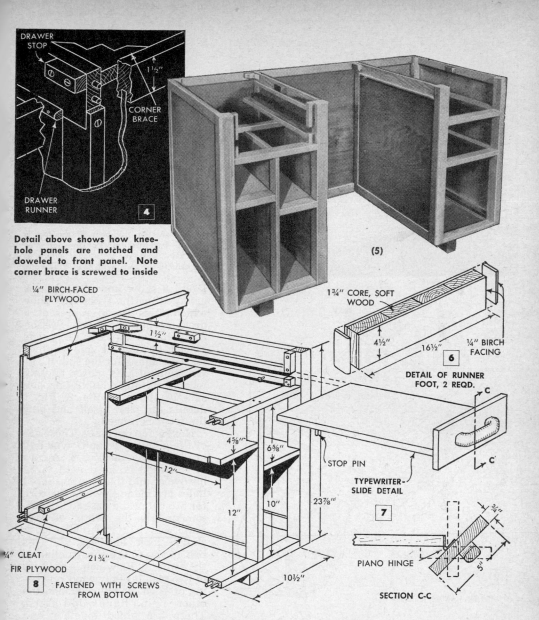

DRAWER STOP

1½"

CORNER BRACE

DRAWER RUNNER

4

Detail above shows how knee-hole panels are notched and doweled to front panel. Note corner brace is screwed to inside

(5)

¼" BIRCH-FACED PLYWOOD

1½"

1¾" CORE, SOFT WOOD

4½"

16½"

¼" BIRCH FACING

6

DETAIL OF RUNNER FOOT, 2 REQD.

4⅝"

12"

6⅝"

12"

10"

23⅞"

STOP PIN

TYPEWRITER-SLIDE DETAIL

C

C

¾" CLEAT

FIR PLYWOOD

21¾"

8 FASTENED WITH SCREWS FROM BOTTOM

10½"

7

PIANO HINGE

¾"

5"

SECTION C-C

a ¾-in. member notched to fit over the lower rail, Fig. 3. Fig. 4 shows how a notch is formed at the top, after which the piece is doweled to both rails at the top and bottom.

Start assembling the parts by gluing and clamping together the rear ends of the units. Follow this by gluing and clamping the outer end panels to them. When this is done, place a brace diagonally from post to post and nail temporarily to hold the assembly square while the glue is drying. Next, put in the dustproof bottom panels and then add the kneehole panels. Finally, glue and clamp both assembled units to the

front plywood panel. In doing this, fit the dowel joints of the kneehole panel first. When dry, spring out the corner posts to engage the dowels in the ends of the rails. Your desk should now look like Fig. 3. Note that a temporary wooden brace is placed across the two units to hold the assembly square.

Fig. 8 details the book compartments for the left-hand unit, and you'll notice that these do not extend the full depth of the unit. Here, the shelves are edge-faced with hardwood as before, the facing strips being fastened to the posts with screws driven from the underside and at an angle. Figs.

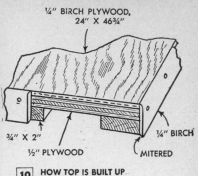

¼" BIRCH PLYWOOD, 24" X 46¾"

¾" X 2"

½" PLYWOOD

¼" BIRCH

MITERED

10 HOW TOP IS BUILT UP

Here is how the thickness of the top is obtained. Two thicknesses of plywood, plus ¾ by 2-in. battens, form core which is faced around the edge wi.h ¼-in. hardwood

9

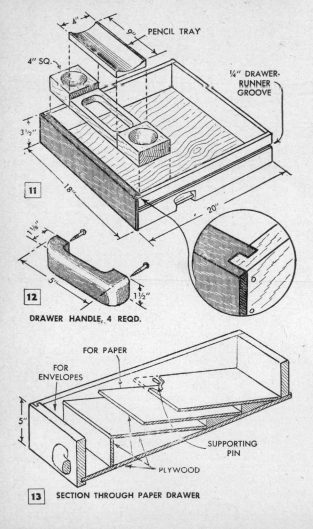

PENCIL TRAY

4"

9"

4" SQ.

¼" DRAWER-RUNNER GROOVE

3½"

18"

20"

11

1⅛"

5"

1½"

12 DRAWER HANDLE, 4 REQD.

6

FOR PAPER

FOR ENVELOPES

5"

SUPPORTING PIN

PLYWOOD

13 SECTION THROUGH PAPER DRAWER

1 and 8 show how the guide is installed for the typewriter slide which folds up to represent a drawer when not in use. Section A-A shows how three strips placed on top of one another form a channel for the slide. Construction of this varies slightly when installing it on the opposite side, as shown in Fig. 8. Fig. 7 details the slide itself and how the front is hinged.

Next come the bases. These are of the popular "island" type and are built up as in Fig. 6. A core of softwood is faced with ¼-in. hardwood and then counterbored holes are made through the core for attaching the base to the bottom and in the center of each unit. At this point the desk should look like Fig. 5. This brings you to the construction of the top, Fig. 10, which is built up of two panels of plywood, one being of ½-in. fir plywood, and the other ¼-in. hardwood faced. These are glued together and backed with five ¾ by 2-in. strips, which run lengthwise to add thickness and provide a gluing surface for a ¼-in. edging.

The drawers are detailed in Figs. 11, 12 and 13. The center drawer has no handle. Grooves cut in the side of the drawer, ride over runners which are bradded to the sides of the kneehole panels. Fig. 9 shows a method of cutting the pencil tray by repeatedly passing the work across a rotating saw blade at an angle.

Chairside SEWING BOX

YOUR sewing accessories for doing those last-minute repair jobs will always be together in this box, which also is large enough to store some unfinished sewing. It is not out of place in any room and goes well with almost any type of furniture. The bottom, back and hinged top are of solid stock, and the sides and curved front are formed from a single piece of veneer, thin plywood or even linoleum. Dowel legs support the box chair-high and are braced with curved dowels located so they are hidden under the box. A lining of quilted fabric gives the box a dainty appearance—Chas. and Bertram Brownold, Woodmere, N. Y.

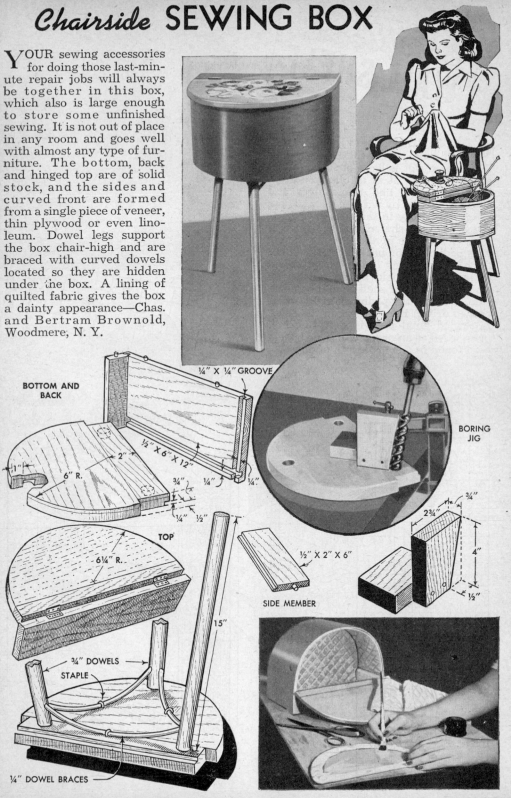

BOTTOM AND BACK

¼" X ¼" GROOVE

½" X 6" X 12"

6" R.

2"

1"

¾"

¼"

¼"

¼"

½"

BORING JIG

TOP

6¼" R.

SIDE MEMBER

½" X 2" X 6"

¾"

2¾"

4"

½"

15"

¾" DOWELS

STAPLE

¼" DOWEL BRACES

Scrollsawed WALL SHELF

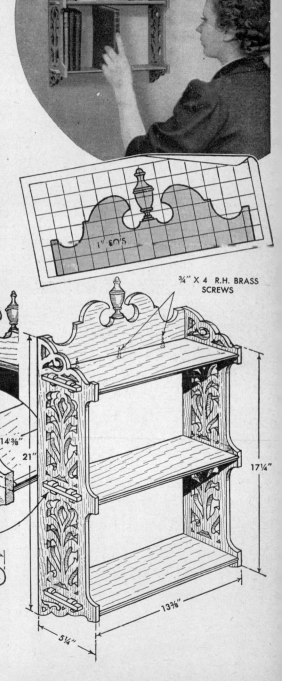

GRACEFUL and serviceable, this wall shelf is just the right size for bric-a-brac, yet is large enough to hold several books. It is scrollsawed from ¼-in. plywood, and the shelves and sides are joined by wooden pegs. These are fitted snugly in slots cut in projecting ends of the shelves and are glued in place as shown in the circular detail. The pediment, of heavier stock, is cut to shape according to the cross-hatched pattern and is held by screws driven through the upper shelf from the underside. To hold the pediment rigid, brads can be driven into it through the sides. A turned finial then is split, one half being used as an ornament. This is held by a tenon or a short length of dowel.

1" SQ'S

¾" X 4 R.H. BRASS SCREWS

14⅜"

21"

17¼"

½"

1" SQ'S

¾"

13⅜"

5¼"

Rumpus-Room Armchair

Strictly in the modern mode, this plywood armchair is easy to make and adds just the right informal touch to a basement rumpus room or front porch. First, saw out the sides and the four pieces for the armrests, Fig. 2, and then cut the bottom and back, and fasten in place by means of cleats, Fig. 1. The armrests are glued and screwed in place. In addition to the bottom cleats, an under-seat brace is required, right-hand detail of Fig. 2. When the sides, back and bottom are assembled, the chair is ready to be upholstered. Pocketed springs are used and are covered with padding and a suitable cloth. If foam rubber is available, it can be used instead of padding with good results. Stain the wood and finish with three coats of shellac. Or by way of variety, you might use a colored enamel finish that contrasts with the pattern of the cloth covering.

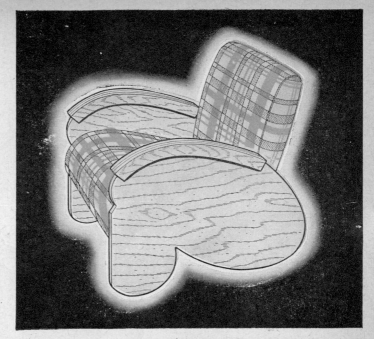

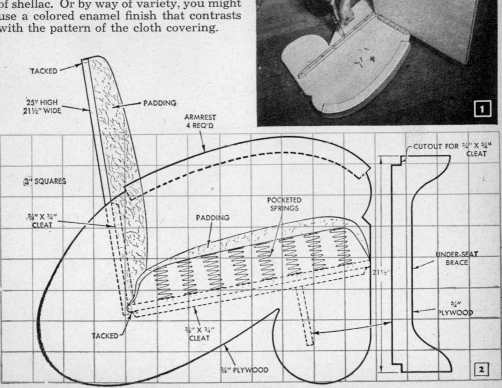

TACKED

25" HIGH
21½" WIDE

PADDING

ARMREST
4 REQ'D

3" SQUARES

¾" X ¾"
CLEAT

PADDING

POCKETED
SPRINGS

CUTOUT FOR ¾" X ¾"
CLEAT

UNDER-SEAT
BRACE

21½"

¾"
PLYWOOD

TACKED

¾" X ¾"
CLEAT

¾" PLYWOOD

HOW TO WEAVE

The completed seat is singed with the flame of a tightly rolled newspaper to remove the reed fibers

By W. Allphin

TO REPLACE an average-size reed chair seat, you'll need about one pound of oval-split reed, which can be purchased from a dealer in seating materials. The reeds must be soaked in water for at least a half hour before using. Tack two strips to the front rail as shown in Figs. 1 and 3. Go under the front rail, over the adjacent side rail,

Warp is begun by tacking two reeds to front rail

and then across to the opposite side rail. Wrap both strips around this rail and make an extra turn around it before returning the warp underneath to the first side rail. Make an extra turn here and go across the top again, as in Fig. 4. Each time you come to a rail, wrap an extra turn of the warp around it firmly before returning to the other side of the seat.

When near the end of a warp strip, shorten it if necessary so that it will end on the underside of the chair. Notch the edges of the old and new strips as in Figs. 2 and 5, and tie with string. A temporary tie is

Detail below at left shows how reed splice is made

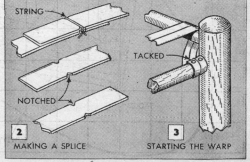

STRING

NOTCHED

TACKED

2 MAKING A SPLICE

3 STARTING THE WARP

A REED-BOTTOM CHAIR

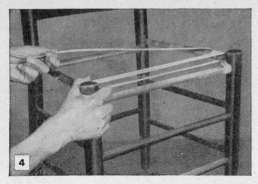

4

Warp strands are given one turn around side rails

5

Splicing warp strands is done on underside of seat

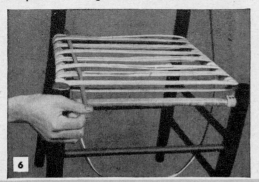

6

Woof strands are passed over and under warp strands

7

Woof is spliced by tucking end under warp strands

made around the rail at the last turn, as shown, to hold the strips while they are being spliced. Crowd the turns a bit wherever necessary so that the last warp on the upper side is back as far as possible. Start the woof across as a single strip at right angles to the front rail. This will leave a triangular space at the side. Weave under two, over two and around the rail, as in Fig. 6. Tuck the new piece in on top of the old one for a distance equal to two pairs of warp strips, as in Figs. 7 and 8.

When you have completed the square area, fill in remaining areas along the side rail as in Fig. 9. Start a short piece by pushing it into the smallest opening through which it will pass, and weave it around to the bottom, finishing by cutting off the strip and tucking in the end. Repeat with a shorter strip until the area is filled. Let the reeds dry overnight and then singe off the loose fibers. Be careful not to scorch the reeds. Singeing can be done with a newspaper torch.

Weaving woof is fun, just over two and under two

Fill-in areas at sides are woven with short strands

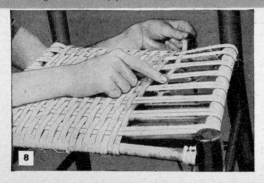

8

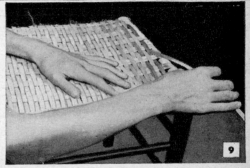

9

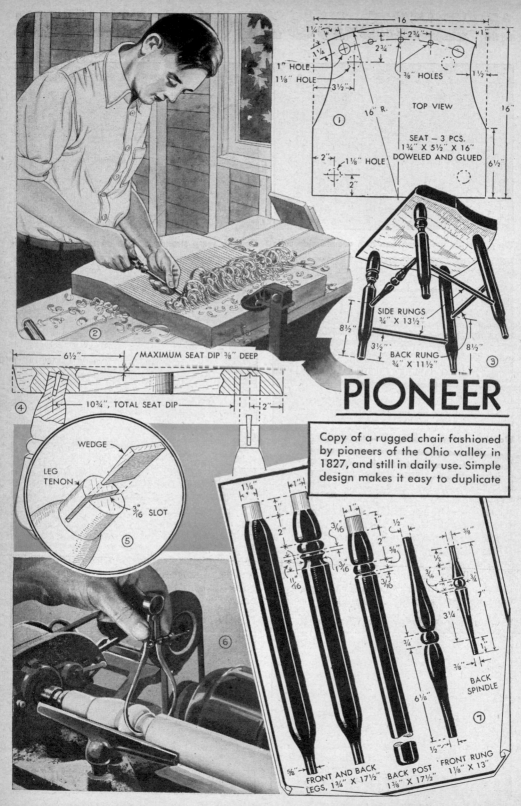

②

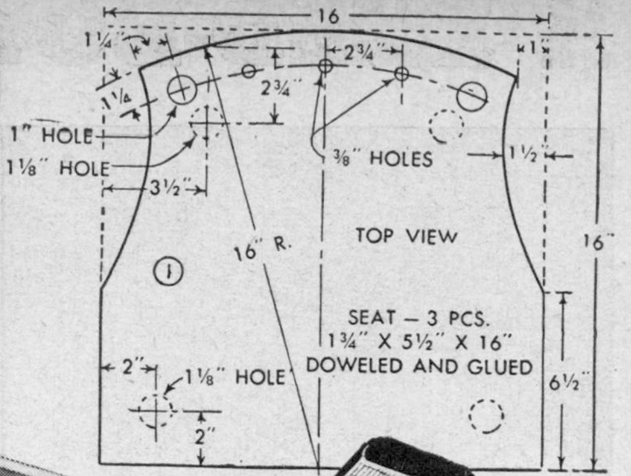
16
1¼
1"
2¾
2¾
1¼
1" HOLE
1⅛" HOLE
⅜" HOLES
1½
3½"
16" R.
TOP VIEW
16"
①
SEAT – 3 PCS.
1¾" X 5½" X 16"
DOWELED AND GLUED
2"
1⅛" HOLE
6½"
2"

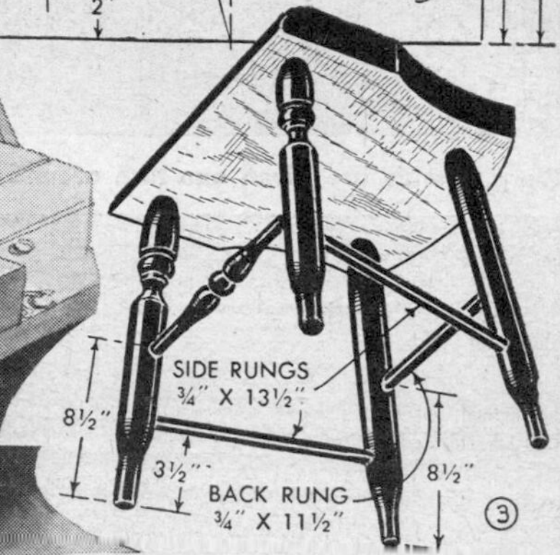
SIDE RUNGS
¾" X 13½"
8½"
3½"
BACK RUNG
¾" X 11½"
8½"
③

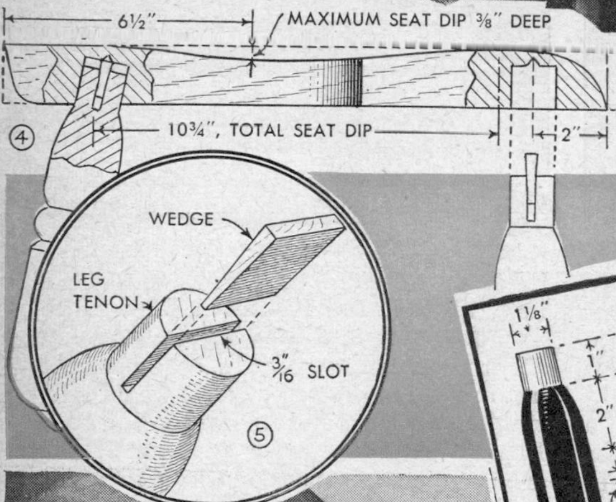
6½"
MAXIMUM SEAT DIP ⅜" DEEP
④
10¾", TOTAL SEAT DIP
2"
WEDGE
LEG TENON
3/16" SLOT
⑤

PIONEER

Copy of a rugged chair fashioned by pioneers of the Ohio valley in 1827, and still in daily use. Simple design makes it easy to duplicate

⑥

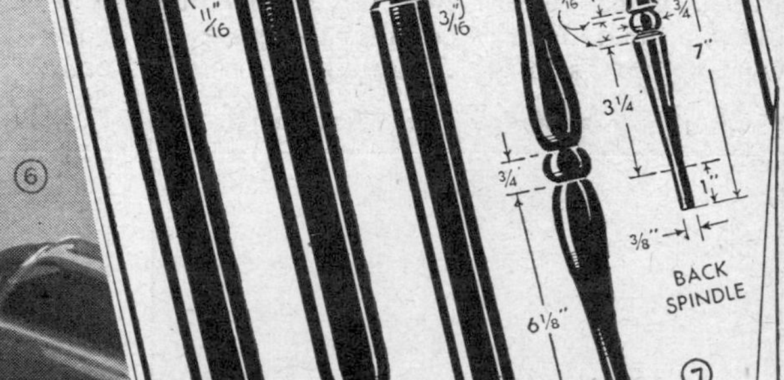
1⅛"
1"
1"
2"
1"
3/16
1 3/16"
11/16
1"
1"
2"
5/8"
3/16
½"
⅜"
½"
3/16
1"
¾
7"
3¼
¾
1"
⅜"
6⅛"
½"
⑦
5/8"
FRONT AND BACK LEGS, 1¾" X 17½"
BACK POST 1⅜" X 17½"
FRONT RUNG 1⅛" X 13"
BACK SPINDLE

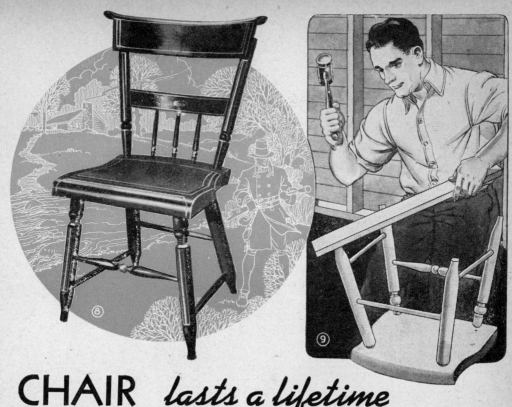

CHAIR *lasts a lifetime*

By Alexander Maxwell

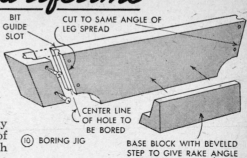

(10) BORING JIG

BIT GUIDE SLOT

CUT TO SAME ANGLE OF LEG SPREAD

CENTER LINE OF HOLE TO BE BORED

BASE BLOCK WITH BEVELED STEP TO GIVE RAKE ANGLE

REPRESENTING the design of no one cabinet maker but rather the incorporated designs of many, the quaint chair shown in Fig. 8 is typical of those fashioned and used by the settlers of the Ohio Valley. Like most early pieces of furniture, the plain ruggedness of this chair makes it easy to reproduce with few tools. And, if care is used in fitting the parts together, it will last a lifetime.

Maple, birch and mahogany are the best woods to use. Start by making the seat first. For this you will have to glue and dowel together edgewise three pieces of 1¾-in. stock to build up the 16-in. width required. Place the pieces so that the grain of each runs in the same direction and use a waterproof resin-type glue to assure strong joints. Fig. 1 shows the plan of the seat. You will find it easier to carve the dip in the seat before bandsawing as the contour of the dip is drawn on the straight edge of the work. Using a chisel, block plane, spoke shave and a scraper blade, the seat is worked down to the guide lines as shown in Fig. 2, after which the front and back edges are rounded according to Fig. 4 and then the seat is given a good

sanding. Referring back to Fig. 1, you now lay out the position of the holes for the legs. Boring these to provide the right spread to the legs is simplified by using a jig like the one detailed in Fig. 10. Each end of it is cut and grooved at an angle of 98 degrees, which represents the sideward spread or slant of the legs. See Fig. 17.

In use, the bit is held in line with the slanting end by a grooved block which fits around the bit shank and over the end of the jig as shown. This block will do for both ends of the jig. To give the bit the correct backward rake for boring the holes for the back legs, a base block is required having a rabbet cut in it at a 102-degree angle. This block is placed under the jig to which it is clamped with C-clamps and, in turn, the two parts are clamped to the

117

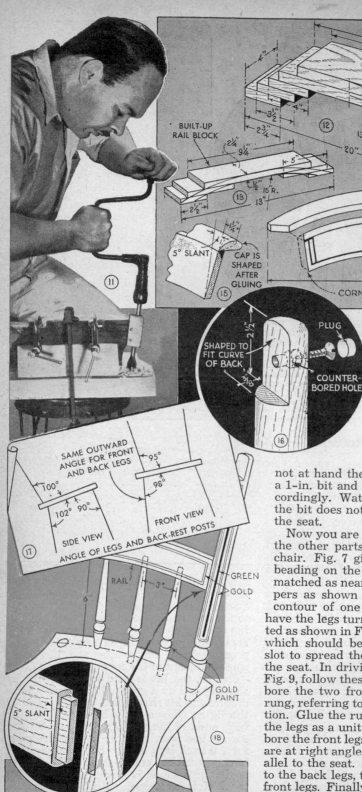

BUILT-UP BACK BLOCK

9" 12¾"

4"

12

3½"
2¾"

13" R.

1"

20"

¾

4"

BUILT-UP RAIL BLOCK

2¼ 9¼"

5"

13

1½" 15 R.

2½ 13"

1½

GOLD STRIPING

14

21½

CORNERS CUT BACK

5° SLANT

CAP IS SHAPED AFTER GLUING

15

1¼

PLUG

SHAPED TO FIT CURVE OF BACK

2½

⅜

COUNTER-BORED HOLE

16

SAME OUTWARD ANGLE FOR FRONT AND BACK LEGS

95°

100°

98°

102° 90°

SIDE VIEW

FRONT VIEW

ANGLE OF LEGS AND BACK-REST POSTS

17

RAIL

3°

6"

GREEN
GOLD

GOLD PAINT

5° SLANT

18

seat across its width as shown in Fig. 11. As the front legs slant only sideward, the use of the base block under the jig is not necessary in boring the front holes. The leg holes, being 1⅛ in. in diameter, require the use of an expansive bit, although if one is not at hand the holes can be bored with a 1-in. bit and the leg tenons turned accordingly. Watch to see that the spur of the bit does not pierce the top surface of the seat.

Now you are ready to turn the legs and the other parts needed to complete the chair. Fig. 7 gives their size. Duplicate beading on the legs and posts should be matched as nearly as possible, using calipers as shown in Fig. 6 to transfer the contour of one to the other. After you have the legs turned, their tenons are slotted as shown in Fig. 5 to take short wedges, which should be slightly wider than the slot to spread the latter when forced into the seat. In driving the legs in place as in Fig. 9, follow these progressive steps: First, bore the two front legs to take the front rung, referring to Fig. 3 for the exact location. Glue the rung in the holes and drive the legs as a unit into the seat. When dry, bore the front legs for the side rungs. These are at right angles to the legs and run parallel to the seat. Next, glue the back rung to the back legs, then the side rungs to the front legs. Finally, drive the back legs into the seat, springing in the glue-coated tenons of the side rungs as you go. You probably will have to trim a little off one of the legs to make the chair stand level, as it is almost impossible to drive each leg in the same distance.

To bore the holes in the top of the seat for the back posts, the slanting ends of the jig will have to be recut to an angle of 95 degrees, and another base block having a 100-degree rabbet will be needed to give the desired rake to the chair back. The curved back and rail can be cut economically from blocks of ¾ and ½-in. stock respectively, built up in the manner shown in Figs. 12 and 13, although if you are able to get stock of the right thickness, they can be made in one piece. Glue one lift at a time, clamp and let dry before adding the next one. The radius is then drawn on the edge as shown and the work is bandsawed, scraped and sanded smooth. The front edge of the curved cap fits flush with the inside face of the back and is shaped as shown in Figs. 14 and 15 after being glued. The chair back is assembled by first driving the three spindles into the seat and then gluing the rail to the upper ends. After this, the post tenons are fitted with wedges as used in the legs and the left-hand post is driven in place, the rail tenon being sprung at the same time into the mortise provided for it. Do the same for the right-hand post and place a bar clamp across both. Fig. 16 shows how the upper ends of the post are notched for the curved back piece, the screws being concealed with wood plugs.

Much of the Ohio Valley furniture was stained a dark red to look like African mahogany and ornamented with fine gold and green hair stripes before being varnished. A stepped maul stick like the one shown in Fig. 19 will help guide the brush in striping the chair. A coach striper's dagger brush is preferred, although a fine water-

FLOWER DESIGN ON CENTER RAIL CAN BE A TRANSFER OR HAND PAINTED

color brush will do. Practice on scrap work first, and see that the gilt is thin enough to flow freely. Try to complete the stripe in one long even stroke, guiding your fingers from the elbow. There is one green stripe on each front leg and on each post, also a band of green encircling the seat. The rest of the striping is done in gold. Of course, if you prefer, you can leave the striping off entirely and apply just a floral design to the center of the back rail for a touch of decoration as shown in Fig. 20. If a varnish finish is applied, rub down each coat with extra-fine steel wool and finish the last one with rottenstone and oil, after which apply wax and polish to a high luster.

Drawer Pulls Fabricated From Copper Tubing and Wire

Neat drawer pulls can be made from ⅜-in. copper tubing polished with steel wool. After the tubing has been cut to the desired length and the ends cut at an angle to fit flat against the drawer front, a length of ⅛-in. wire, threaded at both ends, is inserted into the tubing. Then both the tubing and the wire insert are formed around a large cylinder. The pulls are lacquered in order to prevent tarnishing and are fastened to the drawer front with nuts and washers.

1/8" WIRE

3/8" COPPER TUBE

Alsatian Chairs

THESE continental chairs with their widely splayed legs and attractive, carved backs are worthy projects for the home craftsman and provide distinctive pieces for a hall or dining room. Although each chair back appears difficult to make, actually it is fairly simple because the design first is cut through by scrollsawing. Either of the back designs is cut from a single panel, and the scrolled section finished in low relief with a chisel, veining tool and sandpaper. The seat is mounted on two cleats bored approximately 15 deg. from the vertical for insertion of the legs. The top ends of the legs are saw-cut to receive a wedge driven at right angles to the grain of the cleat. The top edges of the seat are rounded and, by using material 1⅝ in. thick, the seat can be hollowed to form a concave section for greater comfort. In assembling, the back is fastened to the cleats with angle brackets which are recessed flush. Either antique or natural finish, waxed and rubbed to a soft luster, is suitable for this type of chair.

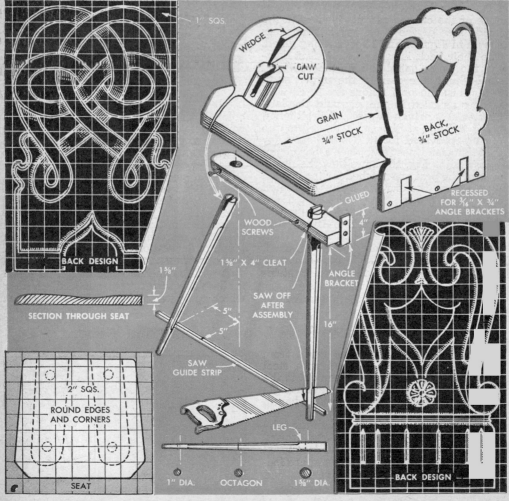

Novel WORK STOOL *has adjustable back*

S UITABLE for use in either your kitchen or home
workshop, the sturdy, well-designed stool shown in
Fig. 1 has a back that can be adjusted quickly by means
of a turnbuckle as in Fig. 2. Oak or maple is the best
wood to use for making it, although other hardwoods
will serve.

Begin construction with the three legs, which are
turned to the dimensions given in Fig. 3, one end of
each leg being turned to provide a ¾-in. tenon. Following this, each leg is sawed and planed to a
straight, octagonal taper which reduces

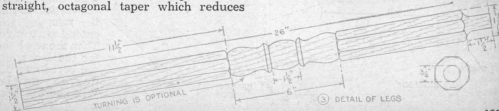

11½"   26"   ¾"

1½"   TURNING IS OPTIONAL   1½"   6"   ¾"   ③ DETAIL OF LEGS

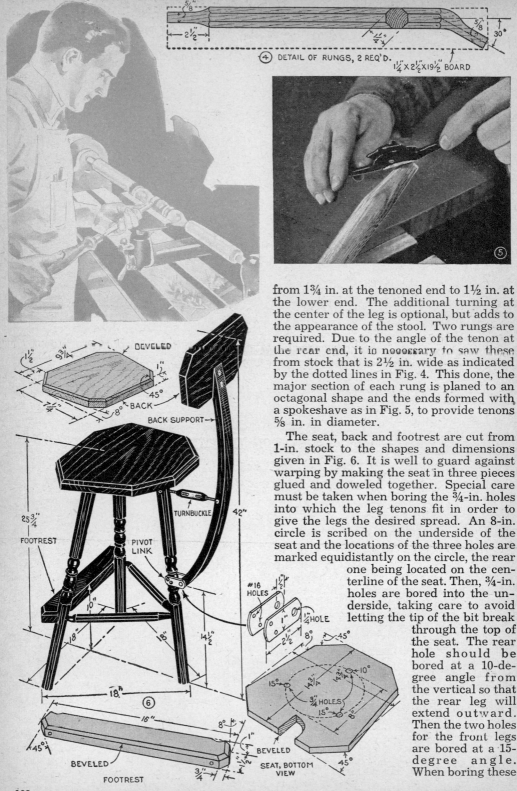

④ DETAIL OF RUNGS, 2 REQ'D. ⅝ 2½ 1½ 30° ⅝
1¼ X 2½ X19½" BOARD

⑤

from 1¾ in. at the tenoned end to 1½ in. at
the lower end. The additional turning at
the center of the leg is optional, but adds to
the appearance of the stool. Two rungs are
required. Due to the angle of the tenon at
the rear end, it is necessary to saw these
from stock that is 2½ in. wide as indicated
by the dotted lines in Fig. 4. This done, the
major section of each rung is planed to an
octagonal shape and the ends formed with
a spokeshave as in Fig. 5, to provide tenons
⅝ in. in diameter.

The seat, back and footrest are cut from
1-in. stock to the shapes and dimensions
given in Fig. 6. It is well to guard against
warping by making the seat in three pieces
glued and doweled together. Special care
must be taken when boring the ¾-in. holes
into which the leg tenons fit in order to
give the legs the desired spread. An 8-in.
circle is scribed on the underside of the
seat and the locations of the three holes are
marked equidistantly on the circle, the rear
one being located on the cen-
terline of the seat. Then, ¾-in.
holes are bored into the underside, taking care to avoid
letting the tip of the bit break
through the top of
the seat. The rear
hole should be
bored at a 10-de-
gree angle from
the vertical so that
the rear leg will
extend outward.
Then the two holes
for the front legs
are bored at a 15-
degree angle.
When boring these

BEVELED 9¾" 1½ 1" 45° 7¾" 8" BACK

BACK SUPPORT

TURNBUCKLE 42"

25¾" FOOTREST PIVOT LINK

#16 HOLES 1½" 1½" 1" ¼"HOLE 2½"

10" 14½"

18" 18"

18" ⑥

16" 8" 1" 45° BEVELED ¾"

45° BEVELED FOOTREST

8" 45° 15° 1¾" 1¾" 10" ¾" HOLES 15° 8"

BEVELED SEAT, BOTTOM VIEW 45°

holes, you must keep the bit lined up with the radial lines drawn from the center of the circle to the points where the holes are started. Also, as an aid in getting the angles correct, you can use small blocks having one edge inclined the desired angle as a guide for the bit. The blocks are clamped to the seat while boring.

Next, without applying any glue, the legs are fitted into the seat holes and are marked to determine the position of the rungs and footrest. The holes for the rungs must be bored at an angle so that the rungs will be parallel to the edge of the seat. Likewise, the footrest is notched to fit the front legs and is doweled or screwed to them. After this preliminary fitting has been done, the parts are reassembled permanently with glue.

The backrest is screwed and glued to a curved support piece, detailed in Figs. 7 to 9. Although it can be sawed from a single piece of hardwood it will be stronger if glued up from ³⁄₁₆-in.

First, two glue-coated strips are sprung around dowels set in a flat board and left 24 hrs. to dry

Then the two strips are removed from the form and additional strips are glued to them, one at a time, letting each one dry before adding the next

strips, using a form to obtain the curvature. Pieces of flat iron screwed to the rear leg provide a pivot link for the back support and a 6-in. turnbuckle permits adjustment.

Doors Between Living and Dining Rooms Fitted With Modern Swinging Bookcases

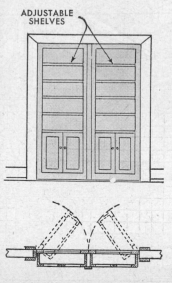

ADJUSTABLE SHELVES

An old-style home with large sliding doors between the dining and living rooms can be easily remodeled without making a major project out of it. The opening can be modernized by fitting it with two new doors in the form of bookcases. Viewed from the living room, the doors will appear to be a built-in bookcase. A large mural can be painted on the dining-room side, thus adding an unusual decorative treatment to that room. Three heavy hinges should be used to fasten each door to the jamb. Note the space left between abutting edges of the doors to permit them to close. A facing strip nailed to one door covers the gap.

Colonial Chairs

By Hi Sibley

JUST the thing to set off your colonial fireplace, these two chairs are not only comfortable but are easy to make, as anyone who has had a little experience in cabinet work will agree. Also, since only reasonably small pieces of wood are required, you should be able to construct the chairs at a relatively small cost for material, which in many cases can be picked up at cabinet shops as scrap.

The larger chair shown in Fig. 1 has a low, wide seat designed for a deep cushion which makes the chair exceptionally comfortable. The front legs and arm supports are simple turnings shaped according to the patterns given in Fig. 2. Tenons are turned on the upper ends, and the lower ends of the arm supports are cut to rest at an angle against the seat frame, to which they are glued and screwed, the screw heads being countersunk and covered with plugs that are cut off to project about ¼ in. Rear legs are jigsawed to shape and are cut so that the upper ends curve back approximately 6 in. farther than the portions of the legs at seat level. Cross members are mortised into these legs to form the back, as is the

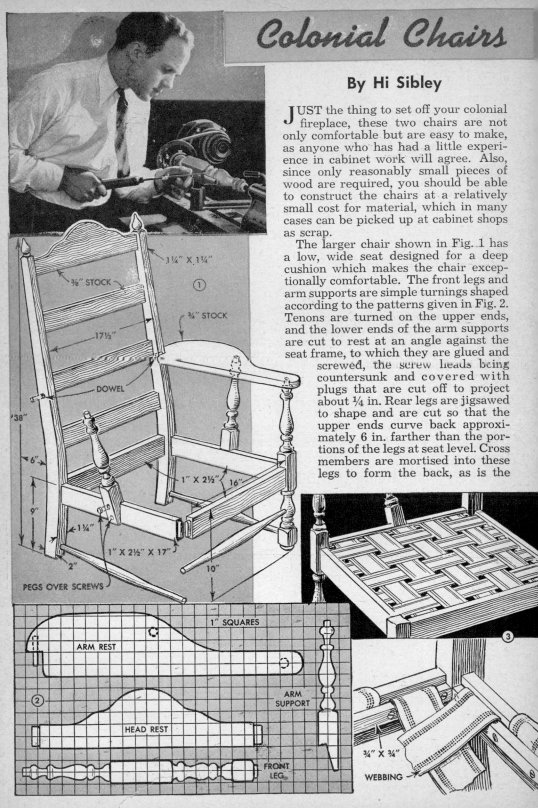

124

head rest, which is cut to the size and shape indicated in Fig. 2. The seat frame is mortised and glued into the four legs. Care must be taken to make mortises and tenons fit tightly, otherwise the chair will be unsteady. Arm rests are jigsawed to the size and shape shown and are drilled to take the tenons on the arm supports and front legs. Notice that holes for the arm supports must be drilled at an angle. Rungs, of course, are simple, tapered turnings.

Installation of the upholstery webbing strips follows the usual procedure. One end of each strip is tacked to the inner surface of the seat frame, pulled tightly and tacked to the opposite side of the frame, the strips being interwoven as indicated in Fig. 3. When completed, wood cleats are screwed over the tacks to act as reinforcement and to help prevent strain from loosening the tacks. Cushions are used in the seat and on the back of the chair.

The sturdy chair pictured in Fig. 4 is of simpler construction. The seat is of solid wood cut as in Fig. 5 and reinforced across the underside with a hardwood spline glued into a groove. Front legs are turnings split at the upper ends to take wedges which spread the ends to bind the legs tightly in place when they are driven into holes in the seat. The rear legs are round and can be turned or shaped with a spoke shave. They are steamed and bent to shape so that the upper ends project back about

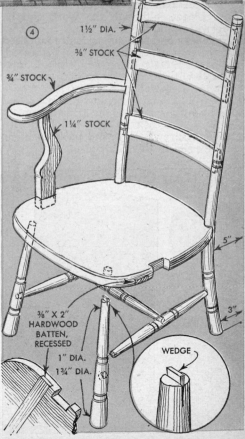

④ 1½" DIA.
⅜" STOCK
¾" STOCK
1¼" STOCK
5"
3"
⅜" X 2" HARDWOOD BATTEN, RECESSED
1" DIA.
1¾" DIA.
WEDGE

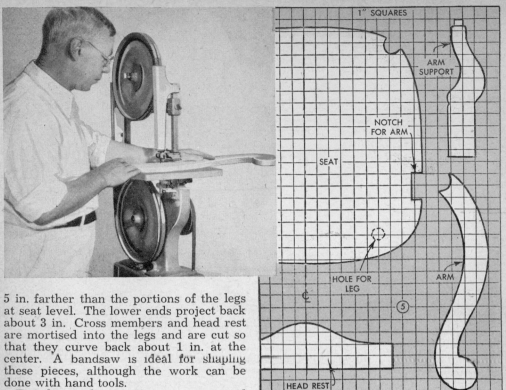

1" SQUARES

ARM SUPPORT

NOTCH FOR ARM

SEAT

HOLE FOR LEG

ARM

⑤

HEAD REST

5 in. farther than the portions of the legs at seat level. The lower ends project back about 3 in. Cross members and head rest are mortised into the legs and are cut so that they curve back about 1 in. at the center. A bandsaw is ideal for shaping these pieces, although the work can be done with hand tools.

Rear legs and arm supports are mortised into the seat edges and glued and screwed, the screw heads being countersunk and covered with plugs. Arms and arm supports are jigsawed to the sizes and shapes given in Fig. 5 and are mortised and glued together. Rear ends of the arms are cut to the contour of the rear legs and joined with glue and screws. Seat and back cushions can be used in this chair also.

All parts of the chairs should be sanded smooth before assembly as this work is easier at this time. After the chairs have been completed they should again be sanded and then finished. They look best when finished in natural wood, but can be stained to match other furniture. Cushions should harmonize with other fabrics in the room.

Old Cedar Chest Converted to Wardrobe for Small Child

If you have an old cedar chest that is not in use it can be made into a wardrobe for a small child. Just remove the feet and attach them to the corners at one end. Then set the chest on end, fit in a clothes pole and you have a substantial closet. If the feet are of a shape that does not permit them to be attached to the end, suitable ones can be made easily.

Shellac Prevents Stain Bleeding

Before applying a light-colored paint to varnished woodwork or furniture, first sand the surface and paint a small test spot in an unnoticeable place to see if the stain will bleed through. Wait a few days and inspect the spot for discoloration. If present, the entire surface should be sealed with two coats of shellac before painting.

REST YOUR FEET

YOU get experience in wood turning, veneering, upholstering and finishing all in one when building this simple footstool. The base is formed of two ¾-in. walnut boards half-lapped at the center. The top is built up of two plywood disks, the center being cut from one to provide the cushion base. Glue and screw the ring to the bottom disk, then true the edge in a lathe. Next, face the edge with straight-grained veneer, using the improvised clamp shown, and, when dry, trim off the surplus veneer flush at the top and bottom. Then veneer the top of the ring and attach to the base with screws. The slip-in cushion is padded in the manner given to fit snugly in the recessed top.

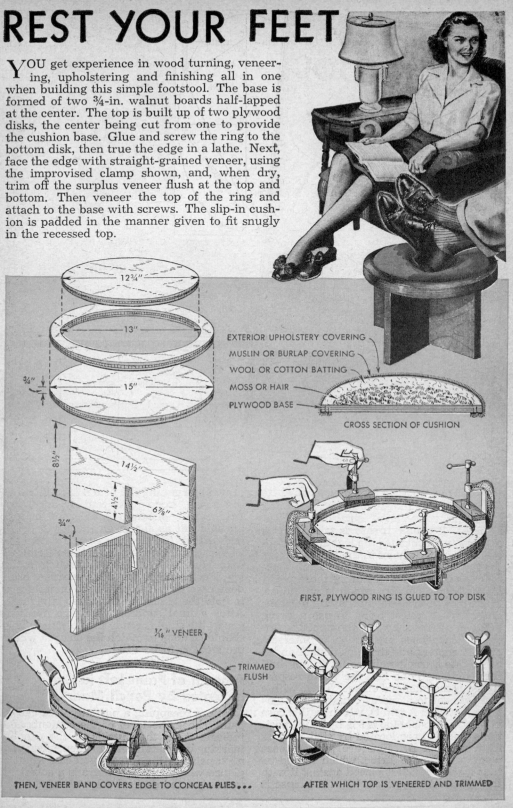

12¾"

13"

15"

¾"

EXTERIOR UPHOLSTERY COVERING
MUSLIN OR BURLAP COVERING
WOOL OR COTTON BATTING
MOSS OR HAIR
PLYWOOD BASE

CROSS SECTION OF CUSHION

8½"

14½"

4½"

6⅞"

¾"

FIRST, PLYWOOD RING IS GLUED TO TOP DISK

3/16" VENEER

TRIMMED FLUSH

THEN, VENEER BAND COVERS EDGE TO CONCEAL PLIES...

AFTER WHICH TOP IS VENEERED AND TRIMMED

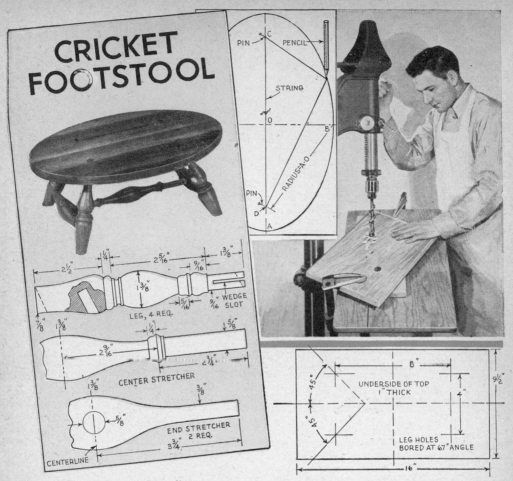

CRICKET FOOTSTOOL

PIN · C · PENCIL

STRING

RADIUS A-O

PIN
D
A

2½"
¼"
2⁵⁄₁₆"
9⁄₁₆"
1³⁄₈"
1³⁄₈"
5⁄₁₆"
9⁄₁₆" WEDGE SLOT
LEG, 4 REQ.
⁷⁄₈"
1³⁄₈"

¼"
⁵⁄₈"
2⁹⁄₁₆"
2¾"
CENTER STRETCHER
1³⁄₈"
³⁄₈"

⁵⁄₈"
END STRETCHER 2 REQ.
3¾"
CENTERLINE

45°
45°
8"
UNDERSIDE OF TOP 1" THICK
9½"
4"
LEG HOLES BORED AT 67° ANGLE
16"

MADE of wood to match your favorite chair, this footstool is just the thing to set off your period furnishings. Construction is simple if care is taken. First, saw out the blanks for the legs and stretchers, and drill the holes in the leg blanks for the stretchers before turning them. Templates will aid in duplicating these parts. Next is the stool top, which is an ellipse. There are several ways of laying out this, one of the simplest being to use a string and two pins as shown in the upper center detail. Two lines are drawn to intersect at their centers, and then positions A and B are located, using radii equal to one half the length and one half the width respectively of the intended ellipse. Then, with a compass set to a radius equal to the distance between A and O, which in this case is 8 in. as the stool top is 9½ by 16 in., positions C and D are located by striking arcs from position B. Pins are put at these points to take the string, which should be taut when a pencil is placed against it with the point set on position B. The ellipse is

drawn by running the pencil around inside the string, keeping it taut at all times. After sawing out the top, holes for the legs are laid out as shown in the lower detail and drilled. The leg tenons are slotted for wedges, after which the stool is assembled with glue, wedges being driven into the leg slots for a tight fit. If the work has been done carefully, clamps will be unnecessary to hold the assembly while the glue dries. After a final sanding with fine abrasive paper, the stool is ready for finishing. This should be done to match the chair at which the stool is to be used.

Amount of Paint Left in Can Indicated by Pencil Mark

Before recapping a partially used can of paint, check the level of the contents and indicate it on the outside of the can by marking with a red pencil. Then, when you need paint in the future, you can tell at a glance whether or not there is a sufficient amount of the desired color on hand.

OCCASIONAL CHAIR in Sheraton styling

By Henry E. Belden

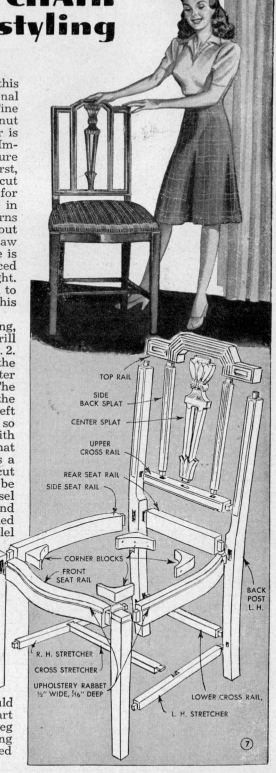

THERE'S just enough handwork on this fine chair to give it the professional touch of the individual craftsman. Fine cabinet wood such as mahogany or walnut should be used. If more than one chair is desired, simply duplicate the parts. Important steps in the construction procedure are shown in Figs. 1 to 6 inclusive. First, full-size patterns of the back posts are cut from heavy paper or thin cardboard for transferring to the work. You'll note in Fig. 9 that the right and left-hand patterns are duplicates; one will serve to lay out both posts by merely turning it over. Saw cuts "A" are made first, then the waste is tacked back on, the second pattern traced and cut "B" is made. Edge "C" is straight. Before making cut "B" it is a good idea to drill a ⅜-in. hole as shown in Fig. 6. This assures a well-rounded notch.

The posts now are ready for mortising, which can be done by hand or with a drill press and mortising attachment as in Fig. 2. Use a ⅜-in. hollow chisel and adjust the fence so that the cut will be in the center of the wood and parallel with the edge. The seat-rail mortises also are cut with the ⅜-in. hollow chisel. Use the scraps left from bandsawing to block up the work so the face of the mortise will be square with the chisel. The front legs are somewhat longer than the back ones, which gives a slight rake to the back and seat. Next cut the mortises for the stretchers. It will be necessary to block up the work so the chisel will cut at right angles to a center line and parallel with the floor line of the assembled chair. The mortise should be cut parallel with the straight or outside edge of the back post, this edge being held against the fence. The mortise for the lower cross rail is cut with the straight or outside edge of the leg resting directly on the drill-press table so that the chisel is at right angles to this surface.

Each chair requires two side rails made from 2-in. stock in accordance with the pattern in Fig. 9. The tenons on the side rails measure ⅜ in. wide, ⁷⁄₁₆ in. deep and 1½ in. long. The mortises on the front legs, Fig. 9, should be cut before the legs are tapered. Start each mortise ¼ in. from the top of the leg and 3⅞ in. from the bottom. Before cutting the lower mortise be sure you have selected the correct face of the leg.

TOP RAIL

SIDE BACK SPLAT

CENTER SPLAT

UPPER CROSS RAIL

REAR SEAT RAIL

SIDE SEAT RAIL

CORNER BLOCKS

FRONT SEAT RAIL

BACK POST L. H.

R. H. STRETCHER

CROSS STRETCHER

UPHOLSTERY RABBET ½" WIDE, ¹⁄₁₆" DEEP

LOWER CROSS RAIL

L. H. STRETCHER

⑦

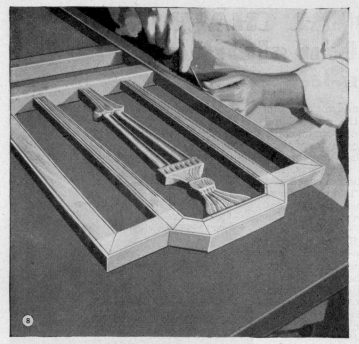

The front legs are tapered on the circular saw by the "notched-stick" method. Take a piece of stock slightly longer than the leg and nail a block near one end. This block should have two step-like notches cut in it. The first one is ⅜ in. and the second ¾ in., both measured from the inside face of the stick. Place the lower end of the untapered leg in the first notch with the stick next to the ripping fence. After the first cut is completed turn the leg completely over so the saw engages the opposite edge and place the lower end of the leg in the second notch. In each instance the fence should be adjusted so that the saw engages the leg at a point 2⅟₁₆ in. below the upper end, as in Fig. 9.

Next, an upholstery rabbet is cut in the seat rails and across the front legs, Fig. 7, making it slightly deeper on the legs. The front legs now can be glued to the front seat

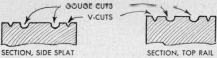

GOUGE CUTS
V-CUTS

SECTION, SIDE SPLAT   SECTION, TOP RAIL

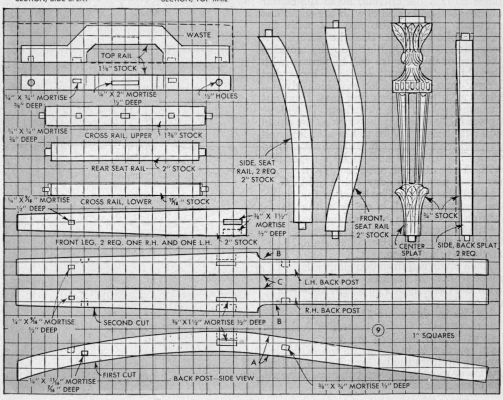

WASTE

TOP RAIL

1⅛" STOCK

¼" X ¾" MORTISE ⅜" DEEP   ¼" X 2" MORTISE ½" DEEP   ½" HOLES

¼" X ¼" MORTISE ⅜" DEEP   CROSS RAIL, UPPER   1⅜" STOCK

REAR SEAT RAIL — 2" STOCK

SIDE, SEAT RAIL, 2 REQ 2" STOCK

¼" X ⅝" MORTISE ½" DEEP   CROSS RAIL, LOWER   1⅝" STOCK

⅜" X 1½" MORTISE ½" DEEP

FRONT LEG, 2 REQ. ONE R.H. AND ONE L.H.   2" STOCK

FRONT, SEAT RAIL 2" STOCK

¾" STOCK

CENTER SPLAT

SIDE, BACK SPLAT 2 REQ.

B

C   L.H. BACK POST

R.H. BACK POST

¼" X ⅝" MORTISE ½" DEEP   SECOND CUT   ⅜" X 1½" MORTISE ½" DEEP   B

⑨   1" SQUARES

¼" X 1⅟₁₆" MORTISE ⁷⁄₁₆" DEEP   FIRST CUT   BACK POST—SIDE VIEW   A   ⅜" X ¾" MORTISE ½" DEEP

rail and the back posts glued to the lower cross rail, the seat rail and the upper cross rail. It's a good idea first to try assembly without glue. Do not glue any other parts at this time. Two side back splats are required, which are tapered, as shown by the dotted lines in Fig. 9, to leave a ¼-in. shoulder around the tenon at the lower end of the splat. The back-splat pattern, Figs. 9 and 11, is traced on a piece ¾ by 3 by 16¹³⁄₁₆ in., then sawed to shape. In carving the splat, work from the sectional views in Fig. 11.

The top rail, Figs. 7 and 9, is cut from 1⅛-in. stock. The offset over the center splat is cut out first, then ½-in. dowel holes are drilled 1 in. from each end and mortises are cut for the splats, after which the sawing can be completed. Do not cut this to exact length until after assembly. After drilling the top of the posts for dowels, the parts are ready for gluing and clamping to the rest of the back. When the glue has hardened, the back assembly is clamped to a bench so that the back may be fluted as in Fig. 8, making the cuts as indicated in the sectional views. Use a very shallow veining to simulate the mitered effect in the top rail. After the stretchers, Fig. 12, have been fitted, assemble the chair in clamps for a trial fit as in Fig. 10. Then apply glue and clamp the parts together. Corner blocks glued and screwed in the seat complete construction.

To finish, coat the wood with an oil stain. Allow to dry for 24 hours, then seal with a coat of thinned white shellac or prepared sealer. Next fill the grain with a paste filler colored a shade darker than the stain and thinned with turpentine to the consistency of thin varnish. The filler should be well rubbed in and wiped off across grain with a coarse cloth. The wiping is done when the filler begins to flatten. If one coat does not fill the pores completely apply a second coat. The "heel" of the hand is good to pack the filler level with the surface before wiping. Let dry for 36 hours, after which any rough spots should be sanded lightly. Follow with a full-bodied coat of white shellac and when dry rub with fine steel wool. Finish with several coats of paste wax rubbed to a fine gloss. A hair-bristle brush will polish the carved surfaces. The simplest upholstery job is a foam or sponge-rubber cushion supported on a bottom of ⅜-in. plywood. This is covered with a layer of muslin and tapestry in whatever pattern you wish. The edges of the top covering are nailed in the upholstery rabbet and the job is finished with upholstery gimp applied to the edge of the seat to conceal the tacks and provide a neat finish to the raw edges of the covering on all sides.

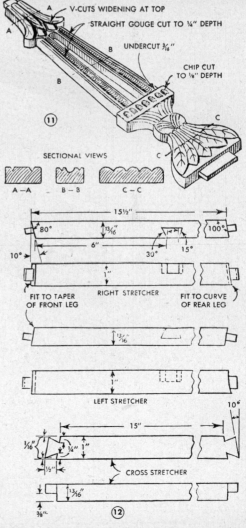

SECTIONAL VIEWS

A—A   B—B   C—C

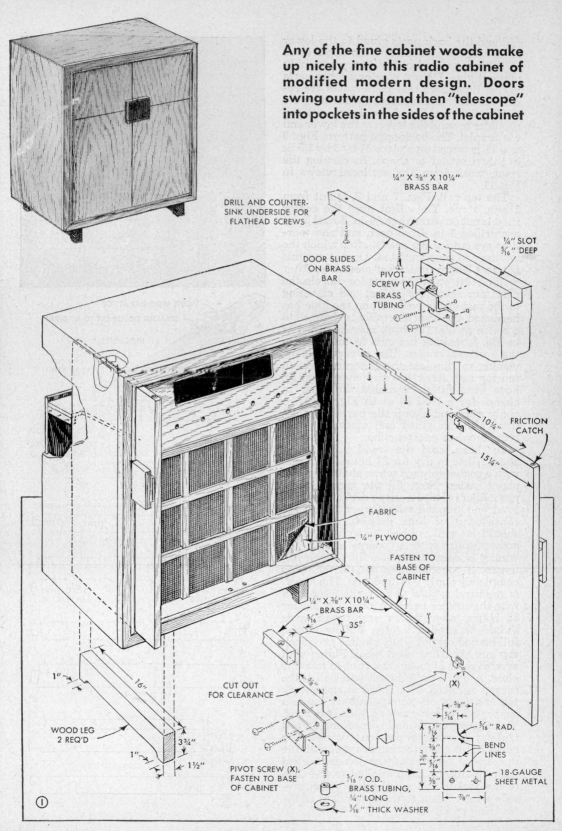

Any of the fine cabinet woods make up nicely into this radio cabinet of modified modern design. Doors swing outward and then "telescope" into pockets in the sides of the cabinet

¼" X ⅜" X 10¼" BRASS BAR

DRILL AND COUNTER-SINK UNDERSIDE FOR FLATHEAD SCREWS

¼" SLOT
5⁄16" DEEP

DOOR SLIDES ON BRASS BAR

PIVOT SCREW (X)

BRASS TUBING

10¼"

FRICTION CATCH

15¼"

FABRIC

¼" PLYWOOD

FASTEN TO BASE OF CABINET

¼" X ⅜" X 10¼" BRASS BAR

5⁄16"

35°

5⁄8"

(X)

1"

16"

3¾"

1"

1½"

WOOD LEG 2 REQ'D

CUT OUT FOR CLEARANCE

PIVOT SCREW (X), FASTEN TO BASE OF CABINET

5⁄16" O.D. BRASS TUBING, ¼" LONG

1⁄16" THICK WASHER

5⁄8"
5⁄16"
5⁄16" RAD.

BEND LINES

5⁄16"
5⁄16"
⅜"
1⅜"
5⁄16"
⅜"
⅜"
7⁄8"

18-GAUGE SHEET METAL

①

②

MODERN RADIO CABINET

By Gene Russell

WITH the exception of the novel "telescoping" doors, which open out and then slide back into pockets, this floor-type radio cabinet is almost as simple and easy to build as a box. Character and individuality of design are added by beading around the double-door opening, built-up door handles and one-piece inset wood legs or feet. Absence of curved parts on the exterior of the cabinet gives the whole job a pleasing plumbness of line that appeals to both the craftsman and the home decorator.

Due to the width of the sides, top and bottom, it will be necessary to build up to the required widths by edge-gluing several pieces together. Select the wood for quality and grain and cut all the pieces slightly longer and wider than the finished

dimensions to allow for fitting. The kind of wood to use depends on the finish you desire. Plain oak will take a beautiful limed finish, which is especially popular on this modified modern design. Any of the other fine cabinet woods are, of course, suitable for finishing in the natural color, bleached or stained. However, if you like an enamel finish, then use a close-grained wood such as birch, gum or poplar.

When clamping edge-glued work, you can save a lot of time and extra sanding by making sure that the edges are flush. Draw the bar clamps tight and then even up the edges by tapping lightly with a hammer. Wipe off excess glue with a damp cloth. Allow plenty of time for the glued joints to dry before releasing the clamps. Doors are built up to width in the same manner, making them slightly oversize all around so they can be trimmed to fit accurately.

This done, the pieces must be sanded smooth. On glued-up work such as this it often is necessary to go over the surface with a jointer plane in order to get it perfectly flat. After planing and sanding all pieces, you're ready to cut to size and join the parts. Cut a rabbet in the back edge of the sides and the bottom piece to take the back. Mitered joints at the corner of the cabinet give the best appearance but are more difficult to make. Clamping can be done by making four clamping cauls from 1 by 4-in. stock, each piece cut slightly longer than the width of the cabinet side pieces. Nail two 1 by 4-in. pieces together at right angles to make one caul. Then make the miter cuts on the four pieces which comprise the top, bottom and sides. Spread glue on the joining surfaces, set the parts together, block them in position and place a caul over each corner. Then draw up with eight bar clamps, two across each panel lengthwise.

Next, glue on the facing strip and beading, Fig. 1. Screw the back panel in place and the inclined shelf for the radio chassis, then the instrument panel and framework for the grille. A look at the three views in Fig. 3 will give you dimensions and location of these parts. Finally, "hang" the doors. Fig. 1 gives the details, Fig. 2 shows the doors open and Fig. 3 gives the position of the door in section. The pivot screw X is shown in position in Figs. 1 and 3. It likely will be necessary to make a trial fit in order to get the doors to work smoothly. Doors should be fitted with allowance for free movement and then finished on both sides and the edges. This adds to appearance and prevents absorption of moisture which might cause the wood to swell.

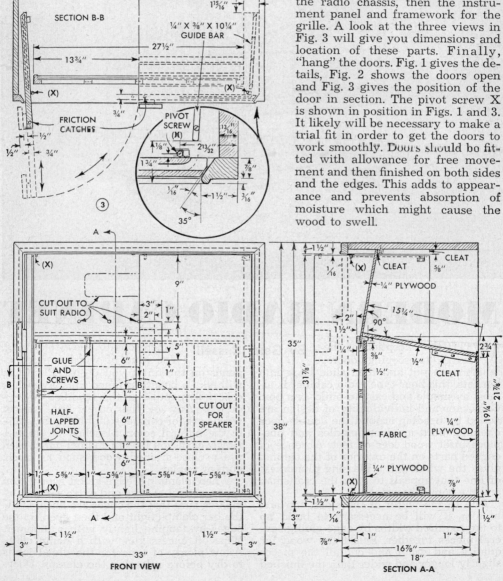

PERIOD CLOCKCASE

By Ralph A. Hinde

THIS SMALL clockcase is just the project for the craftsman who likes to work with fine veneers. The original case was made from flame-grained rosewood veneer glued to a core of ¼-in. pine with a backing veneer of mahogany. The case is proportioned for an electric movement having a 3-in. dial. First, cut the pine core stock ¾ in. oversize. Next, select the face veneers and trim roughly to the size of each piece of core stock. Also, cut the backing veneers to size. Then glue the veneers to both sides of the core. Scrolled parts of the broken-pediment top are of ¼-in. plywood which is faced on one side with a matching veneer. When the work is dry, cut the opening for the dial and run a ⅜-in. rabbet along each edge of the front piece of the case, the depth of the rabbet being equal to the thickness of the piece less the face veneer. Then join the sides to the front with a butt joint as in the lower left-hand detail, using glue and glue blocks. Finish the corner of the joint by sanding carefully. With this method of joining, the end grain is not exposed. The scrolled parts of the base are veneered with the grain running vertically to match the case and the pediment top. Use ¼-in. plywood as a core and join at the corners in the same manner as described above. Pressed moldings add decorative detail but plain, straight moldings can be used. Finish the wood in the natural color and add the finials which are the brass type used on table lamps. These are attached to the case in the positions shown with dowels which are turned into the threaded holes of the finials.

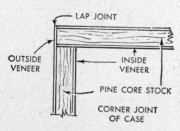

LAP JOINT

OUTSIDE VENEER

INSIDE VENEER

PINE CORE STOCK

CORNER JOINT OF CASE

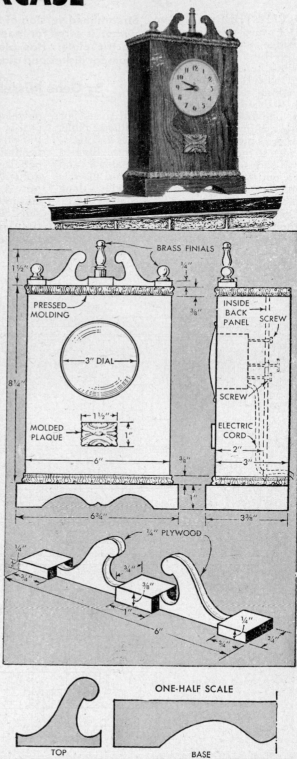

BRASS FINIALS

1½"

¼"

⅜"

PRESSED MOLDING

3" DIAL

INSIDE BACK PANEL

SCREW

8¼"

MOLDED PLAQUE

1½"

1"

SCREW

ELECTRIC CORD

2"

3"

6"

⅜"

6¾"

1"

3⅜"

¼" PLYWOOD

¼"

¾"

¾"

⅜"

1"

6"

¼"

¾"

¾"

ONE-HALF SCALE

TOP

BASE

WHETHER it's your turn to entertain at bridge or you're just having the neighbors in— that's when you'll want to wheel out this smart looking serving cart. It's just the thing beside the bridge table for coffee and light snacks, or to assist in serving at a small dinette table. There's plenty of space for dishes and glassware as indicated in Fig. 4, and the divided top slides back to reveal a metal tray and an outlet to plug in a toaster and electric plate as shown in Fig. 3. The whole thing closes up into the neat little cabinet in Fig. 2 which can be pushed into a corner out of the way when not in use.

Construction is a fairly simple joining job as detailed in Fig. 1. Although standard 1 1/16-in. solid stock is called for, which allows 1/16 in. for dressing, construction can

Streamlined version of the tea wagon is wired for toaster and electric plate. Has plenty of room for dishes and glassware

By Gene Russell

be of 3/4-in. plywood if the dimensions are changed and minor alterations are made in the assembly. Panels for the sides and bottom of the cabinet are built up in width from several pieces doweled and glued edgewise. From the pull-apart view in Fig. 5 you can see how the pieces go together. Note that a small beading is run on the inner edges of the panels. If the mitered corners specified are difficult for you to cut, the pieces can be butted and fastened with screws driven at an angle through the bottom and into the side. If mitered, nails can be driven up from the bottom without showing. Four rabbeted rails join the end members at the top, two at the front and two at the back. Note in Fig. 5 that rails J are mitered and rails L are set flush in mortises located ac-

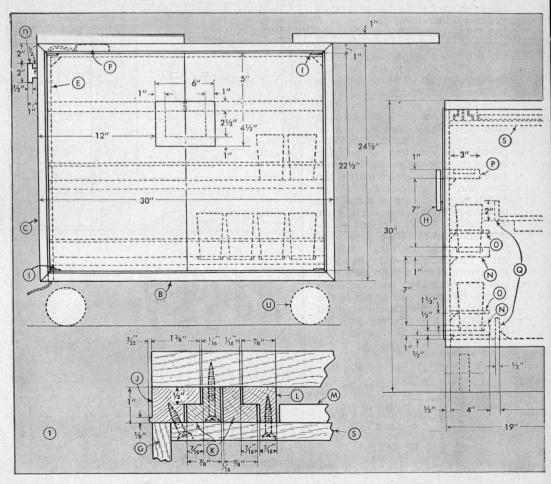

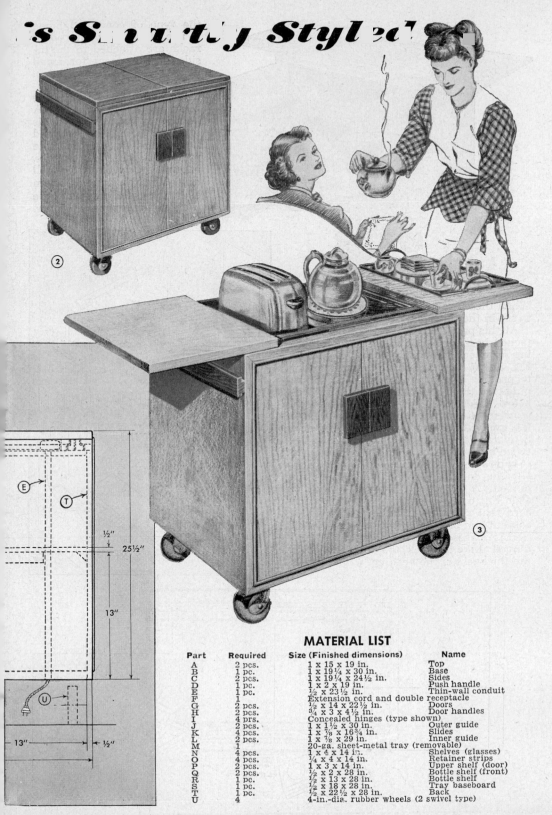

MATERIAL LIST

Part	Required	Size (Finished dimensions)	Name
A	2 pcs.	1 x 15 x 19 in.	Top
B	1 pc.	1 x 19¼ x 30 in.	Base
C	2 pcs.	1 x 19¼ x 24½ in.	Sides
D	1 pc.	1 x 2 x 19 in.	Push handle
E	1 pc.	½ x 23½ in.	Thin-wall conduit
F	1	Extension cord and double receptacle	
G	2 pcs.	½ x 14 x 22½ in.	Doors
H	2 pcs.	¾ x 3 x 4½ in.	Door handles
I	4 prs.	Concealed hinges (type shown)	
J	2 pcs.	1 x 1½ x 30 in.	Outer guide
K	4 pcs.	1 x ⅞ x 16¾ in.	Slides
L	2 pcs.	1 x ⅞ x 29 in.	Inner guide
M	1	20-ga. sheet-metal tray (removable)	
N	4 pcs.	1 x 4 x 14 in.	Shelves (glasses)
O	4 pcs.	¼ x 4 x 14 in.	Retainer strips
P	1	1 x 3 x 14 in.	Upper shelf (door)
Q	2 pcs.	½ x 2 x 28 in.	Bottle shelf (front)
R	1 pc.	½ x 13 x 28 in.	Bottle shelf
S	1 pc.	½ x 18 x 28 in.	Tray baseboard
T	1 pc.	½ x 22½ x 28 in.	Back
U	4	4-in.-dia. rubber wheels (2 swivel type)	

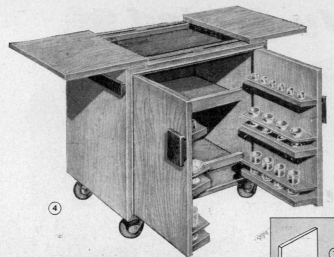

(4)

the type of concealed hinge to use. Finally, counterbored racks are attached to the inside of the doors for small glasses, and a two-part knob, built up of two blocks, is attached with screws from the back, one half to each door. A handle for guiding the cart is attached to the left-hand end near the top. Any suitable rubber-tired truck casters, about 4 in. in diameter, will do, although two of them should be of the swivel type to make the cart easy to steer.

cording to the sectional detail in Fig. 1. When these are in place, the back is fitted to set-in the thickness of the beading.

At this point the sliding top must be attached to slides K, each half of the top being fastened to one set of slides. Notice in Fig. 5 that one set extends past the other to provide a stop so that they cannot be pulled all the way out. Pieces of thin cardboard inserted between the slides and guides before the former are screwed to the top will prevent binding. Next, panel S, which forms a recess for the tray detailed in Fig. 7, is installed. This is screwed to rails J and L as in Fig. 1 and is cut to allow the doors to fit flush when they are hinged. A two-plug receptacle is located as in Fig. 6 and is wired with an extension cord that runs down through a length of conduit and out the bottom of the cabinet.

This leaves the doors to be fitted and hinged. Like the back, the doors are set-in the thickness of the beading. Fig. 5 shows

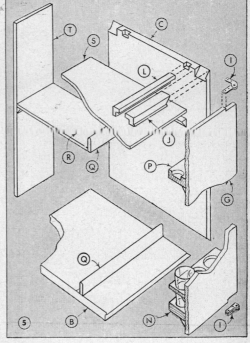

(5) (B) (N) (I)

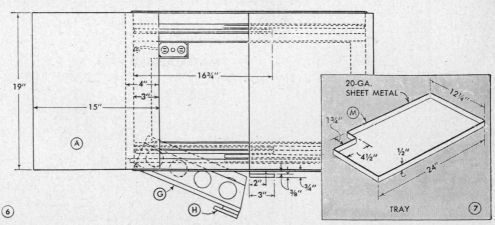

(6) (A) (G) (H)

20-GA. SHEET METAL

TRAY (7)

CURIO CABINET

Colonial both in design and finish, this little curio cabinet provides an appropriate setting for displaying your treasured bits of bric-a-brac. Typical cabinet joinery is used, a right and left-hand side member being cut first from maple or birch and rabbeted along the rear edges for a ¼-in. plywood panel. Except for the shelf above the door, all others, including the top and bottom of the cabinet, are cut the same size. The scrolled valance, which frames the open shelves, is built-up from four separate pieces, the side strips being bandsawed from stock 2 in. wide. The side pieces are joined to the top and bottom scrolled pieces with mortise-and-tenon joints and then nailed to the face of the cabinet flush with the sides. Finally, the top is finished off with a cove molding, and the bottom is fitted with a raised-panel door, being built-up as detailed and hung with wrought-type hinges. A bullet friction catch holds the door shut.

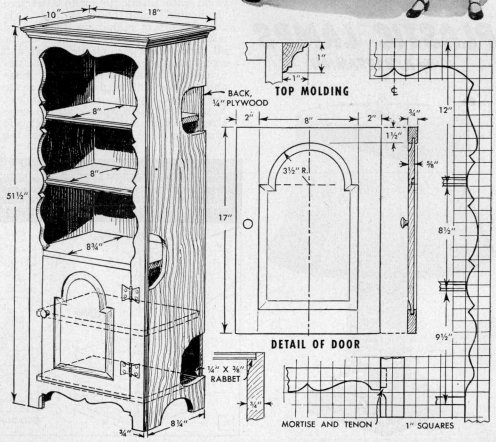

BACK, ¼" PLYWOOD

TOP MOLDING

DETAIL OF DOOR

¼" X ⅜" RABBET

MORTISE AND TENON   1" SQUARES

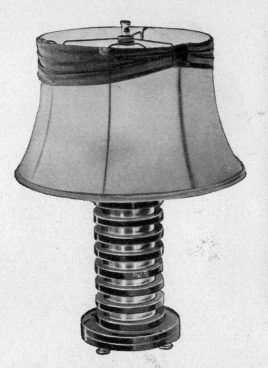

PLASTIC LAMPS

By R. BARSAMIAN

A fast way to cut spacer disks from sheet plastic is to use a circle cutter in a drill-press chuck. Uniformity is had, and, a cutter having a pilot bit of proper size, will form pipe hole at same time

THOSE CHOICE BLOCKS of fancy wood that you have been saving from other jobs will do nicely in combining wood with plastic to make attractive "laminated" lamp bases at very little cost. Layers of aluminum, interspaced with layers of plastic, can be used, or all three materials, plastic, wood and metal may be combined to produce unusual and distinctive bases. Size, shape and thickness of the laminations make the number of variations almost endless. You can cut them square, all the same size, or, every other one can be made smaller to serve as spacers between the

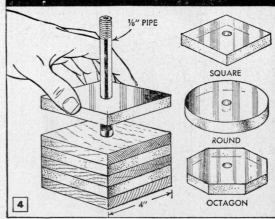

"Disks" may be round, square or octagonal, of plastic, metal or wood. Aluminum or brass spacers combined with clear or colored plastic, or laminations of fancy wood, make attractive bases

plastic. The same applies to bases built up of disks. Variety also is achieved by using, alternately, layers of clear and colored plastic. Still another variation is had by combining thick and thin layers of two different materials as shown in Fig. 8. Here, for economy, the plastic layers should be kept thin as the cost of plastic in thick sheets is somewhat expensive, especially in ¾ and 1-in. sizes.

Figs. 1 to 3 inclusive show progressive steps in mass-producing disk-shape laminations of plastic. Those of one size are cut, drilled and grouped together on a shaft for final finishing all at one time. Assembly of the lamp bases is shown in Figs. 4 and 7 and is typical in building up each base regardless of design. Essentially, the layers, whether round, square or octagon shaped, are coated with cement and slipped over a length of electrical fixture pipe and then clamped. A strong cement for bonding plastic to plastic or plastic to wood and metal is made by mixing ethylene dichloride (available at most paint stores) with fine shavings of clear plastic to a consistency of thick syrup. Do not use until the mixture is entirely dissolved and clear. Pour some of the cement into a shallow container, such as a

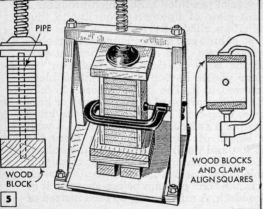

PIPE

WOOD BLOCK

WOOD BLOCKS AND CLAMP ALIGN SQUARES

5

6

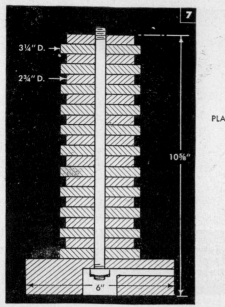

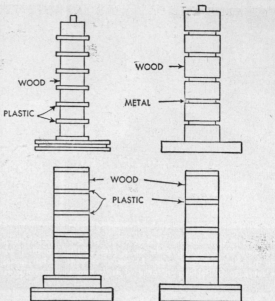

saucer, and coat the surface of each lamination by dipping it into the cement. Work fairly fast as the cement has a tendency to dry quickly. In clamping the assembly, apply sufficient pressure to eliminate air bubbles, but avoid squeezing out all of the cement. A veneer or paper press is ideal to provide uniform pressure, but you can use a couple of large C-clamps. In clamping square-shaped laminations, the setup shown in Fig. 5 should be used to align the edges. Remove the wooden guide pieces before the cement sets, however. Any unevenness too great to remove by hand sanding can be trimmed flush with a fine saw blade or a cutoff wheel as in Fig. 6. The base piece of the lamp is drilled according to the sectional view in Fig. 7 for the lamp cord. Then the two parts of the base are held together by a washer and nut fitted to the end of the pipe.

A word about sanding and polishing plastics: Sawed edges of the material must be sanded perfectly smooth and all tool marks removed. If a lathe is available, the edges of disks can be trued and sanded glass-smooth by mounting them on a shaft and chucking between centers. A cloth buffer is used to polish plastic by holding it against a wheel charged with rouge.

Novel Pin-Up Lamp Glows To Light Up Silhouette Encased in Bulb

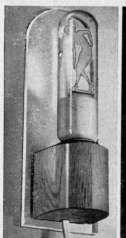

Suitable as a night light, or purely for decoration, this novel pin-up lamp employs a special gas-filled bulb which produces a faint glow of fluorescent quality to illuminate a silhouette inside the bulb. This type of bulb can be purchased at most electrical stores. The sconce or bracket part of the lamp consists of a "reflector" of clear plastic having a socket-fitted block screwed to it. The block is bored to take the inside portion of a regular push or key-type, drop-cord socket. Remove the brass shell and switch buttons and wire it with a length of lamp cord. Then press the socket and its fiber sleeve into the hole in the block, running the wire out through a hole in the bottom. Be sure that the switch is in the "on" position before encasing it in the block. A mirror may be used instead of plastic.

LAMP COSTUMER
For Children

LITTLE folks soon learn to keep playrooms in order when they have this novel lamp costumer which not only provides four hangers for child-sized garments but serves as an attractive floor lamp as well. Four elephant cutouts stand patiently on the base with heads bracing the lamp column. Note that the column is made from two strips, each grooved lengthwise to take ⅛-in. pipe which holds the assembly together and houses the wire, the strips being glued together to form one piece. Join the parts of the base as shown in the pull-apart detail. Round or chamfer all exposed corners and assemble and wire the lamp as indicated. Bandsaw the elephant cutouts and join them to the base and column with dowels and glue. Paint or stain to suit.

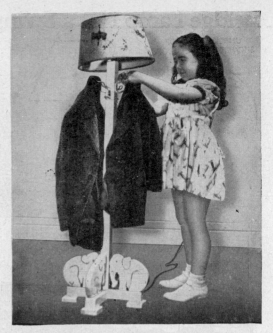

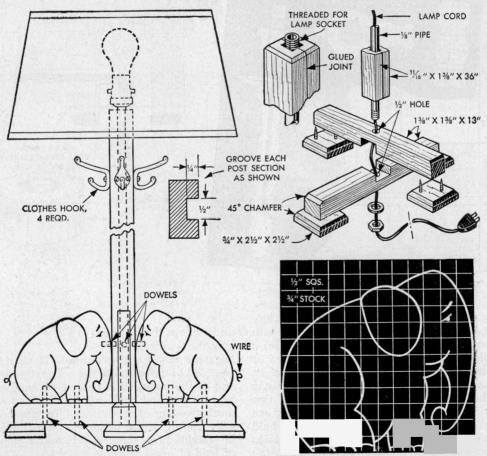

CLOTHES HOOK, 4 REQD.

DOWELS

WIRE

DOWELS

GROOVE EACH POST SECTION AS SHOWN

¼"

½"

45° CHAMFER

¾" X 2½" X 2½"

THREADED FOR LAMP SOCKET

LAMP CORD

⅛" PIPE

GLUED JOINT

1¹¹⁄₁₆" X 1⅜" X 36"

½" HOLE

1⅜" X 1⅜" X 13"

½" SQS.

¾" STOCK

Bridge Lamp Has a Swing Top and Handy Tray

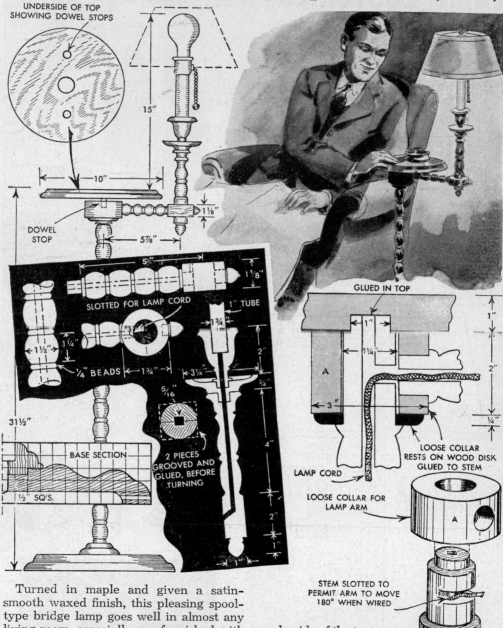

UNDERSIDE OF TOP SHOWING DOWEL STOPS

15"

10"

DOWEL STOP

1⅛"

5⅞"

SLOTTED FOR LAMP CORD

5"

1⅛"

1" TUBE

1¾"

2"

1½"

1¼"

¼" BEADS

1¾"

3¼"

¾"

5/16"

31½"

BASE SECTION

½" SQ'S.

2 PIECES GROOVED AND GLUED, BEFORE TURNING

4"

2"

1"

GLUED IN TOP

1"

1"

1¼"

2"

A

3"

¼"

LAMP CORD

LOOSE COLLAR FOR LAMP ARM

LOOSE COLLAR RESTS ON WOOD DISK GLUED TO STEM

A

STEM SLOTTED TO PERMIT ARM TO MOVE 180° WHEN WIRED

Turned in maple and given a satin-smooth waxed finish, this pleasing spool-type bridge lamp goes well in almost any living room, especially one furnished with period pieces. The base is turned from a block built up by gluing together two or three pieces of wood with the grain at right angles. Each of the spool-shaped parts that carry the lamp cord consists of two pieces which are grooved before they are glued together. The swinging arm is held on a wooden collar, detail A, that rotates on the standard and two stop pins on the underside of the tray prevent the arm from swinging more than halfway around. To permit the cord to move inside the collar, the top end of the standard is slotted. A candle-type socket and shell can be obtained at most five-and-dime stores. To prevent easy tipping of the lamp, the base should be weighted by recessing it to take a piece of lead or other suitable weight.

Spool-design FLOOR LAMP

In making this attractive lamp, short sections are turned to the shape shown in the upper detail, and glued together to form a standard that appears to be a long, continuous turning. This method of assembly is easier than turning a long standard and boring it for the electrical cord. When fitting the sections together, the grain of the wood should be matched as nearly as possible so that the standard looks like one piece of wood. The top end is fitted with a ¼-in. nipple to which the lamp head is attached, and the bottom end is turned to fit a hole in the base. If a new head is not available, you can use one taken from a discarded lamp

If material thick enough for the turned base is unavailable, it may be built up. A recess is turned in the underside to take a 5-lb. lead weight, which may be taken from an old floor lamp

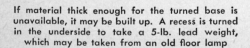

The interesting maple feet are turned at one time, shellacked and polished while in the lathe, then marked off and scrollsawed as shown. These are glued to the base, using 5/16-in. dowels

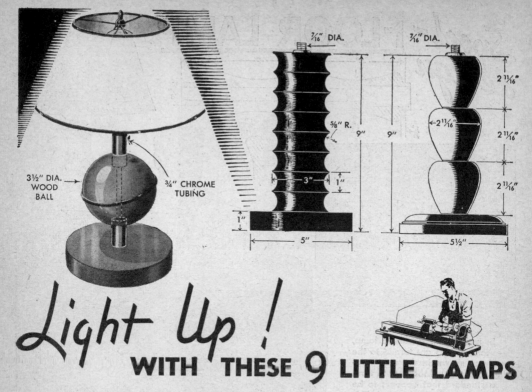

3½" DIA. WOOD BALL

¾" CHROME TUBING

7/16" DIA.

¾" DIA.

5/8" R.

9"

9"

3"

1"

1"

5"

5½"

2 11/16"

2 11/16"

2 11/16"

2 11/16"

Light Up!

WITH THESE 9 LITTLE LAMPS

IF YOU'RE a woodturner at heart, here's a chance to make the chips fly. Take your choice of nine little table lamps that can be made of scraps of fancy wood, plastic, or both, some being made and finished completely in a lathe. With the exception of the fluted lamp below, the component parts of all lamps are "tied" together by a ⅛-in. fixture pipe. The fluted lamp consists of a solid block, counterbored at top and bottom for locknuts, the top nut being concealed by a brass washer. The pipe extending above the base is encased in a ⅜-in. tube and the socket is screwed tightly against it. A hole is drilled through the side of the base for a lamp cord. If necessary, the fluting on the base can be done by hand, using a ¾-in. gouge and then sanding smoothly with a round-nose block.

By Wayne C. Leckey

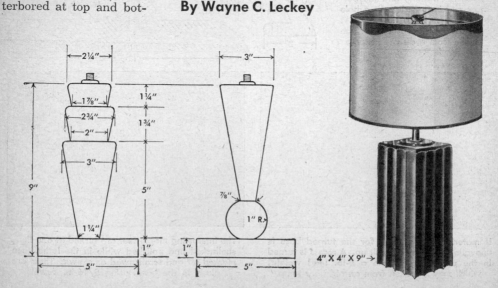

2¼"

1⅞"

2¾"

2"

3"

1¼"

9"

1"

1¼"

1¾"

1"

5"

3"

7/8"

1" R.

5"

1"

5"

4" X 4" X 9"

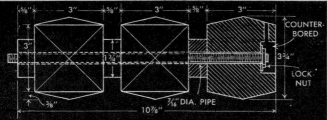

COUNTER-
BORED

LOCK
NUT

⁵⁄₈″ 3″ ⁵⁄₈″ 3″ ⁵⁄₈″ 3″

3″

1¾″

3¾″

³⁄₈″

⁷⁄₁₆″ DIA. PIPE

10⁷⁄₈″

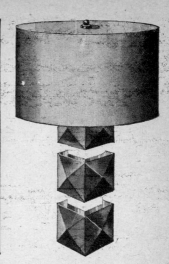

Finished in bone white with spacers of colored plastic, this stunning table lamp takes on a classic-modern appearance. The blocks are shaped identically and drilled through the center for a length of pipe. The bottom block is counterbored for a washer and locknut and then drilled through the side for a lamp cord. With a socket screwed to the top, the whole lamp is held together by the locknut. The diamond effect on the faces of the blocks can be shaped quickly on a disk sander, or the faces may be left plain. The lamp base should be covered with felt or rubber to prevent marring

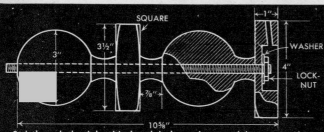

SQUARE

WASHER

LOCK-
NUT

3″

3½″

⁷⁄₈″

1″

4″

10⅝″

Strictly a lathe job, this boudoir lamp is turned in two sections and later connected by a pipe and locknut in the manner previously described. To facilitate centering the pipe hole lengthwise through the pieces, the work can be drilled beforehand, the holes plugged and the work then mounted in the lathe. A cardboard template will be helpful in checking the roundness of the ball turnings and in shaping both alike. Rounding the faces of the square spacer and base of the lamp is done by mounting the pieces on the lathe faceplate. You can counterbore the base at the same time

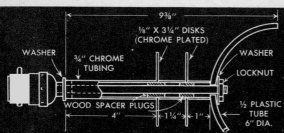

9⅜″

⅛″ X 3¼″ DISKS
(CHROME PLATED)

WASHER

¾″ CHROME
TUBING

WASHER

LOCKNUT

WOOD SPACER PLUGS

½ PLASTIC
TUBE
6″ DIA.

4″ 1¼″ 1″

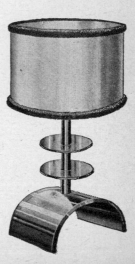

Here plastic and metal are combined. The base is formed of a 5-in. length of plastic tube cut in half and sanded and polished. The other half can be used in making a pair. The lamp post is in three sections with wood spacer plugs serving to align the pieces when assembling. Assembly is made by inserting the plugs half way in the ends of the sections and then placing the metal disks over the plugs. Tightening the locknut after the socket has been wired and fitted to the pipe "ties" the whole thing together like the others

DESIGNED

By Benj. Nielsen

THREE compartments for cigarettes plus an ash tray are all concealed in this attractive hardwood lamp base. When closed, the sections look like a solid wood turning, but swinging the sections to the right or left discloses the compartments for cigarettes and reveals the ash tray in the bottom section. In addition to its usefulness from the smoker's angle, the lamp also provides an excellent hiding place for jewelry and money. Using a good grade of walnut or maple, turn the five sections to an equal outside diameter as shown in the sectional view, Fig. 1. Then round the corners and, while the work is still in the lathe, finish the edges only, by applying a French polish. This is done by dipping a cloth pad in a mixture of sweet oil and shellac and holding the pad against the rotating work. The friction produces a glazed finish which is built up by repeated

TRAYS CLOSED

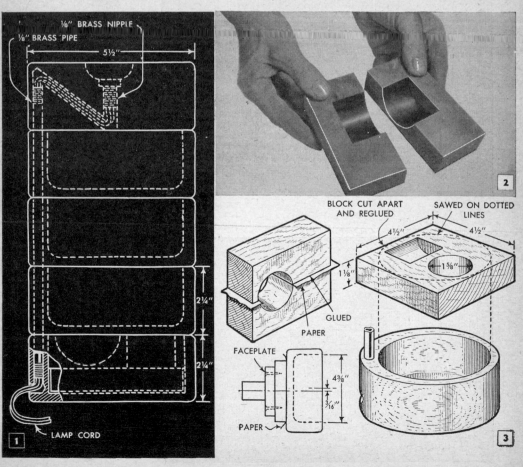

for SMOKERS

applications. Next, glue a wooden disk to the bottom of each of the four lower sections, sandwiching a sheet of paper between the pieces so the parts can be separated easily. Mount each section for turning by screwing the backing disk to the faceplate 3/16 in. off-center, and then turn the recess to the diameter given in Fig. 3. Recesses in the original trays were turned to a depth of 1 7/8 in. but, of course, this can be varied to suit. Note that the recesses in the three center sections are turned with a fillet in the lower corner, but that the corners of the recess in the bottom section are cut square to accommodate a metal ash tray. A wooden cover, having a recess for matches and an opening to the ash tray, fits in the recess in the lower section and rests on top of the ash tray, Fig. 3. Two blocks of hardwood, 1 1/8 x 2 1/4 x 4 1/2 in., are used to make this cover. These blocks are glued together, separated with a sheet of paper, to form a block 2 1/4 x 2 1/4 x 4 1/2 in. Then a 1 3/8-in. hole is drilled about 1 1/4 in. deep at least 1/2 in. in from one edge of the block. This hole must be centered exactly on the joint of the two blocks. The blocks are cut apart along the joint and their edges glued together permanently to form the recess for matches, as shown in Fig. 2. After this, a 1 5/8-in. hole is bored through the blocks between the recess and the edge of the cover, and the block is sawed to a disk shape, indicated by the dotted line. If desired, ash tray and cover may be omitted and the lower section merely recessed in the same way as the other three. To hinge the base sections together, drill registering holes through the thickest portions of the

TRAYS OPEN

sides, forming blind counterbored holes slightly undersize in the top and bottom sections, so the threads of a length of 1/8-in. brass pipe will "take" in the wood. To assure perfect alignment of the holes, the three sections should be stacked and drilled at one time, and then one of these sections should be used as a guide to drill the blind holes in the top and bottom sections. Drill a hole for the lamp cord through the side of the bottom section, and drill and recess the top section as shown by the dotted lines in Fig. 1. Assemble the parts and wire the lamp socket, fishing the cord through the slanting hole with a bent wire.

Colorful Table Lamp From Bottle Gourd

A colorful Mexican scene painted on a dried bottle gourd provides an unusual and attractive base for a small table lamp. To make the lamp, cut off the top of the gourd and turn a wooden plug as shown to fit in the neck of the gourd. The shoulder should be flush with the outside. Then drill the plug to take a piece of brass tubing and wire a lamp socket, running the cord through the tubing and a hole drilled near the bottom of the gourd. Weight the gourd with gravel or sand and secure the plug to the neck with adhesive tape. A brightly colored shade completes the lamp.

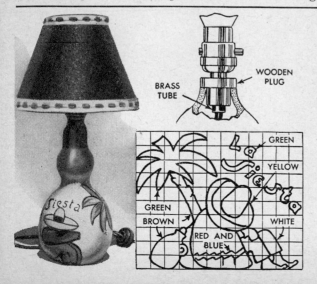

BRASS TUBE

WOODEN PLUG

GREEN

YELLOW

GREEN

BROWN

WHITE

RED AND BLUE

fiesta

LAMPS FANTASTIC

By Norbert Engels

IT IS FANTASTIC to think that lamps like these bring fancy prices in expensive shops, but even more so when you realize that they are made from old pewter jugs and pitchers, ornamental tobacco cans and painted glassware which, in many cases, are simply tossed out. There's practically no limit to what can be used for the lamp bases. It's a case of giving your imagination free rein. Combined with standard fittings or ones salvaged from old lamps, the parts required cost practically nothing. The examples given here show what can be done. The smart copper lamp shown below at the left was made from a 1-gal. oil measure, polished and lacquered and wired for a socket. The base for the nautical lamp shown below at the right is made from a decorative tobacco can and odd parts of several old lamps.

Above, left, a decorative candy can used for the base of this lamp is fitted with a socket fixture taken from an old lamp. The end of the fixture is attached to a wood block fastened to the bottom of the can. Above, right, shows an old-fashioned oil lamp that has been converted to an electric one by replacing the wick unit with a standard socket assembly

Distinctive BOOKSHELF includes a lamp

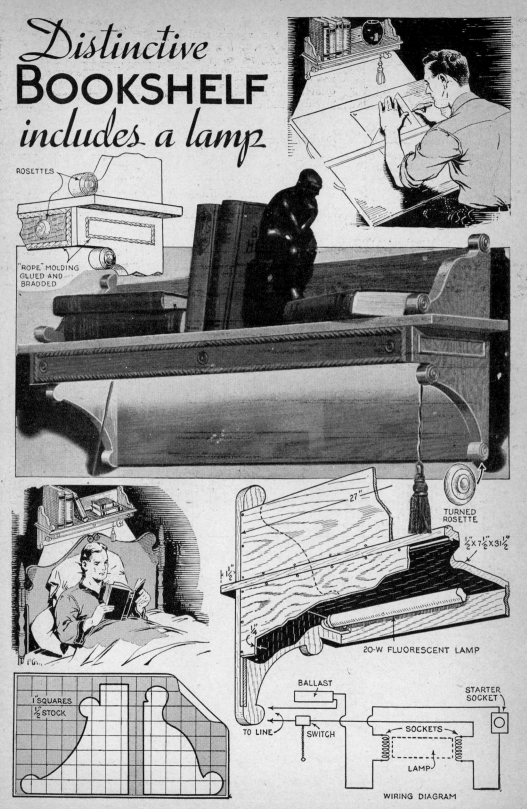

ROSETTES

"ROPE" MOLDING GLUED AND BRADDED

27"

TURNED ROSETTE

$\frac{1}{2}'' \times 7\frac{1}{2}'' \times 31\frac{1}{2}''$

1½"

¼"

20-W FLUORESCENT LAMP

1" SQUARES
½" STOCK

BALLAST

STARTER SOCKET

TO LINE

SWITCH

SOCKETS

LAMP

WIRING DIAGRAM

ROTATING BOOKCASE

TAKING little space in comparison to its large capacity, this rotating bookcase is made to order for the limited study quarters of a high school or college student. It features a novel "ball bearing" base on which the bookcase itself rotates on five wooden balls which roll in a track turned in the surface of the base. With the balls spaced to distribute the load uniformly, the upper part can be rotated very easily for quick selection of books from either side.

The book section is constructed first, preferably of hardwood, such as maple, birch, walnut or mahogany. Fig. 4 gives

By Norbert Engels

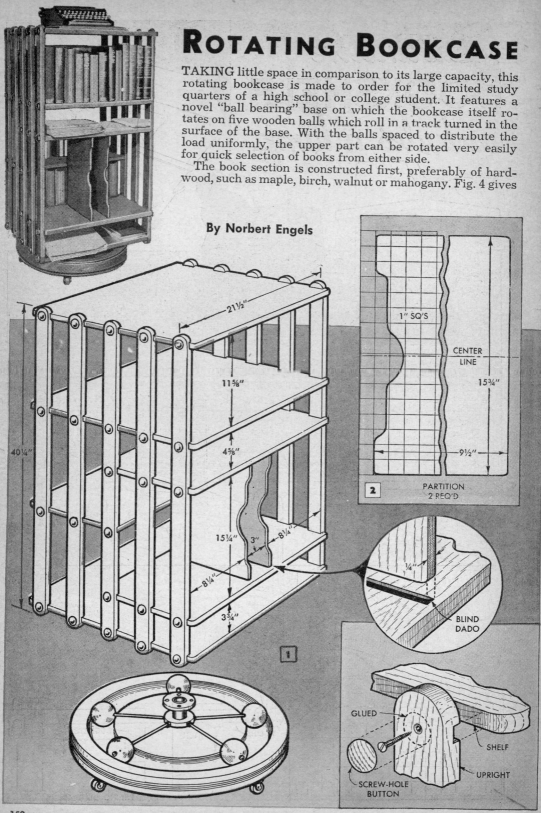

1" SQ'S

CENTER LINE

15¾"

9½"

2 PARTITION 2 REQ'D

21½"

11⅝"

4⅝"

40¼"

15¼" 3" 8¼"

8¼"

3¾"

1

¼"

BLIND DADO

GLUED

SHELF

SCREW-HOLE BUTTON

UPRIGHT

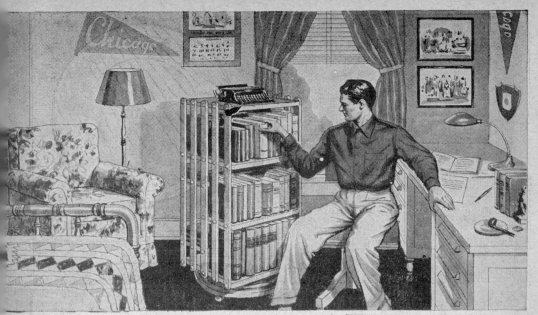

the size and shape of the 10 side members and indicates where each one is notched to receive the shelves. Each member is keyed with the assembly drawing in Fig. 3 to show just where it goes. The wide shelves can be made of plywood, or of solid stock by gluing edgewise several pieces of random widths. Note that between two of the shelves there are two scrolled partitions, Fig. 2, which form a compartment for magazines and newspapers. These are glued vertically in blind dadoes, 3 in. apart. Top surfaces of the shelves, and all other parts, should be sanded smooth before assembling. Holes for flathead screws are bored through each side member, at the notch, and then countersunk slightly so that the screwheads will be flush. Use glue in addition to screws in assembling the parts, and check the whole unit for squareness. Each screwhead is covered by a wood screw-hole button, made for the purpose. Wooden dress buttons will do also, as well as metal furniture glides. The wooden buttons are simply glued over the screwheads. In the case of the bottom shelf, it will be necessary to stain or paint it before it is screwed in place.

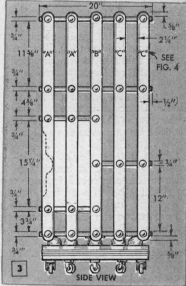

3 SIDE VIEW

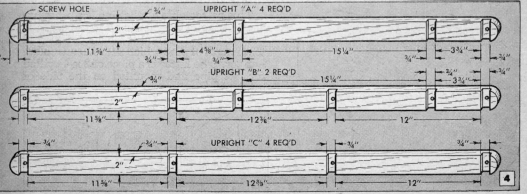

SCREW HOLE UPRIGHT "A" 4 REQ'D

UPRIGHT "B" 2 REQ'D

UPRIGHT "C" 4 REQ'D

4

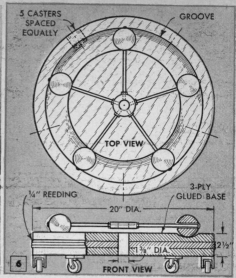

The base is built up of three wood disks totaling 2½ in. in thickness. Cut each slightly oversize and glue all three together with the grain at right angles, one to the other. To turn work of this size, it is necessary to mount it on the left-hand end of the lathe headstock as shown in Fig. 5. The ball track in the face of the base is made 1¾ in. wide and ½ in. deep and ¼-in. reeding is turned in the edge as shown in Fig. 6.

The rotating device is detailed in Fig. 7. It consists of a threaded length of 1-in. pipe, which turns freely in a hole bored through the base at the center, and has a floor flange at one end for fastening the pipe to the bottom of the bookcase. The axles or spokes on which the five wooden balls rotate, are ¼-in. bolts turned into tapped holes equidistantly

spaced in the edge of a metal collar. This collar slips over the pipe kingpin like a wheel, after which the base is locked in place by a pipe cap as shown. Five swivel plate casters are screwed to the base. You can use balls from an indoor croquet set and turn the ball race in the base to suit.

Retractable Clothesline for Low Basement Stored Against Ceiling Joists

This retractable clothesline is pushed up against the ceiling joists after the wash is taken down. Each end of the line is fastened to a length of pipe which slides in a wooden hanger. The latter is a piece of 2 x 4 drilled for the pipe and mounted on the side of a joist.

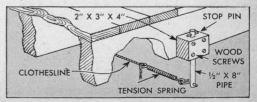

MAGAZINE RACK
Swings Into BOOKCASE

HOUSED in the lower section of this bookcase, a hinged rack holds your current magazines in order, out of sight, yet instantly available. It swings outward like a bin to show its contents, but when closed, its front side comes flush with the front of the case. Hardwood, such as walnut, will produce a beautiful case, but you can use oak, gumwood or oven pine, depending upon how you want to finish it. Both side pieces can be sawed out together, then mortised for the shelves, which are not all of the same thickness. The lower one is of heavier stock so that it can be recessed for

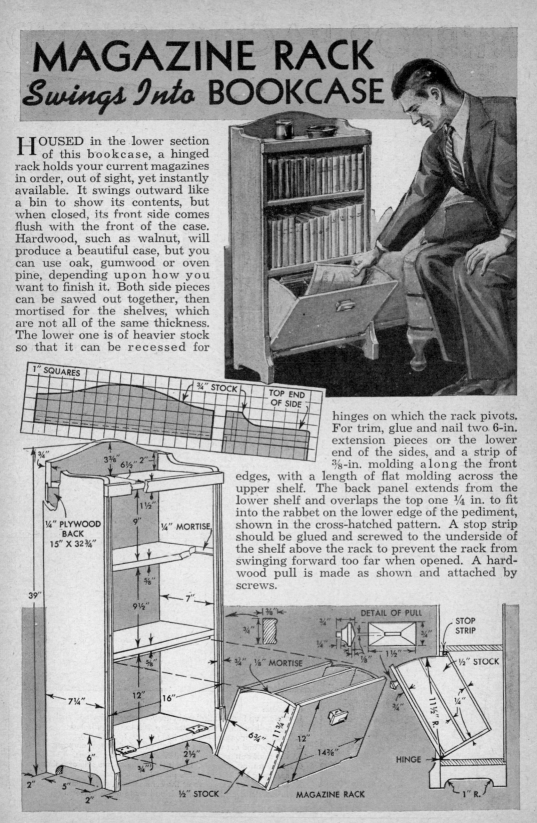

hinges on which the rack pivots. For trim, glue and nail two 6-in. extension pieces on the lower end of the sides, and a strip of 3/8-in. molding along the front edges, with a length of flat molding across the upper shelf. The back panel extends from the lower shelf and overlaps the top one 1/4 in. to fit into the rabbet on the lower edge of the pediment, shown in the cross-hatched pattern. A stop strip should be glued and screwed to the underside of the shelf above the rack to prevent the rack from swinging forward too far when opened. A hardwood pull is made as shown and attached by screws.

MIRROR-BACKED STAND

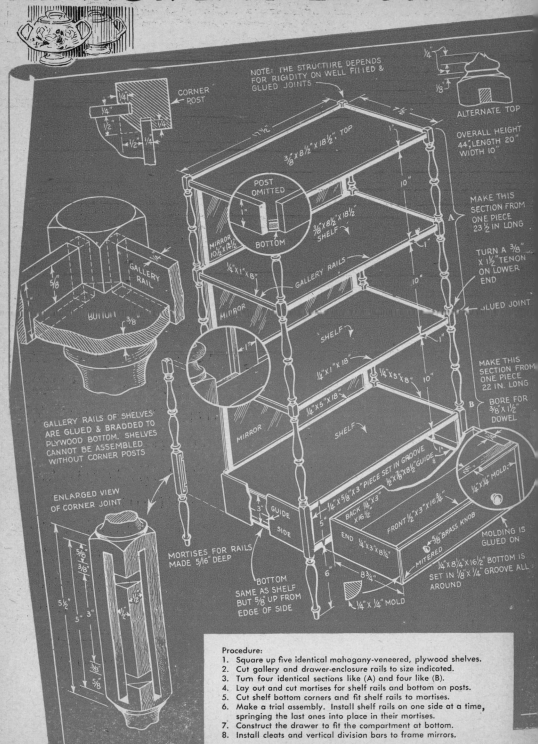

NOTE: THE STRUCTURE DEPENDS FOR RIGIDITY ON WELL FITTED & GLUED JOINTS

CORNER POST

ALTERNATE TOP

OVERALL HEIGHT 44", LENGTH 20" WIDTH 10"

MAKE THIS SECTION FROM ONE PIECE 23½ IN LONG

TURN A ⅜" X 1½" TENON ON LOWER END

GLUED JOINT

MAKE THIS SECTION FROM ONE PIECE 22 IN. LONG

BORE FOR ⅜" X 1½" DOWEL

POST OMITTED

⅜" X 8½" X 18½" TOP

⅜" X 8½" X 18½" SHELF

BOTTOM

MIRROR 10½" X 12½"

GALLERY RAILS

¼" X 1" X 8"

MIRROR

SHELF

½" X 1" X 18"

¼" X 5" X 18"

¼" X 5" X 8"

MIRROR

SHELF

GALLERY RAIL

⅝"

BUTTON

⅜"

GALLERY RAILS OF SHELVES ARE GLUED & BRADDED TO PLYWOOD BOTTOM. SHELVES CANNOT BE ASSEMBLED WITHOUT CORNER POSTS

ENLARGED VIEW OF CORNER JOINT

⅝"
3/8"
5½"
5" 3"
3/8"
5/8"

MORTISES FOR RAILS MADE 5/16" DEEP

BOTTOM SAME AS SHELF BUT ⅝" UP FROM EDGE OF SIDE

6"

8¾"

¼" X ⅝" X 3" PIECE SET IN GROOVE
½" X ⅜" X 8½" GUIDE

3" GUIDE

SIDE

BACK ¼" X 3" X 16¼"

END ¼" X 3" X 8¼"

FRONT ½" X 3" X 16¾"

MITERED

⅝" BRASS KNOB

¼" X ¼" MOLD.

MOLDING IS GLUED ON

¼" X 8¼" X 16½" BOTTOM IS SET IN ⅛" X ¼" GROOVE ALL AROUND

¼" X ¼" MOLD

Procedure:
1. Square up five identical mahogany-veneered, plywood shelves.
2. Cut gallery and drawer-enclosure rails to size indicated.
3. Turn four identical sections like (A) and four like (B).
4. Lay out and cut mortises for shelf rails and bottom on posts.
5. Cut shelf bottom corners and fit shelf rails to mortises.
6. Make a trial assembly. Install shelf rails on one side at a time, springing the last ones into place in their mortises.
7. Construct the drawer to fit the compartment at bottom.
8. Install cleats and vertical division bars to frame mirrors.

for Your RARE CHINA

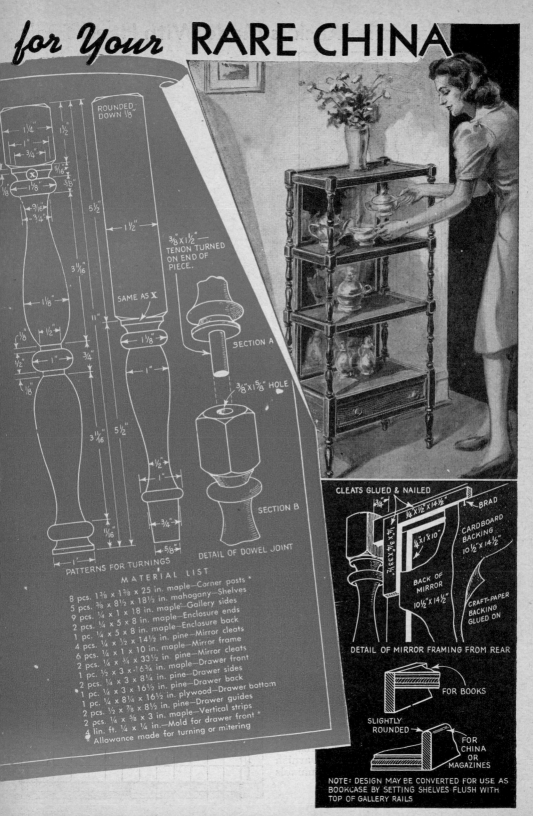

ROUNDED DOWN 1/8"

1 1/4"
1"
3/4"
1 1/2"
5/16"
3/8"
1/8"
1 1/8"
9/16"
3/4"

1 1/2"

5 1/2"

3 11/16"

1 1/8"

3/8" x 1/2" TENON TURNED ON END OF PIECE.

SAME AS X

11"

1 1/8"

1"

SECTION A

3/8" x 1 5/8" HOLE

SECTION B

1 1/8"
1/2"
1/2"
1"

3 11/16"
5 1/2"

3 11/16"
5 1/2"

11/16"

1"
3/4"
5/8"

1"

DETAIL OF DOWEL JOINT

PATTERNS FOR TURNINGS

MATERIAL LIST

8 pcs. 1 3/8 x 1 3/8 x 25 in. maple—Corner posts *
5 pcs. 3/8 x 8 1/2 x 18 1/2 in. mahogany—Shelves
9 pcs. 1/4 x 1 x 18 in. maple—Gallery sides
2 pcs. 1/4 x 5 x 8 in. maple—Enclosure ends
2 pcs. 1/4 x 5 x 8 in. maple—Enclosure back
1 pc. 1/4 x 5 x 8 in. pine—Enclosure back
4 pcs. 1/4 x 1/2 x 14 1/2 in. pine—Mirror cleats
6 pcs. 1/4 x 1 x 10 in. maple—Mirror frame
2 pcs. 1/4 x 3/4 x 33 1/2 in. pine—Mirror cleats
2 pcs. 1/4 x 3/4 in. maple—Drawer front
1 pc. 1/2 x 3 x 16 3/4 in. pine—Drawer sides
2 pcs. 1/4 x 3 x 8 1/4 in. pine—Drawer back
1 pc. 1/4 x 3 x 16 1/2 in. plywood—Drawer bottom
1 pc. 1/4 x 8 1/4 x 16 1/2 in. pine—Drawer guides
2 pcs. 1/2 x 7/8 x 8 1/2 in. maple—Vertical strips
2 pcs. 1/4 x 5/8 x 3 in. maple—Vertical strips
4 lin. ft. 1/4 x 1/4 in.—Mold for drawer front *
* Allowance made for turning or mitering

CLEATS GLUED & NAILED

3/4"

1/4 x 1/2 x 14 1/2"

BRAD

1/4 x 3/4 x 33 1/2"

1/4 x 1 x 10"

BACK OF MIRROR 10 1/2" x 14 1/2"

CARDBOARD BACKING 10 1/2" x 14 1/2"

CRAFT-PAPER BACKING GLUED ON

DETAIL OF MIRROR FRAMING FROM REAR

FOR BOOKS

SLIGHTLY ROUNDED

FOR CHINA OR MAGAZINES

NOTE: DESIGN MAY BE CONVERTED FOR USE AS BOOKCASE BY SETTING SHELVES FLUSH WITH TOP OF GALLERY RAILS

Novel Magazine Rack Is Made With Hand Tools

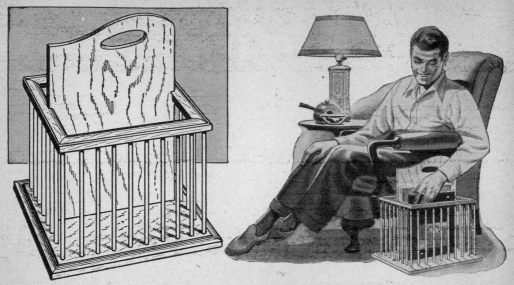

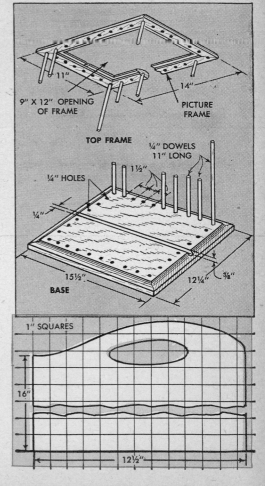

A BREADBOARD, a picture frame, a piece of ½-in. plywood, and a number of ¼-in. dowels are the principal parts of this unusual magazine rack. The design fits in nicely with the furnishings of a den or basement recreation room. Although a breadboard or kneading board from an old kitchen cabinet makes a good base, you can build up a base by gluing together several wooden strips to make the required width. The base is detailed with molded edges but if no shaper is available it can be simplified by merely rounding the edges evenly. Holes for the ¼-in. dowels are spaced and drilled to a uniform depth in the base as indicated. Groove the base as shown. Top frame of the rack is a hardwood picture frame of the dimensions given. Holes are drilled in the back of this frame to register with those already drilled in the base. Cut all the dowels to an equal length and insert in the holes in the picture frame. A spot of glue on the end of each dowel will hold it in place. Next, place a drop of glue in each hole in the base. Then invert the picture frame over the base and insert the dowels one by one into the holes. Finally, tap the top of the frame lightly with a mallet to seat the dowels in the holes. Cut the center panel to the shape and dimensions given in the squared pattern, sand the top edge and the edges of the handhole smooth, notch the top frame as indicated and glue the part in place. Finish in the natural color with shellac and varnish or clear lacquer, or with colored enamels to match other furniture.

INDEX

L

Lamp—
  bookshelf, 151
  bridge, 144
  costumer, 143
  floor, 16, 145
  novelty, 150
  pin-up, 142
  plastic, 140, 146
  table, 15, 140, 146, 149
  with ash trays, 148
Living-room suite, 3

M

Magazine rack, 155, 158
Mantel, 98
Mirror-backed stand, 156
Mr.-and-Mrs. chest, 43

N

Nest of tables, 69
Night stand, 43, 75
Novelty lamp, 150

O

Occasional furniture, 17

P

Painting hint, 126
Paint-preservation hint, 59
Paint-storage hint, 128
Pennsylvania Dutch cupboard, 73
Phone stand, 66
Phonograph-record cabinet, 104
Pin-up lamp, 142
Pioneer chair, 116
Polishing hint, 72

R

Rack for toothpaste, 74
Radiator cover, 94
Radio cabinet, 132
Razor-blade dispenser, 154
Reed-bottom chair, 114
Rotating bookcase, 152

S

Sanding, 50
Secretary, 18
Sectional sofa, 10
Serving cart, 136
Sewing box, 111
Shellacking, 50, 126
Sheraton—
  chair, 129
  night stand, 75
Smoking stand, 72
Stand for chinaware, 156
Step table, 7
Stool, 62, 82, 121

T

Table—
  breakfast, 55, 63
  cocktail, 7
  coffee, 53, 57
  corner, 7
  drop-leaf, 25
  Duncan Phyfe lyre, 58
  gate-leg, 60
  nest of, 69
  occasional, 66, 68, 69
  reclaiming hint, 87
  side, 75
  step, 7
  three-tray, 68
Table lamp, 15, 140, 146, 149
Telephone stand, 66
Three-shelf unit, 25
Toning, 50
Toy-storage drawer, 72

V

Vanity, 43
Vanity stool, 49, 82
Varnishing, 50

W

Wall shelf, 112
Wardrobe, 88, 126
Wastepaper basket, 77
Welsh dresser, 70
Wood chest, 111
Work stool, 121